The Tower: Major Poems and Plays

THE TOWER
MAJOR POEMS AND PLAYS

Owen Barfield

Edited by Leslie A. Taylor
and Jefferey H. Taylor

Parlor Press
Anderson, South Carolina
www.parlorpress.com

Parlor Press LLC, Anderson, South Carolina, 29621

© 2021 the Owen Barfield Literary Estate. The editors' contributions to the work © 2021 by Leslie A. Taylor and Jefferey H. Taylor.

All rights reserved.
Printed in the United States of America
S A N: 2 5 4 - 8 8 7 9

Library of Congress Cataloging-in-Publication Data

Names: Barfield, Owen, 1898-1997, author. | Taylor, Leslie A., 1964- editor. | Taylor, Jefferey H., editor.
Title: The tower : major poems and plays / Owen Barfield ; edited by Leslie A. Taylor and Jefferey H. Taylor.
Description: Anderson, South Carolina : Parlor Press, [2021] | Includes bibliographical references and index. | Summary: "The Tower: Major Poems and Plays presents five literary pieces composed throughout Owen Barfield's lifetime. Previously unpublished, these works contribute to the corpus of twentieth century literature and express in literary form the salient ideas Barfield explored in his well-known philosophical works"-- Provided by publisher.
Identifiers: LCCN 2020048498 (print) | LCCN 2020048499 (ebook) | ISBN 9781643171722 (trade paperback) | ISBN 9781643171746 (pdf) | ISBN 9781643171753 (epub)
Subjects: LCGFT: Poetry.
Classification: LCC PR6052.A643 T69 2021 (print) | LCC PR6052.A643 (ebook) | DDC 821/.912--dc23
LC record available at https://lccn.loc.gov/2020048498
LC ebook record available at https://lccn.loc.gov/2020048499

2 3 4 5

Cover photos by Guillaume Flandre on Unsplash (Tower / Church in Cambridge); "Owen Barfield" (1923). Courtesy of the Bodleian Library, Oxford University.
Book design by David Blakesley.

Parlor Press, LLC is an independent publisher of scholarly and trade titles in print and multimedia formats. This book is available in paperback and ebook formats from Parlor Press on the World Wide Web at http://www.parlorpress.com or through online and brick-and-mortar bookstores. For submission information or to find out about Parlor Press publications, write to Parlor Press, 3015 Brackenberry Drive, Anderson, South Carolina, 29621, or email editor@parlorpress.com.

Contents

Foreword *vii*

Preface *ix*

General Introduction 3

Introduction to *The Tower* 15
The Tower 35

Introduction to *Angels at Bay* 77
Angels at Bay 83
   I. The Wall 85
   II. The Human Dynamo 101
   III. The Paranoia Wing 119

Introduction to *The Unicorn* 143
The Unicorn 147

Introduction to *Riders on Pegasus* 171
Riders on Pegasus 179

Introduction to *Medea* 279
Medea 283

Bibliography 315
Index 317
About the Author 319
About the Editors 319

Foreword

Sitting in my study, it seems that every news article is filled with updates about the coronavirus pandemic. We are undoubtedly facing a unique and unprecedented challenge, with millions of souls across the world experiencing some form of enforced isolation due to an invisible, airborne enemy. In so many ways, the situation is one of individual and collective tragedy. However, it is also an opportunity for quietness, reflection – to look within as well as beyond towards a deeper participation in all Creation. This timely collection of Grandfather's most significant poems and plays offers to take us on such a journey into the poetic imagination. The Taylors are insightful and knowledgeable guides on this voyage of exploration, and I am equally grateful for their scholarship and company!

Grandfather wrote extensively across a range of genres – from children's fantasy adventure to science fiction, monographs on economics, and even collaborating with Tolkien on the odd spoof examination paper for the more inactive members of his walking club – the Cretaceous Perambulators, which was largely composed of the Inklings and their friends. But he always thought of himself as a poet at heart – poetry was his first love. I think he would be completely thrilled with this thoughtful and valuable publication.

Owen A. Barfield
Grandson & Trustee
Oxfordshire, England
April 2020
www.owenbarfield.org

Preface

This compilation of Owen Barfield's major poems and plays is the result of a bit of sleuthing. It began with a six-day visit to the Bodleian Library to peruse the Owen Barfield Archive in early 2016 during which we happily encountered some of the literary works included in this collection. A second trip to the Bodleian followed in early 2018. We approached this collection as scholars who were familiar with—and applied to our own scholarship—Barfield's theories on the evolution of consciousness as laid out in his numerous publications over the course of his life.

We are indebted to numerous individuals who have helped bring this project about. Foremost is Owen A. Barfield, grandson and executor of the Barfield Literary Estate, whose encouragement, friendship, and wealth of understanding made this work possible. Gabriel Schenk has provided invaluable assistance over the years in support of the literary estate, including for these texts. Martin Ovens organized the conference on Owen Barfield in Contemporary Contexts in March of 2016 at Wolfson College, Oxford. We are grateful to David Blakesley of Clemson University who readily saw the value in these literary gems and offered Parlor Press as a forum for publication. Over the years members of the Owen Barfield Society (OBS) have contributed much to the development of Barfield research and publication, most notably Jane and Terry Hipolito, also Peter Fields, Julie Nichols, and other outstanding scholars—special thanks to John Ulreich who presented on Barfield's *Orpheus* at the OBS session of the Rocky Mountain Modern Language Association conference in Santa Fe in 2015 and distributed copies of his 1983 edition of the play. Other scholars who have laid the foundations for this work include Simon Blaxland-de Lange, Verlyn Flieger, Walter Hooper, Jeanne Clayton Hunter, Thomas Kranidas, David Lavery, Donna Potts, G. B. Tennyson, Raymond Tripp, and others. We have had the comradeship of many friends and colleagues in this endeavor, including students in the Inklings seminar, the Epic Traditions seminar, and

PREFACE

Mythology & Literature courses at MSU-Denver, members of the Grey Havens Society of Longmont, Colorado, and the Original Participants of Denver, Colorado. We offer additional thanks for encouragement to our parents Shirley and Robert Lammert and Velma and Harvey Taylor, and our children, Melian and Andrew Taylor. MSU-Denver provided grants partially funding trips to Oxford in 2016 and 2018.

The Tower: Major Poems and Plays

General Introduction

One of the most original and influential literary figures of the twentieth century, Owen Barfield is known primarily for his many publications on the evolution of consciousness, the interpenetrated polarity of being, and the essential reframing of cultural history that results from this theory. At the center of his philosophy is a deep analysis of mythology and poetics that draws from Coleridge, Steiner, and others to reveal the noetic role of the poetic principle and its salient shifts that map the evolution of conscious experience. Like his companions in the Oxford Inklings group, Barfield wrote from a desire to change the landscape of banality and empirical compulsion that seemed to define contemporary society, and that impulse also included the production of fiction, drama, and poetry. However, though Barfield produced creative works throughout his long life, only a few of those works typical of the mythopoeic creativity of the Inklings authors saw publication, though notably his first published book, *The Silver Trumpet* (1925), is the first *märchen*, or fantasy story, published by any of them. Having lived a little past his ninety-ninth year, it is not surprising that in Barfield's long life much worthy work would be left unpublished, but what is most surprising is that the biggest gaps in the published corpus of the Philosopher of Poetry are most of the major poems and poetic dramas he wrote according to his theories that place poetics at the core of conscious experience itself. In Barfield's life only one major poem/drama, *Orpheus*, saw public performance, and this is also the only such work published in his lifetime, albeit more than three decades after the staging of the play in 1948.

John Ulreich begins his Afterword to *Orpheus*, published by Lindisfarne in 1983, by recounting his visits with Barfield in 1973 when he was researching the Inklings through a grant from the National Endowment for the Humanities. Ulreich laments missing the chance of discussing *Orpheus* with Barfield but also comments that this is somewhat by Barfield's choice: "I learned nothing at all about *Orpheus*. And though I reproach myself for my lack of enterprise, Barfield must share the responsibility, for he scrupulously avoided mentioning any of his fictive offspring."[1] Thankfully, Barfield was enthusiastic with Ulreich's project of publishing *Orpheus* in the early 1980s. Yet, nearly four decades later *Orpheus* serves as the only major precursor of this volume. Ulreich goes on to mention two more "major early poems" that he wishes he could find, *Riders on Pegasus* and *The Unicorn*, and other unpublished plays and novels, noting these as works "only now being given the attention they deserve" (117). Even then any such new attention was limited, and rarely included major poetry, no more of which saw full publication. These two poems, *Riders on Pegasus* and *The Unicorn,* are published here, along with the trilogy of anthroposophical plays collectively called *Angels at Bay*. These texts, written in Barfield's middle years, are all works that have been known about but little known. The play trilogy was written in the early 1940s, and the mythopoeic narratives both around 1950. They represent three distinct modes of Barfield's poetic and dramatic voice, though their interrelationship through theme and purpose is readily apparent. These three are flanked by two remarkable works that in contrast with the other three are little known about: *The Tower*, an early narrative epic, the 'great work' of Barfield's youth remembered mainly in the Diaries and Letters of C. S. Lewis; and one more Greek play, Barfield's *Medea*, completed later in life, indeed, seemingly his last major poetic and dramatic work.

The five major works presented here fall into three distinct periods of Barfield's creative life. The first, *The Tower,* is an introspective narrative poem; it was begun as early as 1922 but did not take its final form until 1927. The early sections of the poem reveal the influence of earlier poets, and Lewis compares it to Browning's *Sordello* and Wordsworth's *Prelude*. The later sections of the poem reveal the extensive changes in Barfield's life and are highly informed by his thought processes related to his studies into the evolution of consciousness and anthroposophy. The correspondence between Barfield and Lewis in the late 1920s reveals that he was preparing *The Tower* for publication, but there is no evidence that he pursued this possibility. One is left pondering why *The Tower* and these other major works have eluded publication until this time. The well-known story of Barfield's life gives the general outline of his often side-lined pursuits of literary production, but the details of these great works reveal a deep desire throughout his life to create active, powerful mythopoesis, though many years often intervened between distinct bursts of poetic/dramatic activity, and hopes for wide reception of his work never saw fruition.

Whatever poetical pursuits filled the years after laying aside *The Tower* in the late 1920s, by the late 1930s Barfield had produced another long poetic work, *Orpheus*, spurred by a deep desire "to write a play in verse" and a casual conversation about the impulse with Lewis in which his friend suggested that he take a traditional myth, such as Orpheus, and give it a try.[2] If Barfield is accurate in his 1982 Foreword in claiming a forty-five-year gap between writing the play and writing about it, *Orpheus* was completed in 1937. The following years were historically challenging as the world descended into war, and Barfield in his program note for the 1948 production mentions the motif of an "increasingly totalitarian and mechanized civilization" and the faint signs of coming disaster.[3] These years were trying on a more personal level, too. Barfield's father died in 1938; his mother in 1940. Perhaps these troubles, general and personal, were a stimulus in the early 1940s to writing *Angels at Bay*, a trilogy of anthroposophical mystery plays that explore "the threshold between the living and the dead" more directly than the mythic treatment of the theme in *Orpheus*.[4] The twentieth century by its midpoint had seen incredible violence and social dissolution, and like most of his colleagues and friends, Barfield had been in the midst of much of it.

In any event, as the world came out of war and into reconstruction, plans were made for a stage production of *Orpheus*, and in September of 1948 it was produced at the Little Theatre in Sheffield by Maud Barfield and Arnold Freeman.[5] This performance and attention for his mythopoeic play was perhaps stimulus to another productive period, for within the next two years Barfield had completed the two mythopoeic works in the middle of this volume, the light-hearted poem *The Unicorn*, and the more dynamic *Riders on Pegasus*, in which Barfield performs a mythopoeic synthesis and transference very similar to his work in *Orpheus*. Ulreich's description of this mythopoeic process in his Afterword tells us much about Barfield's poetic philosophy and production, and Ulreich's analysis fully demonstrates that *Orpheus* resonates strongly with Barfield's whole corpus both theoretical and creative. More pointedly, the mythopoeic processes Ulreich sees in the play are a direct model for the processes and qualities of *Pegasus*.

Ulreich's great desire to publish *Orpheus* stemmed in part from his understanding that Barfield's philosophy of the evolution of consciousness unfolds poetically and dramatically in the mythopoeic experience of the work. "In spite of its being relatively early, *Orpheus* expresses the ideas even of Barfield's most recent work. Because it is a drama, not an argument, *Orpheus* is of course much more than a statement of ideas; it is, rather, their full imaginative realization" (131). That is, Barfield employs his understanding of the evolution of consciousness and the role of myth and poetry in that evolution to create a work that does not just explain or even illustrate his theory but performs the maker's work, wielding the mythopoeic forge to shape our experience toward the paths of final participation. "[*Orpheus*] has to do with the nature of participation itself, not so much because it is *about* participation as because it *is* a symbol to be participated in" (131). It follows that the interpretation of *Orpheus* lies not primarily in ideas represented but rather in "the way in which it *actualizes* ideas," bringing them into the mythopoeic experience, and in the resulting texture of theatricality, "the interpenetration of idea and image, sound and sense" (135). Ulreich affirms that the relationship between Barfield's theories and his poetic productions must be found where the link between theory and art is "most intimate, in the imaginative realm where we participate in the process of thinking itself rather than merely contemplate the products of thought" (135). There is an easy resonance between theory and poetic production if one understands the relationship between the two narrative modes. "What Barfield says in *Poetic Diction* about the nature of mythic consciousness gives only a hint of what is here, in effect, a fully evolved theory of myth—presented, however, not as a set of propositions about mythology, but as the embodiment of mythic consciousness in dramatic form" (136).

Noting that even Barfield's philosophical writings often speak in metaphors, Ulreich unfolds Barfield's own interpretive method, both as it is presented in many published essays, talks, and treatises and in how the experience is created in his poetic and dramatic work. "[A]lthough it contains within itself the principle of its own explanation, the metaphor does not 'explain'; it *is* the meaning to be apprehended by the active imagination. That meaning cannot be inculcated; it will never disclose itself to a passive understanding. The reader must actually participate in making the author's meaning . . ." (135). Ulreich muses that whether one is introduced to Barfield's thought through this mythopoesis or comes to the play well-versed in his philosophy, the author's meaning will inevitably be found in his perennial theme: "At one point I asked the author whether it would be appropriate to describe *Orpheus* as a myth of the evolution of consciousness. I was properly answered: 'Can you imagine me producing a myth of *anything else*?'" (135).

Of course, this rich unity of message throughout his life and work is a familiar trait which Barfield himself often discloses. We must imagine that his other mythopoeic poems and dramas share in the same perennial theme and partake in a similar postmodern mythopoeic transference as in *Orpheus*. "By analyzing in order to re-unify, the play transforms the corpus of Greek myth into a new organism; *Orpheus* makes actual the interrelations between various myths which had been hitherto only potential" (136). Ulreich argues that the intermingling of the stories of Heracles, Aristaeus, Orpheus, Eurydice, the Hesperides, Nereus and others is done authentically and powerfully, synthesizing and filling in tradition according to the patterns on which the Classical world itself built but also bringing the relationships and symbols into sharp relief, revealing the constructions of consciousness rather than merely expressing them or suppressing our participation in them. *Riders on Pegasus* in particular overtly follows this same pattern and methodology, intermingling stories that already overlap and create unexpressed implications in the Classical mythology, releasing mythopoeic potential for the purpose of creating another "embodiment of mythic consciousness" in poetic and dramatic form. The resulting poetry is rich and well-crafted, dynamic and lyrical, and the experience of these texts, as Ulreich suggests, paints within that "felt change of consciousness" at the heart of all Barfield's theoretical work.

Yet, despite the enthusiastic admiration of Barfield's poetry by the few readers with access to it, his major narrative and dramatic works remained relatively obscure in his lifetime. The 1948 production of *Orpheus*, despite Lewis's enthusiasm, did not jump-start a literary career for Barfield. Lewis wrote at the time, "I await with great interest the public reaction to a work that has influenced me so deeply as Barfield's *Orpheus*,"[6] yet the public reaction was minimal, and the grand event quickly became a memory for the few. Written around this same time or soon after, the rhetorical stance of the essay "Poetic Licence" confirms that Barfield clearly understood that he was writing against the poetics of the age; indeed, the essay is both an attack on the bleak landscape of contemporary literature and an *apologia* for his dynamic mythopoeic works. Neither the essay nor the poetry it defends were published. One might also note the publication in 1950 of the first Burgeon novel, *This Ever Diverse Pair*, a book written "out of desperation" in response to great life pressures, about which he told Shirley Sugerman, "I've always thought, looking back, that I avoided a nervous breakdown largely by writing that little book. . . ."⁷ It is not hard to see in these grand poetic works the soul of Burgeon writing against his life's Burden—yet unable to bring these creations to light.

In the 1965 "Introduction to *Light on C. S. Lewis*," Barfield tells the story of the origin of *Pegasus* and its production "somewhere about 1950 (when I was still concerned to write verse)."⁸ His parenthetical note would seem a sardonic admission that his poetic work and theory continued to reside well outside the popular milieu. Barfield wrote smaller poems throughout his life, but it would seem that in 1965 he had not turned to serious poetic production for many years. Yet his developing relationship at this time with the well-known American poet Howard Nemerov would prove one avenue in which his theory of poetics directly impacted the inner-circle of published poetry and offered him external evidence that his theories about poetry were important and meaningful. In *Nemerov and Objective Realism* Donna Potts carefully demonstrates Barfield's direct and transformative influence on Nemerov's poetry and other writings. In turn, Barfield greatly admired Nemerov's work and felt a kindred spirit with this Poet Laureate who would play a major role in Barfield's several sojourns in US academia. "In December 1967, Barfield wrote to Nemerov to describe the impact that 'The Blue Swallows' had had on his philosophy and referred to Nemerov as his 'ambassador at the court of contemporary poetry, with which my relations are somewhat strained.'"⁹ The humor of the diplomatic conceit nonetheless underscores the claim to poetical power unrecognized by the literary elites. There are hints of cynicism that at times arise when Barfield notes the marginalization of his poetic endeavors but never a retreat from theory and practice, never a loss of faith in what he knew about poetics and the power of his mythopoeic work.

In the late 1970s, three decades after its original composition as a Preface for *Pegasus*, Barfield's revival and expansion of "Poetic Licence" for one or more talks in North America finds Barfield defending his poetic theories as emphatically as ever. The argument is sharpened somewhat and then expanded but fundamentally makes the same case, though the tone of the later material is perhaps more strident. This work coincides with his interactions with John Ulreich that would lead in time to the publication of *Orpheus* and a new opportunity to write about its poetic principles and power in a new Foreword. Barfield also must have been working on *Medea* around this time, at last turning to another mythopoeic drama. Yet once again the chance to bring attention to his mythopoeic work mostly fizzled. The published *Orpheus* made little impact beyond his typical audience and did not lead to much increased interest in his work as Ulreich and Barfield had intended and hoped. Simon Blaxland-de Lange notes this disappointment in a letter Barfield wrote to Thomas Kranidas in January of 1984: "I am sorry *Orpheus* looks like turning out what Lewis once called one of his books—a *flop d'estime*," noting that it will be reviewed only by the usual anthroposophical publications and expressing disappointment that there was nothing about it in the new issue of *Towards*, but these, he says, are "chicken feed of course in the publicity stakes," and he then expresses guilt that others have put so much effort into another failed attempt to bring his mythopoeic work to the world. "Whether based on experience or on self-conceit, and you can take your choice, I have become accustomed to meet absence of *réclame* with the reflection: 'Oh well, it will find its readers in ten or twenty or thirty years or so'" (140-41). We must assume that this was not just a salve for disappointment but a real hope he shared with a few others, such as Nemerov, Ulreich, and Kranidas, that the day would come when the world would be ready for these powerful pieces of mythopoeic poetry and drama. Through the long efforts of Kranidas, Jeanne Clayton Hunter, and others, *A Barfield Sampler* was published in 1993, in Owen Barfield's ninety-fifth year, which contains a good amount of smaller poems, some fiction, and notably a selection from Act 2 of *Orpheus* and the last eight stanzas (sixty-four lines) of *Riders on Pegasus*, the only previously published material from the poem. In the Introduction, written by Hunter and Kranidas, Barfield's life and work are outlined with emphasis on the strange irony that his "poetic canon remains unexplored to an extent unusual for a man of his literary influence."[10] Hunter and Kranidas note Barfield's "vigorous defenses" in poetic form "of the English language and its capacities and of a romantic poetic defiantly hurled in the face" of a "self-paralyzed" literary age. They do point out that the Philosopher of Poetry was not wholly removed from the literary establishment, noting "the enthusiasm that major figures such as Auden, Bellow, Eliot, and Nemerov have expressed for his thought," and yet the enigma remains: "here is a heralded man of letters, part of whose *oeuvre* is ignored, if not actually quarantined" (12-13).

Blaxland-de Lange also notes the unaccepted challenge of Barfield's powerful poetry as described by Kranidas in "The Defiant Lyricism of Owen Barfield," an essay published in the journal *Seven*. "Kranidas makes the thoroughly valid observation that Barfield's creative, poetic work was, as it were, forced into a backwater of obscurity because of his refusal to follow the predominant fashion of the time, typified as it was by the intellectual ironicism and detachment of much of Eliot's poetry and drama" (267). Indeed, this is not just Kranidas's perception, for the unpublished "Poetic Licence" presents just such a case against the leading poetry of the time, though it must be said that Barfield grants great value to Eliot's poetic perceptions bespeaking the bleakness of the age and finding retreat in stark core values. "The crowning achievement of poetry is to make water taste like wine; but it is also an achievement to turn sour wine back into pure distilled water with no taste in it. The light of common day is the visionary gleam when it is let in on the imbecilities of auto-intoxication."[11] Barfield's own careful defense of his art and the theories behind it are an argument that he believed his works had great worth, however currently obscure, and that they would someday fit audience find. Blaxland-de Lange considers such in his concluding remarks: "Barfield, however, was not content with lyrical outpourings of one kind or another but was . . . actively transforming his 'backwater' into a whole new line of development for cultural and, most especially, social evolution" (268).

Barfield offers analysis of his own mythopoeic methods in his 1982 Foreword to Ulreich's edition of *Orpheus*. Claiming the gap of forty-five years mitigates his natural reluctance "to write anything of a hermeneutic nature" about his own work, he proceeds to describe two themes, the perennial "evolution of consciousness" theme, which he respectfully relegates to Ulreich's full and understanding analysis in the Afterword, and the second theme of love. "And there is, secondly, the theme of or enigma of the relation between man and woman" (8). This theme he unpacks in basic form, and notes various social issues that one might consider, but these are put aside for a more direct and metaphysical synthesis, for the two themes are the "diachronic" and "synchronic" of the same question: "What is the relation between knowing and being?" (9). Barfield's following claim to be writing mythopoesis from a personal inability to give a more straightforward answer to such questions seems pre-subverted by his reframing of the metaphysical within his chosen mythopoeic frame, chosen not whimsically, but purposefully to get to the core of meaning arising from our relationships with nature and each other. The two themes, both the postmodern and the perennial, are one: "Possibly it is from here, deep down in the mystery of cognition, that the interweaving of the two main themes begins. How, if knowledge without imagination is not knowledge at all, but only a kind of cataloguing? And if knowledge without love cannot be knowledge with imagination?" (9).

Perhaps most fascinating in this analysis is Barfield's insightful musing on King Minos attempting figuration beyond his age and in despair turning to build the labyrinth instead—and this becomes a metaphor, or perhaps narrative device, for his own turning away from attempting one kind of answer and settling instead for writing a mythopoeic play. Yet device and pointed turn it must be, for his answer is to claim mythopoeic power, if only beyond his days: "If one cannot answer questions, or solve enigmas, one can at least write, or re-work a myth around them. And since the solid stuff of authentic myth is pretty sure to be wiser than I am, there is always the chance that in my handling of it I may, without knowing it, throw up something that will one day, when the times are riper, help wiser heads than mine to arrive at answers and reach conclusions" (10). The humility offered is perhaps also device but surely acceptable as faith in future days and the potential for a movement toward final participation. Indeed, the context of these remarks shows Barfield in his mid-80s still deeply invested in both his philosophical and mythopoeic productions and their interrelationship. The Foreword is signed and dated February 1982 in South Darenth, Kent. Barfield was still well into one more phase of trying to reignite consciousness through poetics that had included this new work on *Orpheus* and the revival and expansion of "Poetic Licence" for presentation.

In addition, by February of 1982 Barfield had already written one more mythopoeic drama, his *Medea*, and had it rejected by the BBC (in 1980), but he may have already shared it with Martin Moynihan, who would send him two letters discussing the play, one undated, and one dated February of 1983.[12] Barfield could see the power of the unifying synthesis in which he worked, but he could also see the perennial and increasing dangers of the disjointed and myopic modern consciousness that continues to dominate the world, a vision starkly revealed in the sci-fi novella *Night Operation*, written in 1975. Barfield's *Medea* posits toxic masculinity in its most basic desire for misogyny and the resulting social collapse. The ending at best wonders if there might still be absolution and hope in old tropes of power. Barfield would produce one more major work in the late 1980s, the diptych novella *Eager Spring*, one of his last and best works, posthumously published in 2008, which juxtaposes a contemporary story of activists resisting illegal toxic dumping with the protagonist Virginia's attempts to detangle the story of consciousness from the cultural clues in medieval and renaissance literature and art. This last novella plumbs the material destructions of our poisoned age and traces these destructions directly to the folly of consciousness firmly immersed in the empiricist, positivist thinking and social competition that has long transformed us into atomized points of camera-consciousness, "a shivering little biped with pneumonia waiting for him round the corner," as he quips in a late addition to "Poetic Licence" (16). Even much earlier Barfield clearly saw the real dangers of the isolated, empirically bent consciousness of the modern lens. At the end of his program note for the 1948 production of *Orpheus*, Barfield intones on the ominous motif of social dissolution as consciousness descends into meaningless processes propelled by social coercion and violence: "Whether it was equally natural to relate this place [Hades] as closely as I have done to the *upper* world, as we know it today, the world of our highly abstract and therefore increasingly totalitarian and mechanized civilization, may be disputed. The play was written before 1939. Those who can accept the convention will, I hope, feel with me that for us too, there are signs, faint enough no doubt, of an imminent crumbling of the stern barrier between that dreary place and what corresponds with the 'upper air' of myth" (116). Such ominous signs increasingly dominate the world stage in our day.

Yet at the core of all these works is the hope that instead of isolation and social dissolution people will choose rich, participated lives, deepened by a fuller understanding of consciousness and its journey, and empowered by pioneering mythopoeic productions such as those of Owen Barfield and his literary friends. Hunter and Kranidas declare: "Barfield's intellectual vision spans the intellectual vision of the twentieth century, including its darkest corners. But the hope of the saving remnant illuminates all of his portrayals of the human condition" (13). Indeed, here within these long-sought works is mythopoeic power in full measure, a rich exploration of Barfield's life and thought, and incomparable examples of the agents of expansion, that "felt change of consciousness," that poetry can be.

NOTES

1. John C. Ulreich, Jr., "Afterword," in Owen Barfield, *Orpheus: A Poetic Drama*, ed. John C. Ulreich, Jr. (West Stockbridge, MA: The Lindisfarne Press, 1983), 117. Further citations of this work are given in the text.

2. Owen Barfield, "Foreword," in Owen Barfield, *Orpheus: A Poetic Drama*, ed. John C. Ulreich, Jr. (West Stockbridge, MA: The Lindisfarne Press, 1983), 7. Further citations of this work are given in the text.

3. Owen Barfield, "Program Note for the Original Production," in Owen Barfield, *Orpheus: A Poetic Drama*, ed. John C. Ulreich, Jr. (West Stockbridge, MA: The Lindisfarne Press, 1983), 116. Further citations of this work are given in the text.

4. Simon Blaxland-de Lange, *Owen Barfield: Romanticism Come of Age: A Biography* (Forest Row, UK: Temple Lodge Publishing, 2006), 262. Further citations of this work are given in the text.

5. Barfield, "Program Note," 113.

6. Barfield, *Orpheus*: "Note By C. S. Lewis" is given on the back cover.

7. Owen Barfield, *This Ever Diverse Pair* (Oxford: Barfield Press, 2010), xviii. Originally published in 1950, the 2010 Barfield Press edition of this novel includes the original Foreword by Walter de la Mare, one of Barfield's favorite poets, and a new Introduction by Frederick Dennehy which includes this quotation from Sugerman's volume. See also, Shirley Sugerman, ed. *Evolution of Consciousness: Studies in Polarity* (Middletown, CT: Wesleyan University Press, 1975), 21.

8. Owen Barfield, *Owen Barfield on C. S. Lewis*, ed. G. B. Tennyson (Middletown, CT: Wesleyan University Press, 1989), 22.

9. Donna Potts, *Nemerov and Objective Realism: The Influence of Owen Barfield* (Columbia, MO: University of Missouri Press, 1994), 1.

10. Jeanne Clayton Hunter and Thomas Kranidas, "Introduction," in Owen Barfield, *A Barfield Sampler*, ed. Jeanne Clayton Hunter and Thomas Kranidas, (Albany: State University of New York Press, 1993), 12. Further citations of this work are given in the text.

11. Owen Barfield, "Poetic Licence," 12. References to "Poetic Licence" are to a twenty-page typescript in the Bodleian archive (Dep. c. 1155), which includes page numbers and is dated 1979.

Further citations of this work are given in the text. The Bodleian archive also contains the original manuscript in a blue exercise book from 1949 (Dep. c. 1116) and an orange exercise book (Dep. c. 1139) from Barfield's revival of the essay for presentation in 1979.

12. The Bodleian archive for *Medea* (Dep. c. 1097) includes an early draft of the play, a typescript with corrections, the BBC rejection letter, and the two letters from Martin Moynihan.

Introduction to *The Tower*

Owen Barfield's extended narrative poem *The Tower* exists as fifty-eight type-written pages in the Owen Barfield archive in the Bodleian library, Oxford, Shelfmark: Dep. c. 1102. Comprised of 1341lines, the poem is divided into thirteen sections covering the intellectual and spiritual development of the protagonist who experiences childhood revelries, the violence of war, love, heartache, and enlightenment. The poem serves as a poetic expression of the foundations of Barfield's philosophy, and within it one recognizes the thinking that informs his great early works, namely *History in English Words* and *Poetic Diction*. Despite the literary and philosophical significance of the poem, it has been largely unknown and unstudied to this point. Lingering clues to the poem's existence have come down to us through the eventual publications of C. S. Lewis's early diary, *All My Road before Me*, and the Barfield-Lewis correspondence in the third volume of Lewis's *Collected Letters*. The earlier sources indicate that Lewis was initially an encouraging reader and responder to Barfield's poem, though his later critique of the poem is more tempered. After considering the development of the poem based on the textual evidence provided by Lewis, we examine the significance of the poem in light of Barfield's developing philosophy on the evolution of consciousness.

I

Much of what we understand about the development of *The Tower* is due to what Lewis recorded in his journal and through letters. The first reference to Lewis's knowledge of an early partial draft of *The Tower* appears in a diary entry from June of 1922. Lewis reacts favorably, but also compares *The Tower* to Browning's *Sordello*, one of the more obscure poems composed in English. It seems there was a lapse in Barfield's composition of the poem; no mention occurs again until letters from Lewis to Barfield in 1926 and 1927. In the 1927 letter, Lewis refers to "a rather serious break between the two periods of composition."[1] This and other clues in the Lewis materials help us understand the development and evolution of this remarkable poem.

In his diary entry from Wednesday 21 June 1922, Lewis writes:

> After tea he [Harwood] brought out Barfield's 'Tower' and some new pieces of his own, while I gave him the new Canto of 'Dymer' to read. The 'Tower' is full of magnificent material and never a dead phrase: the new part strong and savage—'Big Bannister' is splendid—but very hazy at present. The story is (to me) as hard to follow as *Sordello*. But what genius! The metre *too* eccentric for me, but on that subject Barfield has probably forgotten more than I ever knew.[2]

From this excerpt it is apparent that the "Bannister" episode of the poem—Section II of our current version—was already composed by this date. We also realize from the phrase "the new part" that Lewis was probably already familiar with Barfield's poem. It is also significant to see Cecil Harwood as an early reader—this poem is not secret meanderings, but a bold venture known to Barfield's close friends.

The next reference to *The Tower* occurs more than four years later in a letter from Lewis to Barfield dated October 1926. The "break between the two periods of composition," referred to by Lewis in 1927, most likely occurred sometime between 1922 and 1926, and a great deal had occurred in Barfield's life between these two dates. In 1923, Barfield married Maud Douie and joined the Anthroposophical Society. In 1925, he published *The Silver Trumpet*. His first philosophical work, *History in English Words,* followed in 1926.

Lewis's 1926 letter contains his most extensive critique of *The Tower*, and it seems that for the first time Lewis is responding to a complete version of the poem. It is clear from remarks in the opening of this letter that it is meant to replace an original letter that went missing. Lewis jokingly begins: "How tiresome about the letter. I had trusted to acquire fame by it" (1505). He continues by lavishing praise on the poem:

> The chief points were: (a.) . . . That this is, so far, a great poem—in the unequivocal sense—the sense which those words ordinarily bear in literary criticism. It challenges comparison with the Prelude, and keeps its end up. I think spiritually it is not as high as the Prelude (it does not cover so large nor so momentous an experience): on the other hand it is more consistently poeti-

cal. . . . I have no doubt at all that you are engaged in writing one of the really great poems of the world. (1505)

What follows in this letter is a critique of what Lewis both admired and found wanting in the 1926 version of *The Tower*. The current version of the poem in the Bodleian archive is a later version, for revisions have occurred, many based on Lewis's critique.

Lewis's comparison of *The Tower* with Wordsworth's *The Prelude* is apt. If his comparison of the early sections of the poem to *Sordello* suggests difficulty of comprehension, his comparison with *The Prelude* emphasizes the overall movement of the poem—the development of a consciousness by tracing its experiences and influences. A significant difference between Wordsworth's poem and Barfield's, however, is the perspective of the narrator. Wordsworth composes *The Prelude* in first person, and Barfield composes *The Tower* in an extremely interior third person. Lewis writes in his 1926 letter: "You have contrived to keep all the time within the labyrinthine fidgety world of the inner mind, and yet not lost the soaring, winged *movement*—the *cantabile*, as of Milton or Marlowe" (1505-6). Like Wordsworth, Barfield follows a chronological development of the protagonist and divides *The Tower* into thirteen sections, the same number as the 13 books of the 1805 *Prelude*.

Despite the praise heaped on *The Tower* in his 1926 letter and the apt comparison with *The Prelude*, Lewis is quite direct about what he does not like in the 1926 version of the poem. He states, "two parts as a whole seem inferior" (1506), and proceeds to argue his criticisms of the original opening section and the British Museum Reading Room section. Based on Lewis's discussion and the current version of the poem, we come to realize that Barfield gave Lewis's critique definite weight and revised accordingly. The most extensive revision seems to be a reworking of the opening section. Lewis writes:

> I can't feel you have entirely solved the problem of dealing with emotions at once primitive and reticent without being mawkish. Need the man think of his child (whether born or unborn) primarily as 'my image'? Again it opens with a picture—the sky etc. Pictures (I mean the more completely picturable kind of image) are not really your long suit: and this, with its aureole etc. remains to me literary and uninteresting. . . . I should advice a complete breaking up and rewriting of this section with the powers you now have. (1506)

INTRODUCTION TO *THE TOWER*

It is apparent from the current version of the poem that Barfield reworked the original opening by moving it to Section VIII of the poem and presenting it as "A memory" recorded by the protagonist's expectant mother of an evening in the countryside with her companion. The opening of "the memory" preserves the "picture" Lewis critiqued and the reference to the "aureole":

> *The luminous twilight melted into gold,*
> *A clear unruffled lake of gold, that glowed*
> *Behind the hill's low line, and darkened it,*
> *As the serene brow of a saint is darkened*
> *Under the brightness of his aureole* (8.12-16)

"The memory" of that evening also preserves the father's consciousness of the developing child:

> *Did he not know one thing, and, knowing it,*
> *Whisper within himself again, again,*
> *Marvelling softly;—"Even this moment she*
> *Is fashioning my image in her womb—*
> *Even this moment . . ." till he could not think*
> *Of any other thing, nor speak of this?* (8.29-34)

As the original opening is moved to Section VIII, the new opening of the entire poem is quite reminiscent of *The Prelude* and situates the protagonist in childhood, entering a revelry that stretches "back to the baby mists" (1.20):

> Along a footway through a dreaming field
> A boy went loitering slowly. Since midday
> The golden afternoon had hung about him,
> Like a great, sunlit dewdrop gathering
> To fall from a leaf's point; till all that weight
> Dazzled and lulled his mind; and a faint smell,
> Confused, of hawthorn and of little flowers
> Drowsing about the hedgerow, clothed his body
> And drew a warm veil over all his thought,
> With on the veil traced half obliterate
> The pattern of some far forgotten day
> In childhood, when the smell, unmarked, had been
> Caught in his nostrils and deep in his breast

> Imprinted for all lifetime secretly.   (1.1-14)

It is unclear whether this new opening was included in the 1926 version of the poem and simply moved to a new position of prominence, or if this new opening was more recently composed, perhaps to strengthen resonance with *The Prelude*.

The second section with which Lewis found particular fault is Section XI in our current version, what Lewis refers to as the protagonist's "enlightenment in the reading room of the B.M. [British Museum]" (1506). Lewis writes:

> The first paragraph about there being no Eureka cry but 'Sun Turns himself over' is excellent. So is the third about the man who 'moves about within the quiddity of light and sees Seeing itself, and that our eyes are veils Not windows'. But just in between those the thing itself has to come—and it doesn't. The old and not v. profound image of the light in a dark cave is inadequate. You see, the discovery that consciousness is a voyage of exploration, on the purely logical level, needn't lead to any spiritual consequences at all. (1506)

Barfield's solution to this critique seems to have been to delete the second paragraph, as the "quiddity of light" (11.32) quote from above is now a part of the new second paragraph, not paragraph three. It is doubtful, however, that he revised his emphasis on the spiritual significance of this enlightenment, and it is likely that what he is recording in this event resonates with the understandings he had gained on the nature of language and the evolution of consciousness. Barfield describes the protagonist's newly acquired insights, and the following urgent injunction is a postmodern call to comprehend both the inheritance of meaning and its continual change:

> He saw for ever—as when forked lightning
> Shatters the secret night, the flash is vanished,
> But not the bright map in the shepherd's brain
> Of rocks and trees and shapes of hills and sheep—
> That he whose soul would touch the very past
> Must build himself a delicate consciousness
> Out of the dreams of old civilisations,
> Must see with ancient eyes, not wisely peer
> Through glasses of the last half-hundred years;

> And that whose soul would truly touch the present,
> Must first have touched the past; how Truth's a stream
> That hurries on through complicated webs
> Of thought, which meanings of words, ever changing,
> Keep letting down into it for a moment,
> Till the weak webs are torn away and whirled
> On with the rushing torrent.   (11.44-59)

The spirituality of consciousness is boldly declaimed in imagery sharp and powerful, a palpable flash of revelation from "forked lightning" and the "bright map" of the world revealed in the "shepherd's brain."

Lewis's third and final critique of *The Tower* is contained in a letter to Barfield from 10 Sept. 1927. We know from comparing Lewis's 1926 letter to the current version of the poem that Barfield made some substantial revisions to the poem. It seems likely Lewis in 1927 was responding to a version of the poem very similar to the current version in the Bodleian Library and that Barfield made few revisions after that date. Of Lewis's three extant responses to the poem, the 1927 letter is by far the least complimentary:

> I have finished a first re-reading of the *Tower*. The great passages—VI, VII, X—stand absolutely where they did. The later cantos I have enjoyed much more than I did before: but of course this is chiefly due to my increased understanding of and sympathy with the matter.
>
> As to the poem as a whole, I am afraid I feel now a rather serious break between the two periods of composition. . . . I don't know how far you are thinking of ever working on it again. If you do, I shd. (reluctantly) chuck II, III and IV right out. V and the *danceable duet* wd. have to be saved: but I shd. like the *bristles of mechanic thought* etc. to come after the love-tragedy. (1508)

Lewis's response is rather surprising when one considers that Section II, the Big Bannister episode, was enthusiastically received five years earlier. This suggestion, to "chuck" sections II, III and IV, seems to be guided by what Lewis saw as a "rather serious break between the two periods of composition" (1508). The critique is rather reductive, and few criteria are provided for his recommendations. One possibility for this change in enthusiasm might be that by this date Barfield and Lewis were entering a more intense period of their ongoing debate characterized as the "Great War."

At this point Barfield seems to have set the project aside, and it is likely that no further serious revisions were made. There is no evidence that Barfield ever sent *The Tower* to a publisher, nor does it seem to have been circulated beyond a few close friends. The publication of more formal projects developing Barfield's ideas about language and consciousness seem to have taken precedence: *History in English Words* had been published in 1926, and a revision of his B. Litt. thesis, *Poetic Diction*, would follow in 1928.

II

A sensitive reading reveals that *The Tower* serves as a poetic expression of Barfield's emerging philosophy on the evolution of consciousness. It captures in poetry what Barfield expresses about the nature of consciousness in his early prose works and beyond, for we find in *The Tower* not only the significance of words but also the significance of the physical representations which surround us, both natural and constructed. The tower is an image which occurs throughout the poem—the "old stone tower" of a little town that the protagonist encounters as a soldier (3.14), the "Square and un-English, squat and solid" tower the injured protagonist spies from the ambulance (4.75), the tower recorded in his mother's Memory which "became / A filmy drapery of stone that hung, / Having no weight, from nothing in the sky" (8.53-55). In the final section of the poem, through simile the tower becomes a representation of the macrocosmos / microcosmos dynamic polarity that informs much of Barfield's philosophy:

> For, as the Tower uprose out of its floor
> Into the light, and into the still light
> Outgrowing from the Sun—scattering forth
> The din of its high bells, gold into gold,
> So seemed his breath to rise from his round lungs,
> As from a lesser Earth, until it lost
> Itself in a vast heaven of still thought,
> Whereinto brain poured out the forms it drew
> From the dark air beneath it—sounding forth
> Resonant, yet unheard.   (13.52-61)

The image of the tower is a unifying motif in the poem, but there are many other poetic devices that Barfield uses to create meaning and provide a narrative frame. A chronological overview of the sections of the poem provides insight into the poem's development. The first fourteen lines of the revised version of the poem's opening are quoted above. Barfield devotes 150 lines total to developing this opening section of childhood revelries and frames the interior journey within the boy's loitering along a footway on a golden afternoon (1.1-3). There is a pause to the boy's physical wanderings (1.20-22), but the interior wanderings continue "Back to the mists" (1.29). As the boy reflects on his earliest realizations of awareness, the emphasis is on the five senses: "No self at all, but only a loose bundle / Of senses five, absorbing open-eyed / And open-mouthed, dim tidings of a world:" (1.26-28). Barfield beautifully develops this section of the poem, capturing fleeting narratives through memories of sensations: the mysterious smell of a sickroom (1.57); the sound of "a simple melody / So old that it was sad" (1.77-78); the sight of "Beautiful images, lingering like rich arras" (1.84). The boy's afternoon revelry will cover the foundational experiences and years of his development. The last four lines of the section complete the narrative frame with the boy arising to continue his walk:

> The restlessness was on him now; he rose,
> And went, stirring the breathless afternoon
> In fumes about him, like a man who dives
> And breaks the surface of a warm, rich pool. (1.147-50)

The effect signals the intended narrative structure of discrete tableaux that interconnect by building a life among them.

Section II of the poem, Big Bannister, was enthusiastically praised by Lewis in his 1922 diary entry; however, in his 1927 letter, Lewis recommended Barfield "(reluctantly) chuck" this section along with Sections III and IV. Undoubtedly, Bannister is a unique section in the composition of the poem. It is the only section in the entire poem that actually names a character, and perhaps no other character is so concretely materialized as Big Bannister. This section is also unique in terms of narrative voice. As mentioned above, most of the poem is composed in an extremely interior third person. In the Big Bannister section, the narrative voice often steps back from interiority. This is initially seen in the opening lines: "When men are thrown together, cut apart / From women's faces and fine influence, / Their souls rush off, like ants, on different paths" (2.1-3). The narrative voice continues to develop the argument by a description of what "some" do in this situation:

> Some grow more active, some more obstinate,
> Some scarcely can keep back the mawkish tears,
> And some pop out bright heads from cynic tubs
> And nod to the four quarters with a wink.
> Some—with a gesture—woo dear beastliness,   (2.4-8)

This opening serves as a fitting prelude to the character of Big Bannister:

> Big Bannister, the soft-faced Irishman,
> Who wenched and wenched, and felt himself a man
> By talking *sotto voce* with big eyes
> About his women and their secret clothes,
> Has slid into the room;   (2.24-28)

What ensues is an unexpected confrontation between the protagonist and Bannister, for "Tonight the boy / Chances to be too tired to play up" (2.40-41). The narrative voice has set the scene; the interiority of the protagonist has been delayed.

The consciousness of the protagonist is revealed through the senses in the first section of the poem, but in the Big Bannister section there is a shift to consciousness constructed through metaphysics / philosophy. The term "truth" occurs three times in this section. The first is in reference to those "who woo beastliness," (2.8) and "shout that they alone / Are seeing the world very clearly, swimming / Naked the waters of cold Truth" (2.10-12). The second reference to truth is in the context of the unexpected argument. The boy, "too tired to play up" (2.41), "[a]nswers very gravely with the truth" (2.46). This confrontation leads to an epiphany, for "He now in eyes / Of every man saw more than he could tell / Even to himself" (2.63-65), and he perceives "Heart stumbling after heart, the while men spoke / Out of their knowledge and their pain the truth" (2.69-70). The protagonist comes to meanings and consciousness constructed through interactions with others. By the end of this section, he transitions to manhood:

> He was a working, playing, grumbling man,
> A sleeper through the night, a lover of laughter,
> Sweet comfortable laughter that transforms
> Demons to bogeys and long grief to folly.   (2.93-96)

This closing section foreshadows that the "comfortable" existence will not continue: "And so for many months he travelled on, / And so he might have travelled to the grave" (2.97-98).

Section III is one of the briefest in the poem, composed of thirty-four lines. Despite its brevity, these lines significantly advance the narrative and thematic meaning of the poem. Capturing the pause of a group of soldiers marching through a "little town" in the moonlight (3.1), this section contains the first representation of a tower in the poem, "Fairy beneath the moon, an old stone tower / Framed in the archway;" (3.14-15). Barfield subtly identifies the protagonist as one of this group by connecting Section I of the poem with the interior thoughts of the soldier during this pause:

> But there between those chimings of the bells,
> Somewhere in the quietness of that street,
> Where it flowed most adream, the stream of Thought
> Bubbled, and beauty suddenly built her bridge,
> Her rainbow archway cantilevered upon
> Gossamer bastions . . . A day in fields,
> Clear with whole sunlit reverie, and tonight
> Sprang together behind a soldier's face.   (3.26-33)

The "stream of thought" flows until "beauty" triggers consciousness, building the "rainbow archway" of forgetive figuration with memory at the foundation.

Section IV advances the narrative arc of the poem: the soldier has been injured and is traveling some distance in an ambulance. Before focusing on the interior experiences of the protagonist, the narrative approaches from an exterior perspective:

> From his machine
> An airman spied that road—on it a van
> Ran like a small ball rolling down a groove,
> Hurrying westward.   (4.5-8)

From that point, the narrative focus switches to the protagonist:

> It was dusk inside,
> And there was smell of petrol and burnt oil
> In the nostrils of a dozing soldier
> Exempt from pain and terror—not from woe.

> The shattered limb had ceased to ache—not yet
> The shattered spirit.   (4.8-13)

The interiority focuses on memories related to bodily pain, both witnessed and experienced by the protagonist. The narrative's return to immediacy captures the moment in which the protagonist spies a tower from his ambulance window, "Square and un-English, squat and solid, and yet / Beautiful with its northern symmetry," (4.75-76). This sighting is enough to rouse the soldier to sharper thoughts of both gratitude and despair, elucidated by the interior narrative voice.

Section V opens with a narrative tag situating the protagonist in post-war recovery: "Summer and health returned: remembered war / Was not yet deep enough sunk in his being / To canker every dream" (5.1-3). In his 1927 letter, Lewis refers to section V as the first section he would retain after the opening section ("I shd. (reluctantly) chuck II, III and IV right out"). Section V continues to develop the idea of a dual nature in the protagonist, concluding with an image of dual towers: "one slender tower / Whose grace had moved so many loving hearts" (5.128-29) and "the old tower / Looked all awry and stockish" (5.144-45). The dualism of the protagonist results from the development of a higher consciousness (the "slender tower") that exists somewhat in tandem with the more mundane consciousness (the "old tower"). In this highly interior third person narrative voice we see the emerging duality of consciousness familiar from Barfield's philosophical writings:

> Ay, for now this man
> Began to be not one sole soul but two
> . . . .
> At night, if by the end he had succeeded
> In taming down his mind to be receptive,
> Wide-eyed with bodily fatigue, he grew
> Aware as of a faintly singing cloud
> Enveloping his head: and, wearily
> Closing his volume, would feel in his blood
> The pressure of unwritten poetry
> Knocking: "I can all things!" No imagery
> Formed in his mind, no thoughts; and yet it seemed
> His essence and the essence of the world
> Flowed, and that if he could maintain the mood
> Long enough time, the brain must of itself

> Construct new metaphors, and move the world
> To tears and wonder with its terrible art. (5.45-46; 53-66)

Comprehending the interpenetrated polarity of self and world opens the path to the forgetive art of metaphor. Yet, upon waking the protagonist dismisses those "reveries" and "dreams" (5.69) and insists upon a more positivist outlook: "he who knew / That fire burns or seven and two are nine— / This was the real 'I'" (5.72-74).

Yet the power of the polarity grows apace, for Section VI presents the "new metaphor" of the sunrise paralleling the protagonist's interior feelings of discovering love.

> Slowly the glimmering Eastern sky inserts
> The watcher in his visible universe
> With right or left, North, South, until more light
> Discovers cloud and rock and blade of grass
> Distinct, and gives, like love, to everything
> Colour and self. (6.5-10)

As the rising sun allows us to discern the world around us, so too does love. The next paragraph provides a narrative tag, "She sits—she sits beside him—hush!—speak not!— / Think not!—this is the sunrise of a life" (6.28-29), which situates the protagonist as experiencing "a sunrise" of love. Yet, in closing this section Barfield presents the antithesis of this experience—one can fall out of love as well as fall in—personal passion can die:

> and he is on the threshold,
> Threshold of Heaven on earth—but falling out,
> Not climbing in. From now seek earth on earth,
> Heaven in Heaven—wisdom which men learn
> Only by pain and death, the cruel death
> Of personal passion, which, like some low creature
> Whose hideous vitality kicks in spasms
> After the back is broken, shall long years
> After thou deem'st it crushed and starved to death,
> Raise up its beauteous head and bite the soul
> With awful desolations, bitter thoughts
> Of wasted life and of no happiness. (6.48-59)

There is a sort of "wisdom" that is learned from the experience but also regret, for the infection of positivism pulls one into bitter pragmatics and relegates divinity and beauty beyond a threshold deemed uncrossable by the empirical focus of the day.

Section VII follows, but distantly, the protagonist in the aftermath, "What use to follow him through that blind walk / Of pain, incessant pain" (7.4-5). The narrative voice presents the image of "a dark tunnel's mouth" (7.2) but later questions if a more appropriate metaphor would be "a cave / Exitless, damp, where he has left the light / Of day for ever" (7.15-17). Employing the same structure as the preceding section, Barfield opens the second paragraph with a narrative tag, "Behold him, then, on a hot day in June / Wheeling a road through meadows high with flowers / Absorbed in his great misery" (7.24-26). This day seems to echo the opening of the poem when the protagonist, as a boy, "through a dreaming field . . . went loitering slowly" (1.1-2), for nature once again seems to provide comfort and a "sudden sweet solution of all strain" (7.27). The narrative voice then shifts to a dream in which the protagonist experiences the "springing Tower" becoming "A filmy drapery of stone that hung, / Having no weight, from nothing in the sky" (7.49-50). At this point in the poem, Barfield bridges the image of the Tower to the understandings about language that the protagonist will achieve in the reading room of the British Library (discussed above), for within the dream of the Tower, "the rich golden silence . . . conceived / And grew big-bellied with terrific meaning / And the whole dream resounded as with words" (7.53-56). The protagonist cannot yet hear these words, which causes anxiety, and this section ends with the crippling couplet: "Often day smashed the link which night had forged / Betwixt the sick heart and the dungeoned brain" (7.65-66).

As mentioned above, based on the 1926 letter from Lewis, Section VIII seems to have been the original opening of the poem. Barfield composed an eleven-line introduction to the mother's memory before setting the text of the memory apart with quotation marks before every line; we have instead used italics to set off this part. This section captures the interiority of both parents yet focuses more on the mother's experiences both in perceiving the tower and becoming aware of the conscious being developing in her womb. Interestingly, Barfield borrows lines from Section VII to describe the mother's vision of the tower:

> *Out of the green turf of a hill, beyond*
> *The quiet valley, there uprose a tower—*

> *Four slender walls, which, rising from the ground*
> *In straight austerity, far, far above*
> *Burst into pinnacles innumerable,*
> *That seemed to float on air; the mellow light*
> *Softened the stone and entered into it,*
> *And slowly spread a change over the tower,*
> *Making its corners faint against the blue,*
> *Till it began to dream, till it became*
> *A filmy drapery of stone that hung,*
> *Having no weight, from nothing in the sky.* (8.44-55)

The purpose of this repetition may be to strengthen the conscious link between the protagonist and his mother. Soon after the mother's vision of the Tower she is "startled" (8.75) by a "sweet chime" (8.62) which results in wonder and awareness of another consciousness:

> *A wonder that died not, but slowly grew,*
> *Opening its noiseless petals—mingled all*
> *With the strange dawning of a tenderness*
> *Beyond all wonder, which enclasped her heart*
> *With curious tiny fingers. Now she felt,*
> *For the first time, that they were not alone,*
> *And love came, like a great sob, suddenly,*
> *Whispering "Mother!"—but she could not speak . . .* (8.81-88)

The protagonist is so touched by this account that it seems "to become a memory of his own" (8.11).

Section IX, the shortest section at only twenty-seven lines, traces the protagonist's development from awe to darkness. For days the protagonist basks in the joy of discovering his mother's account: "loveliest memories / Hovered around him, and a sense of awe— / Of dim connections not yet understood / Betwixt all human beings" (9.3-6). Yet, even this gives way to an ultra-positivism (i.e., "darkness") that creeps back in to dominate his consciousness: "And all the mystery were dissolved to matter / In the blind workings of his mother's womb" (9.12-13). In such a frame of mind he recasts the Tower as a "romantic vision" which "had buttressed / His peace of mind with mystic-selfish hopes" (9.17-18). Thus, he descends into a positivist mindset:

> *The fairy gold, its magic dream-light dear,*
> *Shrivelled into a litter of dead leaves.*

> Yet, like a prisoner shovelling dead leaves,
> For want of barren tasks, in idleness,
> He went on piling intellectual knowledge
> On intellectual knowledge, fitting fact
> To theory, adding dead thought to dead thought. (9.21-27)

Section X, one of the longest sections of the poem, is also one of the darkest. Barfield employs metaphor and simile brilliantly in this section to convey the protagonist's contracting consciousness. He begins with the image of a house situated in a valley so narrow that sunlight is perceivable for only a few hours each day. This image gives way to a simile comparing spectral companions to "sweet imaginations":

> Even as the Haunted Sailor's ghastly mates,
> Those sweet imaginations of soul-life
> Without himself in Nature—one by one,
> Unmasked by reason, they stood forth revealed
> As ghostly emanations from himself,
> Then dropped dead. (10.38-43)

The resonance with the Old English poem known as *The Wanderer* is palpable, and the desired effect is similar, to describe an appalling isolation and the confusion of lonely figuration. Another similar tableau follows—that of a delirious mountain traveler who believes he has found refuge from a storm only to have his comfortable dwelling fade and find himself "sitting upon a damp stone" (10.61). Darkness grows and "every star / By which until that moment he had steered / His moral course, was blotted" (10.132-34). But within this void, he becomes aware of "an impersonal Force; it was alive, / Solid" (10.139-40). He sleeps and awakes to "a curious calmness in the air," (10.150). Joy does not yet return, but the darkness has been lifted.

Section XI was discussed above in relation to Lewis's negative response to the early paragraphs of this section in his 1926 letter. As mentioned above, Section XI records the understandings Barfield had gained on the nature of language and the evolution of consciousness and places these understandings in a narrative scene similar to the research he was conducting for his philosophical works *Poetic Diction* and *History in English Words*:

> One day, in intimate study of the past
> When his imagination was all steeped, and dreaming

> Its way along those mazy paths of thought
> Which open from contemplating the growth
> Into their present seeming-simple meaning
> Of smallest, commonest words, a blind thing stirred
> Deep in the core of inexpressive mind.   (11.1-7)

The narrative frame places the protagonist in the Reading Room of the British Library—"Under a grey dome / Inscribed with echoes of the past, the names / Of poets dead" (11.39-41)—to present poetically the beautifully realized expressions of the evolution of consciousness quoted above. Leaving the Reading Room, the protagonist faces the onslaught—"The voluble angry chattering of ten thousand / Small, fussy starlings" (11.90-91)—along with the "thousand faces" (11.93) of humanity with "nowhere-looking eyes" (11.95). The onslaught leaves him "Beholding the world only with his eyes, / Crushed by its weight and passion" (11.105-6) until the next week when his assumed return to the Reading Room would usher in "once more imagination— / Like some huge half-fledged bird . . ." (11.109-10). Eventually he becomes stronger and even when "The books are closed," (11.115) the mind goes on "of its own weight" (11.116). Section XI concludes with the strongest poetical representation of the evolution of consciousness thus far in the poem:

> He sees the sharp horizon
> Of man's sense-knowledge suddenly flung out
> All ways to limitless distance—and he feels
> In his own self the future self of Man
> Stirring, awaking, grasping at consciousness
> Of Life, which since creation has been flowing
> Through and through the body unawares,
> Asleep—and asleep—till at a sign
> The sweet, the long long stored Promethean hour—
> Oh, wondering adolescence of the world!—
> Brings in self-knowledge with a rush, and calls it
> To blossom from blind Being into Truth.   (11.126-37)

Section XII is essentially a pause in the narrative frame focusing on the interior philosophical musings of the protagonist. As his consciousness begins to expand, he gains an appreciation for those who had worked along these lines before and "the sad spirits who abandoned faith" (12.46). He also solidifies the emerging understanding that positivism is a hindrance to truth, for though it categorizes and codifies useful knowledge, it cannot represent the truth embodied in life and consciousness:

> For this neat abacus, which put up for truth,
> Was but the husks of dead truths strung together
> By a mechanic joiner: knowledge is not,
> Until it is the thing it knoweth; knowledge
> Is Life incarnating in consciousness. (12.67-71)

This section concludes with a link to Section V in which the narrator, after the war but before love, "would feel in his blood / The pressure of unwritten poetry" (5.58-59). This line is repeated to begin the last part of Section XII.

> The pressure of unwritten poetry
> Which had so furiously knocked at his blood,
> Sitting alone once by the fireside, now
> Dies into tranquil tremors of the spirit
> And ripples into pure joy; for this man,
> Even this man, has spoken face to face
> With the eternal Muse—and ever more,
> Save in the puny hours, it must be
> Matter of accident if himself or other
> Be chosen to indite. He has found peace. (12.72-81)

The conclusion of Section XII—the protagonist at peace—sets the stage for the culmination of the entire poem, for Section XIII begins in linked repetition, "He has found peace" (13.1), serving as the kernel of all before and all after—not a circle closing, but more like the neck of an hourglass. Interestingly, the protagonist first considers the idea of "accident" in relationship to the philosophical concept of necessity: "for he has seen / How the long wisdom of the living spirit / *Uses* its accident—the vine's green tendril / Accepts the loose brick and the rusty nail" (13.4-7). Aristotle's ontology of "accident" is reframed as a having a role in the "essential" rather than spurious to it, for the empirical catalog of being is reframed as the narrative of consciousness becoming. Along these musings, Barfield records the protagonist's voice, pronouncing an anthem of sorts:

> "Henceforth I take
> All that is granted thus and thus, with thanks,
> With reverence, yet not less as mine own right

For use and growth and knowledge—even I,
This whorl of nebulous thinking, whose moist arms
Nodded in circles blindly, till they touched
The Tower, and sucked and gripped and climbed—"
                                    Marvel! (13.14-20)

Prior to this reference above, "the Tower" has not been referred to since Section X, line 114. Five more references will occur in Section XIII, for this is the arch metaphor linking the protagonist's new consciousness to the steps of consciousness that he has built throughout his life. The Tower becomes the metaphor by which he is able to see: "The strong dream of the Tower / Is but a stone into the pool of Life, / Amplifying its ripples" (13.41-43), and also the crux of the macrocosm/microcosm metaphor discussed above: "For, as the Tower uprose out of its floor / Into the light . . . / So seemed his breath to rise from his round lungs" (13.52-53, 56).

This tension of polarity and threshold is finally explored in the relationship among the Tower and "earth" and "sky," for as humanity is "one with earth and sky, being between" (13.63), so is the Tower "Now earth, now sky—by turns" (13.76):

> There is a mystery of this being between
> Hard to be solved by man, who is himself
> That Being. Thus, the light on the grey Tower,
> Which melted earth and sky to a round pearl
> Of peace and summer stillness and calm joy,
> Was rare upon it: at all other times
> It shot bewilderingly, now bright, now dull,
> Now starting solid from the dull dry glare,
> Part of the earth, under the arch of the sky,
> Now mingling in the mist, its fainting corners
> Streaming out into rain, as though the stones
> Were an unreal streak of the soft air:
> Now earth, now sky—by turns—how rarely both! (13.64-76)

C. S. Lewis's youthful ambition for this "truly great" poem is understandable, and Owen Barfield's efforts with it formidable and traceable. The poetry is consistently good, at times remarkably so, and the philosophy of poetics pronounced and revealed by this work is easily recognizable as Barfield at his best, the kernel and scope of his life-long program revealed with ease, passion, and poetic genius. This forgotten work is a true gem—a unique and pleasurable version of Barfield's great mind easily familiar to the scholar of his work and a lovely exploration of being for any who enjoy the forgetive power of good poetry.

Notes

1. C. S. Lewis, *The Collected Letters of C. S. Lewis, Volume III: Narnia, Cambridge, and Joy 1950-1963*, ed. Walter Hooper. (San Francisco: HarperSanFrancisco, 2007), 1508. Further citations of this work are given in the text.

2. C. S. Lewis, *All My Road Before Me: The Diary of C. S. Lewis 1922-1927*, ed. Walter Hooper. (London: Harcourt Brace Jovanovich, 1991), 52-3. Further citations of this work are given in the text. Note: The Foreword to this volume is by Owen Barfield.

THE TOWER

I

    Along a footway through a dreaming field
A boy went loitering slowly. Since midday
The golden afternoon had hung about him,
Like a great, sunlit dewdrop gathering
To fall from a leaf's point; till all that weight
Dazzled and lulled his mind; and a faint smell,
Confused, of hawthorn and of little flowers
Drowsing about the hedgerow, clothed his body
And drew a warm veil over all his thought,
With on the veil traced half obliterate   10
The pattern of some far forgotten day
In childhood, when the smell, unmarked, had been
Caught in his nostrils and deep in his breast
Imprinted for all lifetime secretly.
Therefrom his mind, smooth traveller, stole away,
Rocking the cradle of old memories
And stooping softly over them with low
And private croonings, while it wandered up
The slowly narrowing path of years that stretched
Back to the baby mists.
                      He scarcely knew   20
When he had ceased to move and lain himself
In the long, warm, unwavering grasses down
    For now already he had reached those mists
And entered, groping, there, where loomed no ghost
To be remembered, saying: 'This was I'—
No self at all, but only a loose bundle
Of senses five, absorbing open-eyed
And open-mouthed, dim tidings of a world:
Back to the mists: deeper: his peering mind

Felt the quick touch of flitting shapes, but saw
No light at all: deeper: and all was still.
Wherefore lost memory turned, to seek some light,
Back down the years. Gleamed suddenly the sharp
Glimpse of a moment, when from game to game
Hurrying through an empty room one night
Breathless and eager-eyed with romping joy,
It chanced that he had looked, scarce knowing yet
What thing a mirror was, into a mirror
And seen a face, his own, give back to him
A stranger's smile first, then a stranger's frown,
And seen an eye, whose depths he could not plumb,
A stranger's eye, which drew his steady gaze;
Then, as he looked, grew larger and more strange,
Till he saw nothing else, but was alone
Drowned in its ocean silence: long he stood
With the first infant stammerings of his mind
Trying: 'myself'—but could not understand.

    Now this gleam died, and larger diffused lights
Shone through the gloaming of his memory
With the faint colours of whole months, whole years
Textures of time, whose many-coloured threads,
Each hour and minute, faded long ago
Into one hue—cast garments of the soul
That tell her growth.

    Surprised, he found his lips
Had formed themselves to utter the pet name
A nurse had made for him: then all at once
An old, mysterious smell, a sickroom, and
The paper on its wall, and the long cracks
Across the ceiling, how they ran to meet,
Parted, and met again, changing and sliding
Into each other there, above young eyes
Bright with some fever and a-swim with dreams.

    Now a remembered midnight—one of many—
As once again from short oblivion he
Starts into tortured wakefulness, aware
Of solitude and the vast emptiness
Of night; and peering forward rigidly,

Half-raised in bed, stares with wide eyes into
The leering silence, damped with gradual sweat
At watery shapes, the film of his own eyes,   70
That float before them monstrously. Alone
He lives the night, alone, a tiny fly
Caught in the world—young spirit's insect-wings
Buzzing with terror in the pitiless web
Of elemental nothing.
                    But there came,
Blotting all these, a simple melody
So old that it was sad; and in his heart
The quaint remembered cadences of words,
Little blunt verses, musical endings
Of fairy chapters tolled again, and brought   80
Their stories back to him, with all that time
When he had lived among them, half confused
What things were true or false, and what were dreams—
Beautiful images, lingering like rich arras
That hangs on modern walls in tatters, still
Fresh with the clear childhood of a race:
And one (the brightest coloured): how two children
Were out in a wide city, when the snow,
Already fallen, made the dark night blench
And, falling still, caressed them with shy touches,   90
Until they, wandering onward hopelessly,
Came to a Lion figured huge in stone
And entered magically a carven throat
Found red and warm inside, and soft with life—
Then, by mysterious inward climbings, were
High on the narrow plinth that topped the column
Above their Lion, and among chill stars
Sailing the sky in a perilous barque of stone
Steered by a statue. . . . But the years had lent
Interior meaning to those baby pictures,   100
The white snow, the red gorge, the chiselled stone,
And the straight column tapering in the dark.
          And there were family days—old shouting days
Of echoes through the house, and of a ring
Of small, bright evening faces round the lamp,

With father young, with mother young and ready,
Before the crinkled weariness of work
Sharpened her face and tired her laughter out—
Long, secure days. . . . Yet even at this time
Often in some chance loneliness it came,
The sudden moment of stark desolation,
The choking misery, the lorn dismay,
When life slid and the future, stoutly nailed
To hopes of little joys, tugged suddenly
And fell, discovering darkness and a wind
That blew about him in a wilderness
Of thought, sole, groping for a boundary . . .
Till, at last, for relief, a voice would sound
From the heart's well of anguish faltering up,
A final voice, that firmly said 'There are
'Mother and home': and slowly, like a limb,
Through which a warm beam flung from crimson coals
Spreads radiant fingers—he would be comforted.
      Save for black gulfs like these, the unmusical days
Sped levelly along on happiness,
Drab happiness, not warm with ecstasies,
Dead happiness always, and the safe love
Of many creatures ever at his side,
Till love's own stream, forgot, flowed underneath
The surface of his heart—not beautiful
With ripple and rocky laughter in the light,
But asleep—and asleep—when, at a sign,
Stripped of its callous crust of long school years,
The soul stood naked, splendidly abashed,
Trembling beneath spell-binding fragrances
That danced about girl-faces. He had walked,
Dreaming of kisses, amid household mirth—
Alone again, alone among all, friends,
As pale new wraiths of beauty, curling up
Around his loves—shy tendrils choked with shame—
Pitted their new-born feebleness against
Habitual laughter, like rough, kindly hands
Smearing the fragile bloom from lovely things,
Habitual laughter, till imagination,

Barred within doors, incestuously created
For its own use its own desirous dreams.
     The restlessness was on him now; he rose,
And went, stirring the breathless afternoon
In fumes about him, like a man who dives
And breaks the surface of a warm, rich pool.   150

II

    When men are thrown together, cut apart
From women's faces and fine influence,
Their souls rush off, like ants, on different paths;
Some grow more active, some more obstinate,
Some scarcely can keep back the mawkish tears,
And some pop out bright heads from cynic tubs
And nod to the four quarters with a wink.
Some—with a gesture—woo dear beastliness,
Thinking that way to jettison their dreams,
Then, suffering shipwreck, shout that they alone   10
Are seeing the world very clearly, swimming
Naked the waters of cold Truth, not floating
Upon the surface in a gondola
Of blurred sensation and child-memories
Grown monstrous, and queer patterns in the skull
Wriggled by the dark worms of suppressed lust . . .
Poor grey philosophers, and cannot see
Themselves are dream and all their theories!
    But many drown like lead without a cry.
    Among such fellows the bewildered boy   20
Grew more bewildered, neither understanding
Himself nor them; as dimly, dimly and slowly,
He noticed and remembered little things.
Big Bannister, the soft-faced Irishman,
Who wenched and wenched, and felt himself a man
By talking *sotto voce* with big eyes
About his women and their secret clothes,
Has slid into the room; Big Bannister,
Who was in Connaught in a little hut,
Growing there eighteen years among the pigs,   30
Till Dublin swallowed him and spewed him out
Into a London barber's shop. He pads
Into the hut, sits, fixes his soft eyes
Upon the reading boy. They are alone.
And now he pours out the last episode,
Purring with female, strutting in the puddle
Of his great naughtiness, punctuating
Each pause with laughter that is oh so sly,

And looking to the hearer for applause
Or bashful deference. Tonight the boy   40
Chances to be too tired to play up,
Put on his grin, and make the sound that oils
The jarring wheels of forced companionship.
He does not laugh, he does not look away,
Or down, or blush; but, like one half-asleep,
Answers very gravely with the truth
Each sidelong question; then he quietly
Asks him a question, and big Bannister
Louder and faster and more greasily
Goes talking on and will not answer it   50
And smirks: the boy with sleep's own devilry
Asks it again, and others, takes him up
At every comma: Bannister blasphemes,
Shouts, threatens, rises snarling from his chair,
Then weeps, and pours his uninvited lees
Of tenderness out into the boy's ear
All tingling—mother and the Irish girl.
    Bannister shunned him after: when they met,
A shell came over the gentle of his eyes,
A shell of arrogance. He went on laughing   60
Deliberately, oilily, slyly;
But the boy, listening, heard in it now
The rumbling undersong. He now in eyes
Of every man saw more than he could tell
Even to himself; in pauses of their talking
To him across the stillness the last laugh
Rang like the screech of something in a cage.
Often the misty argument ran high,
Heart stumbling after heart, the while men spoke
Out of their knowledge and their pain the truth;   70
Till slowly self and most most private self
Came creeping nearer for companionship
And nearer—when one, suddenly afraid,
Skittered away behind a quick guffaw
And hid, and peeped, and crept again. Which he
Contemplating for ever was a child
Pitchiting past the hedgerows in a train,

Drowsily watching the wires—how they soar
Higher and higher—will they go up now
Above the small square window, into the sky?
Higher and higher and higher—flashes a pole
Past the window, jerking them down down
Down down, and soon they are creeping again
Higher and higher, and will they go up now
Above the small square window, up to the sky?
Till he awakens and drops back again,
Filling his mind with small things, like a sail
That bulges with the Trade-wind and flees on
Whirled like a leaf over the empty sea
Along with the empty sky, and comes to port,
Where it is furled and sewn into a bag
For housewife's brickabrack. He was like that,
He was a working, playing, grumbling man,
A sleeper through the night, a lover of laughter,
Sweet comfortable laughter that transforms
Demons to bogeys and long grief to folly.
And so for many months he travelled on,
And so he might have travelled to the grave.

III

    The curving high-street of the little town
Went washed in empty brilliance, up the hill,
Past the cathedral; the clear cobble-stones
Threw each a little shadow-pool; the rails,
Rivers of moonlit metal, gleamed away
Silent, where all day long the trams had clacked.
Here at a corner the old sleeping pile
From the light's bright field sickled a sharp swathe
Across the street and up the mouldering wall,
Where yawned an archway leading to the Close.
Behind it shone under the open sky
Chimneys and spires, together ranged in peace.
Lonely among these floated and stood still,
Fairy beneath the moon, an old stone tower
Framed in the archway; and dead silence lay
Like silk upon the street, and noiseless rows
Of grey mysterious lack-lustre blinds
Hid rows of sleepers dreaming different dreams.
Silence was rustled by the far faint ring
Of metal upon stone, the louder beat
Of feet approaching, the loud tramp, tramp, tramp
Of feet—the feet hesitated and stopped.
Silence was broken by cathedral clock
Chiming a quarter and chiming another quarter.
And the feet moved and the sound died away.
    But there between those chimings of the bells,
Somewhere in the quietness of that street,
Where it flowed most adream, the stream of Thought
Bubbled, and beauty suddenly built her bridge,
Her rainbow archway cantilevered upon
Gossamer bastions . . . A day in fields,
Clear with whole sunlit reverie, and tonight
Sprang together behind a soldier's face.
    And the feet moved and the sound died away.

IV

     Sharp as a tennis-ball from a hard court,
The light rebounded from the cambered stones.
The weighted summer air was dark with noon.
The olive foliages of separate trees
Hung still beneath the sky. From his machine
An airman spied that road—on it a van
Ran like a small ball rolling down a groove,
Hurrying westward. It was dusk inside,
And there was smell of petrol and burnt oil
In the nostrils of a dozing soldier
Exempt from pain and terror—not from woe.
The shattered limb had ceased to ache—not yet
The shattered spirit. Eddying memories
Encompassed and bewildered him; he lived
Over and over again so carefully
Through every chapter of the previous day,
Patiently recapitulating all
The secret ruses of trapped will, up to
The hideous moment when it failed—'If I
Can bring those threads together, disentangled,
Up to hell's gate in memory,
I shall be able to carry them through'—when lo!
The bubble of this fatuous thought exploded,
Which his half-fevered brain at once began
To blow again, until the blinding truth
Shouted that action is irrevocable.
He shifted on the stretcher, to shake off
The misery—remembering how, by jerking
The glass bits of a toy kaleidoscope,
The pattern changes—and the pattern changed:
Individual memories stood out
Atrocious. The Familiars of his bed,
Came gibbering back in loving longways dance
From the dark cupboard where they would not stay:
The long-drawn Shriek of agony, the Knife
Twisting in entrails slowly, the pushed Point
Pressing and pressing home among soft veins
Nearer the windpipe, glimpse of upturned Face

Gasping and squirming in such agony
Beneath the stamping boot, the beastlike Mouth   40
Shapeless with malice and sobbing with hate
At me—until the shape of the mouth grows
And it is nearer, and the car itself
And the whole world are in it: Oh, the darkness—
Recognized darkness—rushing to his soul
Blotting all hope and being, and the wind
That blows about him in the wilderness
Alone and groping for a boundary—air
Chiller than breath of spectres—oh, the darkness
Rolled, like a stone, across his spirit's tomb.   50
    Then all at once a spasm of bodily pain
Aroused him, as the ambulance down jolted
Into a hole and out again: fled thought
Leaving thick fumes; and vaguely now he gazed
Through the back curtains shaken to a slit
Upon wide sunny fields, the burnished road
Dropping away behind him like a cable
Put by a travelling drum. The air was clear;
No cloud was in that sky; and yet earth seemed
Dark. As on some October afternoon   60
Black beams shoot down from where the sun must be,
Threatening instead of brightening the earth,
So from within his clear and painless head
A beam of darkness seemed to radiate
Personal, yet eclipsing actual day.
    Into his picture slid a tiny hamlet
With peasant-women stooping over beans
Natural, industrious, immemorial, and
A little child came running to the gate
To gape after the car. He scarce had time   70
To feel how this flit glimpse of fellow-creatures
Was dissolving despair, when they turned
Sharp to the right in the middle of the village,
And the slit shewed him, far on the sky-line,
Square and un-English, squat and solid, and yet
Beautiful with its northern symmetry,
And known already from large picture hanging

Coloured in local shop—there gazed upon
With sense of dim significance—a tower:
Quick witchery! How soon the dreamlight spread 80
Over his world, that dusk interior
Odorous, and those thronging memories.
Noon entered his lax limbs. His blood flowed tingling
As betwixt sleep and waking. Eyes seemed looking
Out over leagues and leagues of wasted acreage
Barren as a sharp landscape of the moon,
Save where earth rose in split and blasted trunks,
Which, staggering beneath forgotten agonies,
Suffered their mineral passion—and this tower
Sullenly pointing to a sullen sky. 90
Oh, desolation of the Spirit of Man!
     Yet—even as he cowered—back it sped
(Which he had once, detached for the first time
From home and love, and mad with loneliness,
Walking the streets of a strange city, known)
Vast, electrical cloud of exultation,
Bursting of childish bonds, huge levity
And condescending power of a Djinn
Uncorked from the small flagon of himself
And towering like a beanstalk, like a cloud 100
Spreading all over heaven—*I come!*—Oh, joy!
Oh, soaring liberty! The very dead
Sang carols in his ears, as though their life's
Sweet stem had been cut off to grant him life,
Life that should tear new meaning from itself,
Life that would in no manner be denied,
Till it had walked about the stars
And made a girdle of the Galaxy . . .
"Till he has bumped his head against the bars
And played the noodle in the gallery!" 110
He nodded, jerking vanity out of dreams,
And sank stonelike into the freezy waters
Of self-contempt. 'Poor wish-fulfilling cog!
Because it has no courage, must it dream
Always of courage, and because no strength,
Must its contemptible imagination

Play Samson in the nursery? Is it not,
Is it not enough the creature is not fit
To eat from the same plate . . . but it must use
Armies for inspiration—it must strut 120
Starched up before its mirror, on the staff
Of the Creator? Fuss, fuss, little flea,
And think thou art the pulse of the machine!'
      Bodily weariness obscured the thread
Of serious argument, but not that sense
Of contradictions unresolved, torn halves,
Which, if he could but strongly re-unite,
Would take the strain and leave him free for sleep.
Yet ere he slept indeed, that journey done,
He was betwixt white sheets, lazily turning 130
The pages of bright, stupid magazines,
And not a vestige in his muddy soul
Either of vanity or aspiration.

V

    Summer and health returned: remembered war
Was not yet deep enough sunk in his being
To canker every dream: and dreams came
Hard on each others' heels. What suffering
They brought was this—their very numerousness,
The fear of dropping each ere it could form
Tangible memories—and the wild impatience.
Oh, that impatience, ruin of youth's joy!
All things are mapped for joy. Within his ear
Nature and poesy begin to chant   10
Their danceable duet. Fresh ears, fresh eyes
Are built into his soul by piercing words
Of Keats or Shelley—all that marvelous Wave
That burst the crust of Reason; now does Fancy
Behold a Nature never dreamed. Oh Boy,
It is enough—and more: drink, oh drink deep!
Be tranquil as old age even at this moment
While sensitive as youth. Thou fool, and blind,
It may not be. The everlasting hunger
For growth, for personal rapture, for some joy   20
To which these hints are but the scraping prelude,
Will not be quiet. Life drives onward fast.
Scarce eighteen times shall Earth have twirled her moon
Ere he has launched on that long agony
Of gradual starvation in the dark
That death which must inform him pang by pang
How these faint noises were the actual tune.
    And *are* they faint? Now, while thy freedom holds,
While love still glimmers low on the horizon
Like some rose-tinted mountain, to whose base   30
Holiday-makers tramp unhurrying
With well-filled knapsacks—even now, not once
But many times, the secret-breathing world
Whispers to thee, yet whispers with a voice
Which memory shall warehouse as a shout:
Mornings in later summer—the cold air
Crudding the heart beneath the risen sun
Flashing over a carpet of thick dew

Which loads meticulously clear each thread
Of perilous cobwebs; level evenings   40
Filling the air with spirit of gold,
Till time itself is crystallized, and hangs
Like a pure grain washed from Pactolus' bed.
Were these *faint* signals? Winking jack-o-lanterns
Not to be trusted? Ay, for now this man
Began to be not one sole soul but two.
He could no longer trace the ligature
That ties an evening to a morning mood.
Often at night, before his hearth, reading,
Alone, or struggling to compose the cauldron   50
Of formless impulses that burst to dreams
Fast as each bubbled to the surface—often
At night, if by the end he had succeeded
In taming down his mind to be receptive,
Wide-eyed with bodily fatigue, he grew
Aware as of a faintly singing cloud
Enveloping his head: and, wearily
Closing his volume, would feel in his blood
The pressure of unwritten poetry
Knocking: "I can all things!" No imagery   60
Formed in his mind, no thoughts; and yet it seemed
His essence and the essence of the world
Flowed, and that if he could maintain the mood
Long enough time, the brain must of itself
Construct new metaphors, and move the world
To tears and wonder with its terrible art.
     But then—when he awoke after ten hours
Of deathlike sleep—shaking it off, he smiled
At all those reveries, and thought those dreams
Worms spiring through a lump of lifeless clay   70
Until the stuff seems living. He who laughed
At fatuous affectation, he who knew
That fire burns or seven and two are nine—
This was the real "I": that other, the dreamer,
Was the poor lunatic court poet, kept
To while away a Prince's tedious hours
By tickling his senses with neat wit

And flattering up his immortality.
Spiritual visions? Bodily states of strain,
Reverberations, delicate overtones   80
Of the quivering catgut of desire!
     As once the live prey of the Inquisition
Was fitted struggling into a harsh robe,
A barrel of steel wedges, which impinged
And hour by hour blotted out bright life,
So had the bristle of mechanic thought,
Entering by tiny punctures unperceived,
Closed on his consciousness through gradual years,
Till now the spikes, nigh meeting, left no space
For flesh and blood. He was beside himself.   90
His mind bowed down to emptiness. Each cracked
And leaky syllogism carried him
Easily over great gulfs of discourse,
Give only that the slick conclusion mocked
His heart's immediate knowledge. The most true,
Most intimate experiences were cast
For self-deceptions exorcising fear.
So one night, waking swiftly, he lay gazing
Upon the furniture of his bedroom
Lit up for company, and two bright eyes   100
Fastened them glittering upon one chair
Senseless and standing still in the same place
Under the lamp—until its stony look
Bruised and bewildered him, and in his brain
It seemed a loud voice prophesied, uttering:—*Dead!*
     These isolated moments of strange life,
These alternating moods, seemed to detach
Himself even from himself, so that he feared
Actual madness. For, at other times,
Awaking in the night to contemplate   110
Majestic constellations through the pane,
He seemed a prisoner gazing through the eyes
Of someone else's body, a rough ape's
Or a dead man's, despairing, choking—struggling
With claustrophobia—bursting with fierce life.
     Yet of all this none knew; for in the day

From those deep roots of humour in his blood
Sprang up a foliage of shame, which made
His own experience seem affectation,
Byronic, not to be believed, until
He doubted his own memory. Meanwhile
A load accumulated on his heart
Secretly, unacknowledged, felt one moment,
Forgot the next; till sometimes it broke through,
Transmuted to pure tenderness, in fumes,
Dense fumes astonishing, which hung around
Whimsical accidental thoughts and things;
And, in especial, round one slender tower,
Whose grace had moved so many loving hearts,
Clustered like a rich swarm of bees. He waited
Its coming into view around some corner
With eagerness each time he walked. He stood
Often exactly at its base and gazed
Up, or was greatly comforted to feel
It soaring up out of him like an angel
Loving and overshadowing and awaiting.
And he would watch the way it took the light
Of morning or of evening, rain or dry,
Autumn and Spring, reflecting or absorbing,
Now blue, now grey, now calm and sunny gold,
As some young lover notes with different thrills
His mistress's various drapery and her moods.
    But when this very image sprang into
Expectant fancy, quickly the old tower
Looked all awry and stockish—a mere peg
For sentimental ravings—and the calm
That brooded on his spirit was churned up
To personal hunger and anxiety.

VI

  See how the day grows on the morning earth,
How forms and masses vague coagulate
Of darker within darkness—the first hope
Of light, while space must still be thought, not seen:
Slowly the glimmering Eastern sky inserts
The watcher in his visible universe
With right or left, North, South, until more light
Discovers cloud and rock and blade of grass
Distinct, and gives, like love, to everything
Colour and self. Now one part of the heavens   10
Is all a lake, and still it is unknown
Betwixt which pair of shrubs He will appear,
And yon cloud-mirror, floating high, glows pink
And yonder after, and the morning creeps
Forward on leaden feet—till, suddenly—
Your eyes!—oh, *one* part of the bright lake blazes
To shooting scarlet, it stirs like a rose
Opening before the watcher's eyes, who knows,
Nor waits a heartbeat ere that burning rim
Shouts over the sharp shoulder of the earth;   20
And his blood leaps with inarticulate sense
Of life, of life to come—yet, in one hour
The little eye of day is up, hard, small,
Screwed in the sky for all to see—no more
Singing Osirean secrets to the heart,
Which all day strives wistfully to feed
On the faint glorious memory of His birth.
  She sits—she sits beside him—hush!—speak not!—
Think not!—this is the sunrise of a life:
Through but this afternoon it shall be bliss   30
Only to be in the same room—he swims
In skies of liquid light—each wee impression
Of world through window, music, happy colour
His thundering heart informs with joyous God;
And all the memories of all hours of peace,
Magic of women's faces, all sweet calms
Rained by a glint of kindness, from their tombs
Deep in the wormy vaults of memory

Arise, they sing, they dance, until Desire
Shakes his great shoulders and sighs and slumbers—only   40
Murmuring on in dreams: 'Let Time stand still!'
And all the while the raving lover listens
To his own fencing voice, with trivial pun,
Jest, quip, opinion, guarding well the secret,
And all the while his blood throbs with a sense
Of an unspeakable fullness yet to come,
Of standing on the threshold of new life
Never yet dreamed—and he is on the threshold,
Threshold of Heaven on earth—but falling out,
Not climbing in. From now seek earth on earth,   50
Heaven in Heaven—wisdom which men learn
Only by pain and death, the cruel death
Of personal passion, which, like some low creature
Whose hideous vitality kicks in spasms
After the back is broken, shall long years
After thou deem'st it crushed and starved to death,
Raise up its beauteous head and bite the soul
With awful desolations, bitter thoughts
Of wasted life and of no happiness.

VII

    As one that swiftly fades into the 'O'
Of a dark tunnel's mouth, he vanishes.
Oh, let him! Though a curious pen had power,
What use to follow him through that blind walk
Of pain, incessant pain—to watch him lying
Abed each morning, longing for the night—
To sleep—only to sleep again—to fly
Consciousness—all exertion—cracking hours
Of will towards ambitions now long dead,
But once held by the forward-looking stranger?   10
Oh, everlasting shifting of inertia,
To gull the watchful enmity of friends
With an explosive phantasm of momentum!
To pretend life and to be a machine!
For still it *seems* no tunnel, but a cave
Exitless, damp, where he has left the light
Of day for ever. Yet, if it were fed
With air and sun!—if discs of gold should lie,
Never so far between, upon the floor
Of that infernal pilgrimage, then we   20
Down the dear shafts may peep and watch him cross
Stooping, and softly sing of how the beam
Touches his rounded shoulders as he goes.
    Behold him, then, on a hot day in June
Wheeling a road through meadows high with flowers
Absorbed in his great misery—and, ah, feel
That sudden sweet solution of all strain,
Melting of misery into the world,
To be rained back again as tenderness,
Beyond all wonder, from the living colours   30
Of flaming buttercups and snowy daisies.
    See him discovering the lovingkindness
Of Sleep, dear Sleep, who laps each conscious being
In the warm mother-ocean of its blood,
As nurse Demeter nightly wrapped her charge
In the glorious fire of the gods
To mend his mortal weakness.
                        Feel with him

The mysterious sense of inner power,
The gleam of light wedged betwixt two huge glooms.
            But, most of all, one evening of still light,   40
When the whole world was as the deep floor
Of a vast ocean, which was the still light:
Petals and twigs thrust out into that light
Sustained like seaweed; until his faint soul
Undulated in it like a starfish
Floating translucent in translucent waves.
And the same light engulfed the springing Tower,
Till it too seemed to float, till it became
A filmy drapery of stone that hung,
Having no weight, from nothing in the sky,   50
And, in his summer dreaming, hung again
Over against that sky, and still was drenched
In the rich golden silence, which seemed gathering
Intolerably—until it conceived
And grew big-bellied with terrific meaning,
And the whole dream resounded as with words.
Words which he could not hear, but quickly woke
Sweating, and wept somewhat for loneliness.
But the next morning that incisive horror
Of self-deception, which was closing fast   60
All avenues to the sounds of the spirit,
Returned upon him and half blotted out
The dream's intensity; which now he thought
Garbled by willing memory to please.
        Often day smashed the link which night had forged
Betwixt the sick heart and the dungeoned brain.

VIII

    And then, one day, he rummaged in a drawer
And found, under a pile of motley goods,
A sheet of folded paper, yellow, writ
Close in his mother's hand, and at the top:
"A MEMORY"; which, as his eye glanced down,
Rushed wonder first, and then amazed delight
Of recognition; and, for days and days,
As he walked to and fro about the house,
The gentle gesture of a bygone age
Throbbed in his being, captured all his fancy,   10
And seemed to become a memory of his own:
    The luminous twilight melted into gold,
A clear unruffled lake of gold, that glowed
Behind the hill's low line, and darkened it,
As the serene brow of a saint is darkened
Under the brightness of his aureole.
But on this Eastern shoulder, gazing out
Across the valley to a distant height,
There were twain lying still: the evening fell
Settling about them, and the long turf lay   20
Under the cool and green air silently.
Even so these two, all wrapped in the great silence,
Lay stretched along the turf, so silently
They gazed, but, as they gazed, held conference
Closer than uttered syllable could yield;
For they drew nearer in this casual hour
Than ever they had been, or ever again
Would be, until death took him from her side.
Did he not know one thing, and, knowing it,
Whisper within himself again, again,   30
Marvelling softly;—"Even this moment she
Is fashioning my image in her womb—
Even this moment . . ." till he could not think
Of any other thing, nor speak of this?
The woman heard the whispering of his mind
So plainly that it needed not his voice
To utter the familiar thought; yet peace
Wrapped her entirely from all wondering,

Great peace, not drowsy, but the peace of trees
That wait a-tiptoe for the wind's first breath,   40
Or of the darkness waiting for the light:
In such a stillness of the dawn her soul
Was hushed, as waiting for no common thing.
    Out of the green turf of a hill, beyond
The quiet valley, there uprose a tower—
Four slender walls, which, rising from the ground
In straight austerity, far, far above
Burst into pinnacles innumerable,
That seemed to float on air; the mellow light
Softened the stone and entered into it,   50
And slowly spread a change over the tower,
Making its corners faint against the blue,
Till it began to dream, till it became
A filmy drapery of stone that hung,
Having no weight, from nothing in the sky.
    The air grew very still. . . . Among the grass
Small insect-noises were so clear, they sounded
Like children shouting afar off. . . . There broke
Forth from the tower, on which her listless eyes
Rested in thought, eight lingering, rich tones,   60
Anciently musical, rising and falling
In a sweet chime, whose undulating din
Floated across the valley sedately, borne
In the still lap of evening, till it sank
Into her ears, and settling silverly
About her waiting soul, astonished it . . .
    As when a painter dawdles on his way
Disconsolate, seeing the common things
With common eyes, and scornful of himself,
Some tiny thing pours a delicious change   70
Over his senses, and he sees again
That they are beautiful—then all at once
Loses that vision, and goes seeking it
In emptiness of soul for days and days—
So startled was the woman by this chime,
Till, as she looked, the greenness of the grass,
The curving outline of the hill, the tower,

The sky's unfathomable clarity
Troubled her with their dumbness, and she lay
Full of the evening's beauty—wondering. 80
     A wonder that died not, but slowly grew,
Opening its noiseless petals—mingled all
With the strange dawning of a tenderness
Beyond all wonder, which enclasped her heart
With curious tiny fingers. Now she felt,
For the first time, that they were not alone,
And love came, like a great sob, suddenly,
Whispering "Mother!"—but she could not speak . . .
Night rustled softly down. . . . At last they moved,
Breaking the spell, and rose, and slowly went 90
Whispering together down the darkened hill
Into the valley, where the cottages
Sent up straight wisps of smoke, and shut their door.

IX

    For days and days that far-off evening
Was vivid to his brain, and the still light
A constant presence; loveliest memories
Hovered around him, and a sense of awe—
Of dim connections not yet understood
Betwixt all human beings—kept him warm,
Shutting the night out—
                      But then with slow pace
Darkness crept back, darkness crept back, darkness,
The loving minion, the pluperfect friend,
And for the first time even upon the Tower
Did leer, because the wonder and the sweetness
And all the mystery were dissolved to matter
In the blind workings of his mother's womb.
    Yet this he hardly knew yet: his stripped soul
Beyond a naked woman was abashed,
Seeing as in a glass how far the vision
Of a romantic Tower, yes, had buttressed
His peace of mind with mystic-selfish hopes.
    Thus did the Tower, high hope's last refuge, crumble
Into hereditary rubble, thus
The fairy gold, its magic dream-light dear,
Shrivelled into a litter of dead leaves.
Yet, like a prisoner shovelling dead leaves,
For want of barren tasks, in idleness,
He went on piling intellectual knowledge
On intellectual knowledge, fitting fact
To theory, adding dead thought to dead thought.

X

    At last he came into a narrow valley
So steep, that from the windows of the house
Wedged in its bottom an outlooker saw
Not sky but rock. The sun slipped overhead
In a few hours only every day
And all the rest was evening; the caged eye
Nowhere might rest in distance; the hot head
Ached with the evil hammering of itself
Reflected on itself from vertical
Walls—it throbbed with the pressure of the air   10
Of the close valley corked by a huge Peak
Squatting there dead . . . Inhuman tons of rock!
Christened (for so he dreams) by some old lover
Who, with eyes sharpened by the inner shock,
Looked out on a strange world, and did discover
A maiden in a mountain—a sweetheart
Nor warm, nor cold, nor proud, nor meek, nor vain—
Nothing—oh, sexless *Jungfrau!*—wandering heart
Bashing its soft self on a stone . . .
                                The pain
Swelled like a tumour, till it touched his brain,   20
So that the past and future were shut out,
So that the light itself seemed hideous,
So that to say a kind word to a friend,
To smile or bid Good morning!—these were tasks
Beyond the utmost powers of his will,
Tearing the stomach.
                        The hard, hollow rocks,
Like corpses of soft earth! And every night
Through large round shining eyes he watched the Moon
Glowing, till hypnotised imagination
Had hoisted his gross flesh on to its crust,   30
And with last gasps he crawled upon its crust
Scorching and hackling in the pitiless glare
Of the kind sun that warms us here, and thought
Of all those kindly atmospheric veils,
Human illusions, which himself had stripped
Severally from himself, till now the soul

Stood parching naked: one by one they had dropped,
Even as the Haunted Sailor's ghastly mates,
Those sweet imaginations of soul-life
Without himself in Nature—one by one,   40
Unmasked by reason, they stood forth revealed
As ghostly emanations from himself,
Then dropped dead. Even the long pain of love
Dissolved in thought's sharp acid—he mistrusts
Some half-willed Rosicrucian exercise
Done by the dim Self working out its way,
Some web of self-enlightenment, unwound
With spider instinct from domestic bowels.
"It is not true!" he cries, "I did not raise
This spectre out of all my own desires   50
And fit it on the first female—they lie!"
But to him shouting only his own voice,
Faint, like the screech of something in a cage,
Came echoing round out of the chill stones.
    As some delirious traveller in a storm
That howls all night upon the mountain-side
Enters a chamber, richly tapestried,
Warm, glowing with soft bulbs, and sinks down sighing
In a deep feathery couch, to find the cushions
And all the wood frame and the hangings mist   60
And himself sitting upon a damp stone:
Such seemed his love—such the whole world—unreal—
Nothingness! Nothingness! Yet ever *fear*—
Oh, fear of *what*? Satanic irony!
Fear of the mountains, fear of his own ghost,
Of matter without spirit—horror of Death
Closing in on him on all sides at once,
Choking his physical throat, till all day long
Breath comes in jerks and the heart thumps eccentric
Pinned under private mountains of oppression.   70
    One respite only from this state he knew,
One instant of release, no sooner felt
Then finished, and himself clapped back with weights
Into the lazar-house:
                Ran down that cleft,

Eternally poured from eternal snows,
A torrent, whose roar drumming down the rocks
Bombled the listening ears all day, all night:
There, as he leaned upon a wooden bridge
And watched the sliding platform of dark waters
Vanishing underneath for ever and ever— 80
Once—in the aimless void of misery—
It seemed the moment blossomed into years,
It seemed the whole world changed into his world:
The awful will-strain tugging at his stomach
Is pulled from under like a water-weed
And whirled down seaward: music of life flows
Through and through suspended limbs
Like water through a grid, while aeons pass.
      So sometimes, when men dance upon the ground,
The music and the motion of his limbs 90
Mix for a second, while a dancer's soul
Stands in extreme bliss outside both, dead still,
Upon the mighty Rest that entertains
The motion of the Planets and the Stars.
Dear God, that such a moment will not stay
Even in the memory: it is, and then
Oblivion closes utterly: no fragrance
Hovers to mark the smooth spot where it sank;
Only blank thoughts, while gulls, wheel screaming round
Empty and hungry, without strength to dive. 100
      Darker and darker grow the short days: now
The valley seemed to be shutting up its jaws
On him, and solemnly out of the unknown region
Through his thin skull there marches a procession
Of speaking dreams . . . A bed in a dim room
And on it a draped Figure: by his side,
Standing, the dearest of all friends, who stirs
To lift the white sheet, which he would forbid,
Both knowing and not knowing what it hides:
But she has lifted it, and from that bier 110
The dreadful symbol from its glaring sockets
Shoots forth the hated truth that both must die
And be apart for ever . . .

                          At the tail
Of all these nightmares rose the Tower's self,
Resonant, lovely, and with from its cope
Bells chiming, whose far-welling waves of sound,
Grown visible, all lapped upon his soul
Particularly, like incoming hopes
Of revelation: yet at the same moment
In which he (chosen from all other men   120
For his calm strength and royal dignity
And his great sorrow) was to learn the Secret,
They turned a regiment of little imps
Who frisked about—each was a clack of laughter,
Habitual, wooden laughter, like rough hands
Smearing the fragile bloom from lovely things.
And they had dogged and mocked him all his life
And kept him from his home. And he awoke
To actual thunder spreading through the heavens
Like roots of a huge tree, and lay there still   130
Quaking and listening.
                          When in two hours
The storm died and the dawn broke, every star
By which until that moment he had steered
His moral course, was blotted: not a motive:
There was no motive left in heart or brain
To stop him practising but what might bring
Immediate comfort to the senses . . .
                                        And
In this void moment he became aware
Of an impersonal Force; it was alive,
Solid; he felt its weight upon his belly   140
And knew moreover that, while his own brain
Mocked it as automatic, as taboo,
Taunting him with old Puritan standards
Ingrained by blood and class—whether or no
It were indeed these, or some nobler thing,
Or meaner—it would hold him from worst evil,
Or what in lost moods he had once called evil.
          He slept, and, in the morning, when he woke
To go about his tasks, there was a change:

There was a curious calmness in the air, 150
A gratefulness, like rest to weary limbs.
The pain was gone. But when he looked to find
Old hopes of pleasure flooding back to glut
The hollows of the heart, he looked in vain.
He seemed a vessel which had been uplifted
And turned over and drained, and on a hook
Hung dangling empty in the empty air.

XI

    One day, in intimate study of the past
When his imagination was all steeped, and dreaming
Its way along those mazy paths of thought
Which open from contemplating the growth
Into their present seeming-simple meaning
Of smallest, commonest words, a blind thing stirred
Deep in the core of inexpressive mind.
There was no startle, no eureka cry
Of jubilant revelation—none the less
Pivot of lifetime was that moment: Sun   10
Turns himself over down in Ocean's caves:
Earth shivers, and every valley is aware
That a golden head will raise itself
And, looking over the horizon, roll
The white mists back, ha! ha! and drink them up.
For he had dimly seen how Language grows,
Yea, how the noise that thrills out of our mouths
Is a vast voyage of discovery;
And how the thing men call discovery
Is Man's own growing consciousness—pin-point   20
Of radiant light that further flings its beams
And further into the darkness: Ptolemy,
Copernicus and Newton, they are eyes
That carry changing pictures to the brain
Of one slowly growing from boy to man,
From man to poet, and to something more.
    As one whose earnest thought dwells long upon
The form and structure of the eye, working
Within its physical workings, faithfully
Led like a child by sense, till soon his trained   30
Imagination freely moves about
Within the quiddity of light, and sees
Seeing itself and how our eyes are veils,
Not windows: thus it is when a fresh mind
With suffering, with labour, with delight
Streams with the streaming sap of language—lo!
Imagination unawares has learnt
To pierce the veil of consciousness itself

And become spirit.
                  Under a grey dome
Inscribed with echoes of the past, the names   40
Of poets dead, and between double walls
Fashioned of echoes of the past, the thoughts
Of dead men petrified in tomes, he saw,
He saw for ever—as when forked lightning
Shatters the secret night, the flash is vanished,
But not the bright map in the shepherd's brain
Of rocks and trees and shapes of hills and sheep—
That he whose soul would touch the very past
Must build himself a delicate consciousness
Out of the dreams of old civilisations,   50
Must see with ancient eyes, not wisely peer
Through glasses of the last half-hundred years;
And that whose soul would truly touch the present,
Must first have touched the past; how Truth's a stream
That hurries on through complicated webs
Of thought, which meanings of words, ever changing,
Keep letting down into it for a moment,
Till the weak webs are torn away and whirled
On with the rushing torrent. At such times
The caged intensity   60
Of inarticulate, surging thought would drown
His whole rapt soul and swallow up his brain
From reading a word more out of the book,
Would raise his breathing body from its chair
And pace it softly round the huge hushed hive
Of books and buzzing minds, picking its way
Catlike between the inexpressive shoulders
Of hunched, incurious readers—and then out
Through the mute oscillation of swing doors.
        Then, as he walked through stony galleries   70
Peopled with statues of old myths and gods,
The constant-crystallizing vegetation
Of man's unfolding dream, congealed in stone,
Those forms began to melt and pass, sliding
Into each other there before his eyes
Bright with intenser thinking, until Time

Sprang into life in his imagination
Incarnate in a visible procession
Of cloudlike shapes. It seemed that a warm vapour
Moved, as he moved, wholly enveloping him   80
From his surrounding, like the magic mist
Poured by Athene round the wanderer
Walking into Phaeacia; and the floor,
The walls, the statues, and the passers by
Slipped back like shadows, but his furious thought,
That was the real world through which he moved.
    Outside the door the shock of the winter air
Wrapped itself round his face, and drew their warmth
Out of these blooded thoughts. And in his ears
The voluble angry chattering of ten thousand   90
Small, fussy starlings from the high eaves drowned
The singings that had fill them from within.
Then, in the street itself, the thousand faces
Hurrying past on business important,
Thick mouths, low foreheads, nowhere-looking eyes,
Dark lines drawn by fatigue and suffering,
Dark lines drawn by unending hungriness,
Soft curves drawn by complete stupidity
And lust, and opulent power, lines and curves
Which were the perfect signature of minds   100
That never never could receive such thoughts,
Made those thoughts seem unreal, till at last
They ebbed along the roaring stream of buses
And lost themselves in London—he walked on,
Beholding the world only with his eyes,
Crushed by its weight and passion; but next week
(As if they had but ebbed to flow again)
The thoughts would start to build themselves once more
Into his mind: once more imagination—
Like some huge half-fledged bird, with clanging wings   110
Too stiff to lift its bulk, which flies at last
By taking from the top of scaffoldings
Laboriously erected—soared up sunwards
Over bright fields of green and shimmering life
That lie this side the brain.

                        The books are closed,
But still the mind, of its own weight, goes on
Challenging, groping, excavating dim
Experiences out of his own past
And of the vast past of the mind of Man,
Till, freed from senses by some accident,
High mood, a glimpse of beauty, the sooth fragrance
Of steaming tea—they fluctuate and begin
Forging a body and rhythm of their own
Which fits itself into the Stream of Thought,
So that his own mind buds from history
As part of Life. He sees the sharp horizon
Of man's sense-knowledge suddenly flung out
All ways to limitless distance—and he feels
In his own self the future self of Man
Stirring, awaking, grasping at consciousness
Of Life, which since creation has been flowing
Through and through the body unawares,
Asleep—and asleep—till at a sign
The sweet, the long long stored Promethean hour—
Oh, wondering adolescence of the world!—
Brings in self-knowledge with a rush, and calls it
To blossom from blind Being into Truth.

XII

    And now, as time flowed onward, normal mood
Came to confirm with more assured consent
Dear inspiration—if this were a dream,
Then what was the true waking? Thus, detached,
He asked himself—and, even detached, could feel
The force of the quick growth of the world's store
Of knowledges, to feed comparison,
Knowledge of earth, of languages, beliefs,
Civilizations, customs, dreams—could mark
Dispassionately his individual place.   10
As one of many minds, purged, from the start,
By the star-cold perspective, of all dreams
Of grossly personal immortality,
Not needing, like his fathers, or like those,
The first philosophers, bred up in myth
As being the air they breathed, to spend much spirit
In puffing his soul clear of mantled fumes.
    And he was grateful for that mountain air
Which wrapped and chilled his childhood; for the dawn
Was coming over the mountain, and behold!   20
The far-spread plains beneath, the scarp of Earth,
The works of man, the rivers and white roads
With men upon them walking, who could not see
Past the next rise or corner, and all eager!
    Oh, in such high moods, all that mass of fact,
Which sat on his crushed spirit like the stones
Of vast Egyptian tombs, began to lighten,
To stir like loosened wax, to melt, to float,
And the house of the dead, the great museum,
The tomb of expressed dreams, was like a shell   30
Waiting till life should crack it from within.
As busy coral masons in their dark
Labour and pullulate and leave behind
Their limy corpses for a million years,
Until the placid ocean shows its teeth
Found a new reef, and one of them beholds
The blue Pacific heaving in the sunshine,
So did he seem upraised on generations

Of hooded scholars and sharp men of science
Who fed on Aristotle in the dark 40
And on his mother Nature.
                           Yet not long,
And all this arrogance was pricked with pain
At thought of the great cost—with speechless thanks
To those who had gone on working by their light,
But not by this great light, and above all,
To the sad spirits who abandoned faith,
Not with that truculent glee which brings support,
But out of the pure flame—even though they knew,
Being wise, that most of what they loved must die,
Cowardice and self and pride o'erwhelm the world 50
And the last healer, Art, be starved to death.
        He had re-lived himself part of that woe,
Dying his death; but he had risen again
In this world—they had sunk into the tomb
To live there, die there.
                         Thus, as thought on thought
Came flooding, dream on dream, unfolding petals,
He saw how these, their thoughts, were but slant sections
Of a vast shape beneath it, which each soul
Was working out. The firmament of time
Rushed back, as once before men's startled eyes 60
The firmament of space: and souls were stars:
And worlds on worlds of fresh discovery
Opened before blind eyes which late had seen
One rigid framework with some unfilled gaps
Scarce worth the labour of completing—now
Endless—say rather not even begun;
For this neat abacus, which put up for truth,
Was but the husks of dead truths strung together
By a mechanic joiner: knowledge is not,
Until it is the thing it knoweth; knowledge 70
Is Life incarnating in consciousness.
        The pressure of unwritten poetry
Which had so furiously knocked at his blood,
Sitting alone once by the fireside, now
Dies into tranquil tremors of the spirit

And ripples into pure joy; for this man,
Even this man, has spoken face to face
With the eternal Muse—and ever more,
Save in the puny hours, it must be
Matter of accident if himself or other 80
Be chosen to indite. He has found peace.

XIII

    He has found peace: gazing upon the world
No longer from without, but from the core
Of self-discovered Being, he can stare
Even accident in the face; for he has seen
How the long wisdom of the living spirit
Uses its accident—the vine's green tendril
Accepts the loose brick and the rusty nail,
The spider trails her web from the dark coign,
And hollows of all shapes are hives for bees:
"So let my spirit grow upon this symbol—"
(Which, since he found those musical, haunting
Words written by the mother, had been laid
Tacitly by, as into a sealed hole
Chalked up 'Heredity') "Henceforth I take
All that is granted thus and thus, with thanks,
With reverence, yet not less as mine own right
For use and growth and knowledge—even I,
This whorl of nebulous thinking, whose moist arms
Nodded in circles blindly, till they touched
The Tower, and sucked and gripped and climbed—"
                              Marvel!
Even as he speaks, the symbol springs to life
Undreamed of: floats before his soul: not fixed,
Not growing: dream nor picture nor idea.
Is it the vision of some shape outside
Or of dark forms built up in his own flesh
And shadowed forth upon the world? The Tower:
Oh, hearken, hearken, those high bells ring wide
Weaving the web of Life from star to star,
The singing web that beateth down to earth
To join all things discrete in time and space,
Banishing emptiness, throbbing betwixt
Petal and petal, finger and finger, word and word,
Washing the island syllables of verse,
Packing with itself each melodic pause
Of music, till the music is as a sea
In which the soul floats outward: Mighty Nurse
And Mother of Becoming! Ocean of sound

Made visible by magic—yet not sound
But rather welling from one heart of Life
Into all space, glutting the crevices   40
Of the seen world.
                    The strong dream of the Tower
Is but a stone into the pool of Life,
Amplifying its ripples; so that he sees
Them, look! outspreading from the Sun in rays
Of astral light—the blood of God's own heart—
Into each earth-form, ring of trunk of tree,
Spiral of mollusc, whorl of trumpet-flower,
And the slow-breathing orbits of his thinking
Striving to be all these things—to be earth,
And the calm sky above, and the still light   50
That enters into all things equally.
For, as the Tower uprose out of its floor
Into the light, and into the still light
Outgrowing from the Sun—scattering forth
The din of its high bells, gold into gold,
So seemed his breath to rise from his round lungs,
As from a lesser Earth, until it lost
Itself in a vast heaven of still thought,
Whereinto brain poured out the forms it drew
From the dark air beneath it—sounding forth   60
Resonant, yet unheard. Even as in dreams,
Where we *are* all we listen to, so he
Was one with earth and sky, being between.
    There is a mystery of this being between
Hard to be solved by man, who is himself
That Being. Thus, the light on the grey Tower,
Which melted earth and sky to a round pearl
Of peace and summer stillness and calm joy,
Was rare upon it: at all other times
It shot bewilderingly, now bright, now dull,   70
Now starting solid from the dull dry glare,
Part of the earth, under the arch of the sky,
Now mingling in the mist, its fainting corners
Streaming out into rain, as though the stones
Were an unreal streak of the soft air:

Now earth, now sky—by turns—how rarely both!
    Even thus man, knowing, becomes all he knows,
Losing himself—and sleeps—or finds himself
And is cut off from knowledge, from all life
Save his one world of folly: the weak child,   80
That must creep back into its mother's womb
And lose its life in hers, or else must fall
Out of her breast, and die of the steel cold!
He stiffens, falls out, conscious . . . and there come
The demons, shyness, shame, habitual laughter,
Keeping him trivial, shutting him quite out
From the one source of truth, till, lo! he dies
Into metallic, yankee heartlessness
Rasping, or thin disguised as urbane taste,
Seeking only his comfort.
                        Oh, ye gods!   90
Ye gods that bound yourselves on rock and cross
To become our life—only let us want,
Infinitely, nothing for ourselves,
And we shall set you free: let us but feel
And we may be ourselves and be alive!
But when we feel not, we are still unborn,
Asleep, dim embryos of your wombs—or lost,
Drowsing in snow. Torture us back to life,
Even as ye tortured him! Oh, in your shapes
Of cloud and tree and rock—building of man—   100
And form of woman—hide with the old skill
Those cruel memories of the loveliness,
The huge unearthly wisdom, which are ours
While we lie sleeping. Change these curdling hearts,
Even as his was changed, tearing away
All other their supports but this your Life—
This wind that blows about us in the wilderness—
Until we be confounded—till we know not
What can be left to feel for, hate ourselves
For every idiot passion.
                           When he grieved   110
Of old, pride rushed to solace him with dreams
Of his own strength and dignity: where now

Was pride? Or it but raised its charming crest,
And straight he loathed and bruised it, knowing well
Himself, eternally afraid—himself,
Eternally afraid of life and death.
Yet midst this tumult of uncertain passion
Not comprehended—fluctuating—wild—
Stood—like a pharos on its hidden rock—
The meaning of the Tower—still a-building,   120
And he could add new stones, as he found strength,
Drawing foundations of blind life up to
The sky of wisdom—he and all men else,
Rearing a second Babel, wedding earth
And heaven, not now for power, but for love.
Till, as life travelled on its quieter way,
Great confidence came creeping to his heart
That on it also, even as odour
Flits to each opening blossom, and must flit,
Courage would light—from that same Union!   130
  Whose other child was Poesy, and whose pledge
Was the eternal mystery of light
Ever recurring now to memory
Or sinking with new glory into his eyes,
And the calm sweetness, and the singing voice
Of bells that rang rang rang through his whole being,
Answering all the riddles of the world
With—What is Poesy? The second birth!
It is the incarnation of this flesh
Into this consciousness. What is this flesh?   140
It is my hair, my limbs, but it is, too,
My grass, my trees, my splinters of red rock
Folded and crumpled round me: I am Earth:
But I am still asleep: knowledge is waking,
And Poesy the dream that waking brings.
There is a noise of trumpets in the mouth
Of Wisdom, and their voice is Poesy
Expressing incarnation—Dear my Joy!—
Expressing incarnation of wise Earth
Into this conscious self of Everyman,   150
Even thine and mine and all men's, all in one

And one in all—one ring of all the dancers
Shouting in chorus with uplifted mouths
And fast-linked hands, and with what grave precision
Drawing a figured Zodiac from that love,
Selfless, outpouring, which is even now
Our Earth's unlimited soul, which is our sleeping,
And all the hidden meaning of our lives.

FINIS

Introduction to *Angels at Bay*

*A*ngels at Bay is known to the world mainly through a description and summary in Simon Blaxland-de Lange's 2006 biography of Barfield's life and thought. Blaxland-de Lange dates the trilogy as "written probably in the early 1940s," though the extant typescripts were produced "between 1955 and 1970, when the Barfields were living at Westfield, Hartley, near Dartford."[1] The analysis of these plays is part of Blaxland-de Lange's program to demonstrate the "essentially artistic aspect of Barfield's mind" through "the major element in Barfield's explorations as an imaginative writer," in particular through "his poetry and poetic drama." Blaxland-de Lange directly links *Angels at Bay* with the play *Orpheus*, which came before, and *Riders on Pegasus*, which came after (256, 260). At first glance *Angels at Bay* may not seem to have much in common with these two explorations of the human experience through the reworking of Classical myth. Yet themes buried in the richly mythopoeic explorations of the flanking works, are overtly foregrounded, simplified in caricature, and more directly represented in *Angels at Bay*. Blaxland-de Lange comments that in *Angels at Bay* "the passionate concerns about the threshold between the living and the dead which are subtly veiled in *Orpheus* come explicitly to the fore" (262). In the 1982 Foreword to *Orpheus*, Barfield writes: "C. S. Lewis in a Note written in 1948 emphasized, I hope rightly, that *Orpheus* is a mystery drama, not a 'problem' one," though it may "stretch a sort of tentacle here and there" toward socio-political issues.[2] These potentials may arise from the text, but the mythopoeic purpose is to reshape and reframe the foundational meanings that underlie our social problems rather than address them directly. This is undoubtedly also true for *Angels at Bay*, which is overtly a mystery drama and follows Steiner in the genre, and though the settings are mundane rather than mythic, the juxtaposed angel scenes explicitly reframe and redefine the action. The effect is not subtle but pointed, and one need not be reminded that to interpret these plays as anything empirical or problematic to the empirical misses the central point of the angelic reframing.

None of the three plays that make up *Angels at Bay* functions alone—they are a true trilogy forming a single work. The first two plays are divided between a first scene depicting stereotypical action in current society and a second scene of angelic reframing of meaning and being in opposition to the banal realism of the previous scene. The last play presents a future-shock scenario set by Barfield as taking place "Early in the twenty-first century." By the end of the play the two realms are blended in the struggle against the meaninglessness of objectified consciousness in our day. Together the three plays present a highly stylized representation of the ontological wasteland of modern life and the quiescent spiritual awareness to which the world must awaken.

The theme of the first play, "The Wall," is the contemporary Western world's disconnection with death. In a society that rejects meaning and objectifies all existence, death is only the undignified and appalling snuffing out of being, and the only meanings that may be derived from its contemplation are inherently morbid and tragic. Blaxland-de Lange notes that in the first scene, "[d]eath is portrayed as a subject regarding which the only decent thing to do is to keep silence," and he footnotes two connected Barfield essays from 1930, "Psychology and Reason" and "Death," both treatises of significant depth "the meditation upon which found expression in both *Orpheus* and 'Angels at Bay'."[3] The second scene, set in the angelic realm, recasts life and death teleologically and anagogically, the discourse of the assembled angels lamenting "the strongly earthbound thoughts of those who have recently died" and the inability of the living "to form any connection with their loved ones beyond the threshold of death" (262).

Similar to the opening scene of "The Wall," the first scene of the second play, "The Human Dynamo," is also seemingly conventional drama and presents a day in the life—and almost death—of a high-powered publishing tycoon, Sir Charles Ritson. The conventional presentation of admiration for the dynamic and successful man of business is a parody to be reframed by the second scene from the angelic realm—this time even more directly as the action of the two scenes are nearly simultaneous, and Ritson's incredible luck in mindlessly escaping his imminent demise is recast as the true tragedy for his soul and the result of direct intervention of dark forces. The theme of the frenetic energy of human endeavor portrayed by Ritson might resonate with the opening of the fourteenth century poem *Piers Plowman*, yet the concomitant mindless consumption of the natural world's resources aligns more to the ecological concerns of the twentieth century, a theme inherent in Barfield's program throughout his life and most overtly developed in his late novella, *Eager Spring*. Blaxland-de Lange notes: "The angels are deeply concerned about the increasing meaninglessness of the activities of the human beings in their charge, and Serakel, who is one of the angels of the coniferous trees, laments about the destructiveness that they have wrought" (263). Indeed, the irony of casting Ritson's escape from death as tragedy evinces the possibility for human beings to lose their essential humanity to the fixations and processes of empirical causality.

The dehumanizing processes of modern life and oblivious camera-consciousness inscribe Ritson's loss of humanity in proportion to his socio-economic ascent by modern empirical standards. Armaros, the Angel of Sir Charles Ritson, at first resists the suggestion to recall the soul he guards, but when asked to ponder "the dark gulf that yawns before" and look deeply into Ritson's heart, Armaros sees a desensitizing descent into mindless causalities. He reports seeing "whirring wheels / Smooth, unctuous, dead frightening . . . swift, swifter . . . and O my Soul! / As the years pass, they are self-moved, are impulsed by a will / Till the door closes in this face, and I seek entry again in vain!" Blaxland-de Lange notes that much of Barfield's early literary critique drew heavily from the poetry in particular of Blake, Milton, and Keats (257). One easily hears in Armaros's lines Blake's lament in *Jerusalem* for the destruction of human learning, the raging "Loom of Locke" and the mechanical "Water-wheels of Newton" that have objectified and enslaved the life of the mind: "cruel Works / Of many Wheels I view, wheel without wheel, with cogs tyrannic / Moving by compulsion each other: not as those in Eden: which / Wheel within Wheel in freedom revolve in harmony & peace." One might also recall the Oyarsa of Malacandra's pronouncements on Devine in *Out of the Silent Planet*. Speaking of the evils that arise from the 'lord of the silent world', The Oyarsa says: "[A] bent *hnau* can do more evil than a broken one. He has only bent you; but this Thin One who sits on the ground he has broken, for he has left him nothing but greed. He is now only a talking animal. . . . If he were mine I would unmake his body for the *hnau* in it is already dead."[4] It is the great success in worldly matters granted by positivist consciousness that in turn robs us of our humanity and cancels any opportunity to rise above the visceral biology it defines.

However, the destructive power that Ritson wields as a publishing tycoon pales in comparison to the evil that is contemplated by "the board" of powerful men in the final play in the trilogy, "The Paranoia Wing." As the sinister powers increase their efforts and total hegemony is about to be unleashed on society, the higher powers of good emanating through the conduit of angels must choose their moment of decisive action. A traditional theme of good vs evil is at the forefront, and it is not difficult to place this drama in greater literary and social contexts. Anyone might recognize the dystopian theme of empirical science as both the means and excuse for a dehumanizing imposition of control on a mainly unsuspecting population whose lives have been stripped of meaning—a theme prominent in much British literature of the period. Yet the critique in *Angels at Bay* of modern banality and the ruthless arrogance of power has more in common with the other Inklings than with Orwell or Huxley. The stylization is overt, and the tone broadly mythopoeic—with an unabashed assumption of spirituality.

In the second play, the Angel Serakel's vocalizing of the violence of commercial silviculture, and the implications of such for all life, resonates with similar themes in Tolkien and Lewis in both spiritual and environmental themes. Blaxland-de Lange notes the wanton destructiveness of the mindless consumption of forests, but the message is necessarily deeper, more fundamental. Like the perceived living-death of Ritson's descent into mindless impulsion, the trees he farms for paper are alive but not living: "Man's planning, man's calculating thought / Of vat, pulping-machine, paper-mill, works—renders the life of trees / A life lifeless, a sad substance that sends nothing back to earth." Similarly, the crassly reductive positivist discourse from the board of governors of the secret lodge in the third play resonates with the translating of positivist discourse in Lewis's Space Trilogy, revealing the inevitable brutality of objectifying language, or perhaps more directly with the civics discussion at the end of Tolkien's *Leaf by Niggle*. Indeed, one of the more biting passages of *Angels at Bay* is the change in the patient Alexander Reid of "The Paranoia Wing" revealed through recordings of his post-treatment discussions with the hospital Chaplain. When the Chaplain asks if he had been mistaken about his sense of reincarnation, Reid replies:

> Well, no, Sir. I would hardly say 'mistaken'. It's too dignified a word. I don't feel now that I ever got as far as that. There must first be a thing to be mistaken about. Reincarnation, if it meant anything, would mean repeated incarnation; but incarnation is

not a thing. It is just a word. How could anyone ever suppose it meant anything? What size is it? Where is it kept when not in use? How do you paraphrase it? Something like "a not-body becoming a body", I suppose! Honestly!

The almost ridiculously smug tone of positivism is reminiscent of Tompkins in Tolkien's story spouting bitingly reductive scorn for Niggle's attempt to create meaning through artistic homage to primary creation: "He could not have designed a telling poster to save his life. Always fiddling with leaves and flowers. I asked him why, once. He said he thought they were pretty! Can you believe it? He said *pretty!* 'What, digestive and genital organs of plants?' I said to him; and he had nothing to answer. Silly footler."[5] In a sense, the mythopoeic flavor of much Inklings literature directs more critique at the shackles of modern, positivist figuration than the political brutality of the powerful—though Streeter's reaction to the catastrophe at the end of the third play—"Semajay, help!"— hints that not all antagonists are well-meaning scientists misled by a blind and conceited positivism—some are truly agents of evil. In these several respects Barfield's themes resonate strongly with his compatriots among the Oxford Inklings.

Yet more specifically, within the broad circle of Inklings and friends, the mythopoesis of *Angels at Bay* is somewhat unique in its referencing of anthroposophy. A rather overt example from "The Paranoia Wing" is the patient/prisoner Joan Holdsworth's direct rejoinder to Dr. Sedlescombe: "Why do you beat about the bush? I'm quite sure you know very well that nearly everyone kept in the Wing has been actively engaged, in one walk of life or another, or in their spare time, in the pursuit of spiritual science." Blaxland-de Lange clearly discerns that in form, style, and content, *Angels at Bay* "was Barfield's attempt at a modern mystery play . . . clearly inspired by Steiner's four mystery plays," though certainly Barfield was "very far from merely imitating" (265). Yet, it may well be such overt referencing of anthroposophy that has kept *Angels at Bay* more unknown than *Orpheus* or even *Riders on Pegasus*, for without a framing that resists positivist interpretation, the message would crumble as mere ideology. Certainly any who might smirk at presenting Ritson's escape from death as the real tragedy would certainly find little sympathy with Joan Holdsworth's prophecy that "if we are killed—whether by design or accident—we shall only help to make stronger those who remain." Yet, as Blaxland-de Lange reports, Barfield intended *Angels at Bay* as anthroposophical drama, a modern mystery play, not a problem play or strange inscription of ideological myopia; rather it is a considerable revelation of Owen Barfield's "inner questings and strivings around the mid-point of his life" and a significant key to the development of his philosophical thought in artistic expression. (265)

Notes

1. Simon Blaxland-de Lange, *Owen Barfield: Romanticism Come of Age: A Biography* (Forest Row, England: Temple Lodge Publishing, 2006), 262. Further citations of this work are given in the text. In a recent communication, Blaxland-de Lange indicates that he has found evidence that the third play, "The Paranoia Wing," was completed much later, in the summer of 1962. A second edition of the biography is forthcoming.

2. Owen Barfield, "Foreword," in Owen Barfield, *Orpheus: a Poetic Drama*, ed. John C. Ulreich, Jr. (West Stockbridge, MA: The Lindisfarne Press, 1983), 7. Further citations of this work are given in the text.

3. Blaxland-de Lange, *Owen Barfield*, 333, n244. "Psychology and Reason" was originally published in T. S. Eliot's *The Criterion: A Quarterly Review* 9 (July 1930): 606-617. "Death" remained unpublished until 2008. Both essays are now available on the Owen Barfield Literary Estate Website: http://www.owenbarfield.org/articles/ .

4. C. S. Lewis, *Out of the Silent Planet* (New York: Scribner, 2003), 137–138.

5. J. R. R. Tolkien, *Tree and Leaf*, in *The Tolkien Reader* (New York: Del Rey, 1966), 119.

ANGELS AT BAY

THREE PLAYS

I. The Wall
II. The Human Dynamo
III. The Paranoia Wing

I. THE WALL

Characters

A Doctor
Marjorie Mayne
Peter Mayne *Marjorie's brother*
Mr. Cousins *A neighbour*

Remiel *An Archangel*
Shezef *An Angel*
Raquel *An Angel*
Kaüret *Angel of Henry Mayne, father of Marjorie and Peter*
Ramaturel *Angel of Gertrude, Henry's wife*
Melaicharos *Angel of Marjorie Mayne*
Tashkit *Angel of Peter Mayne*

Time: *The present* [mid-twentieth century].
Three months elapse between Scenes 1 and 2.

Scene 1

(The living-room of a medium-sized suburban house. On one side a few steps lead up to a door opening on an inner room. On the opposite side another door.)

DOCTOR *(standing with his back to the audience in the open doorway of the inner room and speaking to someone within it)*

Nonsense my dear man! Before you know where you are, you'll be out in the garden. In a deck chair to start with, you know. And you'd better be getting those golf-clubs cleaned up. Let's see, what's the handicap? Eh? Nonsense! You'll have your ups and downs of course. You must expect that. Well, I really must be getting along now. Good-bye for the present.

(He comes out and closes the door behind him. As he does so, Marjorie enters from the opposite side.)

MARJORIE

Well?

DOCTOR *(gravely)*

I'm glad you are here. I wanted to see you before I went. There's no point in upsetting your Mother unnecessarily.

(She gives him a sudden enquiring look, in reply to which he shakes his head.)

MARJORIE

Do you mean he can't possibly recover?

DOCTOR

I'm afraid not now, Miss Mayne. Actually, I don't think it can last more than a few days.

MARJORIE

Surely there must be *something* we can do! Another specialist—

DOCTOR

Honestly, it's useless.

MARJORIE

Do you want *me* to tell Mother?

DOCTOR

I think it will be best.

MARJORIE

Oh God! Doctor—does he know?

DOCTOR *(shocked)*

Good *lord*, no! *Never* tell a patient anything of that sort. What's the point?

MARJORIE

Has he ever asked you?

DOCTOR

Whether they ask one or not, the only duty I recognize is to tell my patient what will do him the most good.

MARJORIE

But you said—

DOCTOR

And when it's too late to do him lasting good, what will make him most comfortable in his mind.

MARJORIE *(after a pause)*

You know best, Doctor.

DOCTOR *(after a further pause)*

Don't worry too much Miss Mayne. We shall have started keeping him under all the time, well before the end comes. He won't know where he is or what is happening to him.

Marjorie

Mercifully!

Doctor

Well, good-bye Miss Mayne. I'll be along tomorrow at the usual time. *(exit)*

Marjorie *(with one sob)*

Daddy! Daddy!

(Enter Mr. Cousins)

Cousins

I met the Doctor going out. Well, what's the news today?

Marjorie

Oh, Mr. Cousins!

(She goes up to him and speaks a few words in a low voice.)

Cousins

Oh dear, oh dear! I *am* sorry! Poor chap! Shall I go in and see him as usual?

Marjorie

I think he'd like it. *(He goes towards the inner door.)* Cheer him up, won't you? *(Stopping him as he is about to turn the handle.)* You won't say anything to distress him? He doesn't know, you know!

Cousins

No, no of course not! Not for the world! Just the usual little chat about nothing in particular.

(He goes in, shutting the door behind him. Marjorie goes to the other door and calls through it.)

Marjorie

Peter!

(Enter Peter)

PETER

How is he today?

MARJORIE

Not so good, I'm afraid.

PETER *(He looks at her closely.)*

I say, what's the Doctor said? *(She says something to him in a low voice.)* Poor-old-boy! Mother upset?

MARJORIE

I don't think she knows. I say, Peter, what shall we do about Mother?

PETER

Do?

MARJORIE

About telling her—and afterwards.

PETER

Gosh, it'll nearly kill her. She's got nothing else.

MARJORIE

I'll tell her—tomorrow probably.

PETER

We shall have to find ways of keeping her mind off it. The first bit after the funeral will be the worst. We must take her out of herself at all costs. Bridge—parties—anything.

MARJORIE

Funeral! You know how he hated all humbug and ceremony.

PETER

Oh we just can't talk about that now. I don't really want a lot of humbug either. I mean when the house is empty.

(Re-enter Mr. Cousins.)

MARJORIE

Well?

COUSINS

Well of course he is weaker—I don't think he wanted me to stay any longer. *(A pause)* Miss Mayne, are you sure he doesn't know anything? I began to wonder at one point.

MARJORIE

Why? What did he say?

COUSINS

It wasn't what he said. It seemed an effort for him to listen to what *I* was saying. And once or twice I noticed a sort of fixed look in his eyes that rather worried me.

MARJORIE

You didn't say anything to—

COUSINS

No, No, of course not. *(A pause)* Once or twice I had a queer feeling that he was rather hoping I *would* talk about it.

PETER

Talk about what?

COUSINS *(uneasily)*

Well—the future.

MARJORIE

You promise you never will, don't you?

Cousins

Of course.

Peter

Gosh! I know what you mean though. I've thought once or twice he was going to raise the subject. Made me sweat all over. What *can* one say?

Marjorie

What did you say?

Peter

Oh, we never actually *got* on to the subject. I managed to make him laugh. Took his mind off it, you know. And we started talking about something else altogether.

(A pause)

Cousins

Well, I'm afraid I'll have to be getting along. I'm awfully distressed—

(A noise, between a cry and a moan, comes from the inner room. All look at each other for an instant, and Marjorie flies to the door and goes in, leaving the door open. Marjorie's voice and another are indistinctly audible through it. After a short time, Marjorie re-appears at the door.)

Peter

What did he say?

Marjorie

I'm not sure. He mumbled in such a funny way. Seemed to be dreaming he was back at school and then kept asking why the light wasn't left on. *(Closing the door behind her)* Peter, ring up the Doctor and tell him to come back *at once*. He *promised!* I simply can't bear it. He *must* be got to sleep.

(Curtain falls, as Peter turns to leave the room.)

(Music)

Scene 2

(The curtain rises again, disclosing a scene suggesting an irregular plateau surrounded by rocks with waterfalls visible in the distance through clouds. The whole, including the foreground, is enveloped in a light mist. In the centre a large, low rock, roughly rectangular in shape, makes a sort of natural table with its end towards the audience. On both sides of the rock stand a number of angels. At the head, farthest from the audience and facing it, Remiel.)

Remiel

My two Captains, bright Angels, brave eager partisans!
To you, Raquel, and you, Shezef, hail!
     Show me whom you bring,
To share tidings, shape plans and swell further our growing strength.

Raquel

We burn brighter, with love greeting thee, glorious Remiel!

Remiel

Name-speaking and hand-clasping! From each Angel I long to hear
His word sounding—

(Shezef, Raquel, and Kaüret clasp hands.)

Kaüret

   I, Kaüret, guard soul of Henry Mayne
From earth-body freed lately. Oh—

Ramaturel *(breaking-in)*

     I, Ramaturel,
Am Gertrude his wife's Angel.

(Shezef, Raquel, Ramaturel and then Shezef, Raquel, and Tashkit, clasp hands.)

Tashkit

   Tashkit! I guide the soul
Of his son, Peter.

(Shezef, Raquel, and Melaicharos clasp hands.)

MELAICHAROS

        Mayne's daughter! My name, Melaicharos;
Hers, Marjorie. Hail, Master!

KAÜRET

        Oh, this cannot go on!

RAQUEL

Be calm, Brother! We all know, we all feel, the same dismay.
How I felt it, when I gathered my soul a year ago!
For that cause we take care to meet here from time to time:
        For that cause we meet here today.

KAÜRET

Oh yes, yes! I have heard Angels, heard numbers say the same—
But, oh Raquel, I never dreamed death could be like this!

REMIEL

We meet here to share news and shape policy, Kaüret:
Despair strengthens, kept hidden—once uttered, it weakens will:
The one speaking and the one hearing, both falter. I bid you cease.

KAÜRET *(looking round him)*

I crave pardon. But oh, Brothers! . . . You all bid me not despair—
Have *you* tried to reach souls that are drugged deep and bound to earth
By vapid thinking, ever down sinking, stone deaf, as mine has been,
To the pure Sound, and all drowned in the Light round the light of him?
        My poor soul, with his light growing dim!

REMIEL

Be sure, Brother, we all know, we all weep. This very thing
Is the stern task, to speak plain, that the times ask. Our Enemy
From birth-moment to death-moment pours over the souls of men
Earth-stunning sensation, swift emptiness of thought.
Our main purpose in so meeting is soul-waking; our greatest need

Is help coming from earth-dwelling, strong souls. We wait for this,
But while waiting, we pool knowledge; and act also, where we can,
With grace ministered, help tendered, deeds done—and all the time
      We plan battle for time still to come.
Enough then! Begin conference! Tashkit, we call on you!

TASHKIT

Alas, Brothers, I bring little. Thank God, the soul I guide
Is a good soul, a soul truthful, not selfish, fairly kind,
But no more.

SHEZEF

      More's needed, much more, would we keep alive
Man's spirit fast failing. The foe squats everywhere,
His might spreading, his grip growing: Mansoul is occupied,
Our own country! Semjaya, the cold-bringer, holds it down
      With his deft hordes, and we, helpless, watch!

TASHKIT

I know, Brother, and all this, on the deep nights, I whisper while
He lies sleeping, for heart-hearing, but still, so far, he has not heard.

KAÜRET

Son-father! In life, friends! Is there no force to throw in here?
No starved longings, with time turning slowly into ghostly love?

TASHKIT

Not yet, Brother. You ask early: have patience—look, with me
At his will clouded by youth, happiness, hope springing of life to come:
Hard battle with those burdens half-dreaming his spirit does!
He loved fairly, as sons do—but think! Think of all the power
Held over a faint lover by Them! I have nothing yet:
In time, maybe—ten—twenty years later—

SHEZEF

      Too late, too late!

RAQUEL

For the main purpose, I grant: still we must also keep in view
The far goal.

KAÜRET

 My thanks, Brother!

REMIEL

   Proceed farther: Melaicharos,
Can you tell any good news of help hoped from the sister soul?

MELAICHAROS

She hates death.

REMIEL

   They all do, the best even.

MELAICHAROS

    I mean not that—
Not her own death in a dim future—she shuns thinking of death at all.

KAÜRET

She loved deeply: she lived much in him: how can she let him go
without struggling?

MELAICHAROS

   Without struggle? No, No!

KAÜRET

    Then sorrow makes
Her soul's current set deeper and more strong. He needs that strength
And I ask for it. Oh, pass it me!

MELAICHAROS

    Ah, Brother, I did not say
Her soul-current set deeper; truth rather says, it flows

More shallowly.

KAÜRET

      How? Shallowly?

MELAICHAROS

                    Oh, Brother, the foe is strong!
On some nights she came near to me—quite near—because of him.
But day followed, dull custom and light shining on common things,
And she slipped back, as I groped yearning, with love burning. The Enemy
Is strong—terribly: whole lives are his grim prey: he has practised her,
Her life through to shun thinking of death! Shrinking back in fear,
At each try she starts back from the thought, too, of the dead she loves,
Calls morbid the death-dwelling thought: so his image sinks
As if drowned in the roar round, in the bright senses' cataract
Of rapid shocks! Lost, lost is he! Deep longings unfulfilled,
Held pure and faced fearlessly, turn slow to ghostly love,
      But grief stifled grows little and cold.
She is less lively, more trivial: light gratifications fill
The void places of his dear face, use wholly her feeling now,
My poor soul: the bed-comfort, food-pleasure, blazing-hearth,
Skin's greeting to silk sheathing it, nerves' thanks to nicotine,
And that daily, unceasing eye-pasture of printed page!
For spirit-music—low chuckles of mind's brook meandering through
The long novel-drugged fancy, death fearing, fails to rise!
She sleeps well, but far, far from her own Angel—I long to help,
      But find open no way to near her.

REMIEL

      Try still! The hour ripens fast . . . let Ramaturel,
The wife's Angel, join counsel—tell what of gifts he brings.

RAMATUREL

Of grief much: of love more: I bow daily before my Soul
With awe—erring and short-sighted soul! None the less I bring
In my hands truth and strength, lovely firm fruit of constancy,
Tough-rinded and sweet-centred; by long years of married life
Well-ripened—will's habit set, so she cannot help

But seek selflessly his happiness, his good before her own
At each moment—

KAÜRET

                But how comes it, this great good could be so near
And no breath of it rise up—

RAMATUREL

                I have no power to pass it on!

KAÜRET

    Oh dire words! Why, Brother?

RAMATUREL

                Will's habit is helpless here.
We can seek only a known thing: she knows nothing, nor seeks to know
Of his need lately!

KAÜRET

    I fear greatly—feel grief approaching fast!

RAMATUREL

Hurled back by a huge Wall, her thoughts wander about the past—
Lamed mind that would fain find rest somewhere—

SHEZEF

                I know, I know—
"He liked this; he used that; would have wished (if he were here today)"
I know well the dreams, memories, tears, photograph near the bed—
And oh, never a thought, never a stray fancy for what he likes
Or wants now, what he feels now, what he now wishes for, hopes
and needs!
I don't ask they should not grieve, or forget quickly the past: I know
Too well, Brothers, the sweet intimacy that lights up with the to and fro
Of the bright senses (thin fences, themselves linking the lands they part)
As hand-pressure and voice-tamber flick signals from heart to heart.
If they spared only one corner of the love-weighted thoughts, they weave

For us—us and their own dead—we could win worlds—you know we could.

    I ask pardon! I came near despairing.

Remiel

You speak truth. *(A pause, during which he looks from one to the other.)*
    Can none tell of means found to breach that Wall?
(A pause)

Kaüret

No help? Ah!

Shezef

    Record, Raquel: Again failure!

Remiel

                  I think not so
To feel helpless is great grief: we are helpless, I grant it, now,
Till times change and men melt in the Warmth coming. But even so
Not all wasted our deeds fall. It is our winter. Underground
The frost grips, and the seed sleeps, but the seed softens as the spirit awakes,
In the first place our love-union lends strength to our Brother here
To bear woe without weakening: next, all must understand
That at each meeting our main purpose for time being—reconnaissance—
Is borne farther. We learn more. Semjaya's secret ways
Become known. We spy out his main strength and—do not doubt—
His worst weakness. Have patience! For oh, Brothers, underground
Our own strength is fast growing—fast growing! The time will come,
And come soon, to wield all we now gather of truth and will—
    To resist openly—wage active war!
(A pause)
    So let us seal our union, as before.

Kaüret

    I will be patient. Make me one of you!

REMIEL

    Now cast we all our burdens in the lap
Of those Intelligences high, for whom
Our failures are success, and all our jars
Are harmony: Dominions, Virtues, Powers,
And those high Lords of Wisdom, Will, and Love
Who fill us and we them. And now not less
We meekly bow our heads to those below
Through whom we rise, remembering thankfully
That Man, who labours through his cold and dark,
Labours for us too, who are filled with light
And move always in music—in such sort
That joy is mingled with our fiercest pain.

(Each Angel places one hand on the shoulder of the Angel next to him and with the others clasps the hand of the one opposite to him.)

ALL

      Members one of another
        Filled with the Spheres above,
    We bind us, brother to brother,
        To lift Mansoul in Love.

(Music, while the Angels move, passing in and out of one another, about the stage, and eventually return to their places. Towards the close of this movement the music fades, and they recite)—

ALL

      Winged with the Will of God,
        I will carry His making Word
    To Man building a body
        For my Lover and Lord.

(All the Angels kneel round the rock. Remiel turns his back and raises both his arms.)

REMIEL

    Quoniam apud Te est fons vitae.

(Light shines down from above on the surface of the rock.)

ALL
    Et in lumine Tuo videbunt lucem!

CURTAIN

II. THE HUMAN DYNAMO

Characters

Ernest Pratt	*Office junior on the staff of* The Sunday Universe
Miss Hopton	*Private secretary to Sir Charles Ritson*
Sir Charles Ritson	*Governing Director and effective proprietor of* The Sunday Universe, Ltd.
Robert Noakes	*Manager of the Football Pools Department of* The Sunday Universe
Remiel	*An Archangel*
Shezef	*An Angel*
Raquel	*An Angel*
Armaros	*Angel of Sir Charles Ritson*
Anpiel	*Angel of Robert Noakes*
Khif	*Angel of Ernest Pratt*
Chemalion	*Angel of an un-named assiduous reader of* The Sunday Universe
Serakel	*One of the Angels of the coniferous trees*

Time: *The present* [mid-twentieth century].
The times occupied by Scene 1 and 2 are approximately simultaneous, but the end of Scene 2 occurs slightly before the end of Scene 1.

Scene I

(Scene: A very well-appointed room in the offices of The Sunday Universe. *Ernest is dusting and polishing the inkstand and other objects on the large mahogany writing-desk.)*

(Enter Miss Hopton with papers under her arm.)

Miss Hopton

Hurry up and finish! I want to put these papers down.

Ernest

Wattime's the Big Noise coming in?

Miss Hopton

Don't be cheeky! Sir Charles may be here any minute now. *(Putting down the papers and looking through them.)* Oh, dear, I wish he'd come to the office *regularly* instead of popping in on us unexpectedly like this!

Ernest *(watching her)*

Storm expected! *(She does not answer.)* Old Danvers said outside there was going to be hell all over the office this morning. The Great White Chief's browned off 'cos the circulation hasn't gone up again.

Miss Hopton

What are you writing there? and put down Sir Charles's umbrella at once.

Ernest

Gar! it's only 'is spare one. I was only making a note where he got it.

Miss Hopton

Why?

Ernest

Because he knows what's what.

MISS HOPTON

Thinking of buying one like it?

ERNEST

Not just yet.

MISS HOPTON

Oh, I know! You see yourself turning into a Sir Charles yourself some day!

ERNEST *(embarassed)*

Well, what's wrong with starting right and having a go?

MISS HOPTON

That's all right, Ernie, there's nothing like ambition. By the way, do you know what the circulation of the *Universe* was when Sir Charles bought it three years ago?

ERNEST

No.

MISS HOPTON

300,000. Do you know what it was last week?

ERNEST

Yes. Same as the week before. 4,000,000 certified. I say, Miss Hopton, who's the bloke that does the certifying, and how much does he get for it?

MISS HOPTON

Mm! I wonder if you've got the remotest idea that Sir Charles is probably the keenest brain and the finest all-around man in England. You're aiming high enough, young man!

ERNEST *(singing)*

"I worship the ground you *tread* on . . ."

Miss Hopton *(sharply)*

That's enough now! If you've finished, you can go.

(Exit Ernest and, after a final look round, Miss Hopton.)

(Enter Sir Charles Ritson. He goes straight to the desk and turns over the papers left by Miss Hopton, then rings a bell, takes off his hat and begins taking off his coat. Enter Miss Hopton.)

Miss Hopton

Good morning, Sir Charles!

Sir Charles *(hanging up his coat and returning to his desk)*

Good morning, Miss Hopton, I asked you to have ready on my desk the Costings Analyses, Costings Graphs, Copy Analyses, and Circulation Graphs. The Costings Analyses and Graphs and the Circulation Graphs are here, but not the Copy Analyses. Bring them, please!

Miss Hopton

Yes, Sir Charles. I'm very sorry.

Sir Charles

I want them quickly please. *(Exit Miss Hopton.)*

(Sir Charles spreads some of the papers out on the desk. Re-enter Miss Hopton with further papers, which she hands to him. She stands waiting with her notebook open.)

Sir Charles

Thank you, I'll ring. *(Exit Miss Hopton.)*

(Sir Charles continues examining the papers for a time, then he presses a button, which starts a faint whirring noise in the microphone on his desk. Speaking into the microphone):

Is that Sports? Give me Mr. Anderson. *(The amplifier attached to the microphone says something indistinguishable.)* Why is he out? Give me the Assistant Dog-Racing Editor! *(noise from the amplifier as before)* I want two more columns on Dogs next week. I'm telling Make-up. Right. That's all! *(He presses the button again, with similar results.)* I want Mr. Noakes.

(Enter Mr. Noakes.)

NOAKES

Good morning, Sir!

SIR CHARLES

Oh, Noakes, what staff have we got on Pools now?

NOAKES

Fifty-one Sir, counting myself.

SIR CHARLES

How many outgoing letters to readers last week?

NOAKES

Well, I should say—

SIR CHARLES

Don't you know?

NOAKES

Between ninety and a hundred, Sir.

SIR CHARLES

If I give you ten more clerks and two more columns, can you raise it to seven hundred and fifty in three weeks?

NOAKES

I can try, Sir Charles.

SIR CHARLES

Very good. That's settled. I'll tell Make-up. *(Exit Mr. Noakes.)*
(Sir Charles rings the bell. Enter Miss Hopton.)

Miss Hopton, I want *Maison Chic*—the Advertising Manager—no—get me the Sales Manager, he's got more ginger.

Miss Hopton
Yes, Sir Charles. *(Exit)*
(Sir Charles returns to the desk and the papers. The telephone bell rings.)

Sir Charles *(into the telephone)*
This is the *Sunday Universe*. Ritson Speaking. I want to screw up my advertisements appeal . . . Yes . . . I think we can help each other. Are you prepared to let me see a batch of your drawings, whether accepted or not? . . . Yes . . . I'm going to pick out my own and offer you two-thirds rate for four consecutive insertions . . . this afternoon . . . as many as you like . . . yes, both kinds . . . whatever the *usual* proportions are—no, wait—say 10% off over-and on under-clothes . . . that may be, but *you* want them to sell clothes, *I* want them to sell newspapers. . . . Very likely, but it's not only the women I'm thinking of. . . . Yes, I know! That's just why I'm offering the 33 & 1/3 % reduction. You can take it or leave it, you know . . . what? Right, right, right. Good man! Good-bye! *(He replaces the receiver and rings the bell. Enter Miss Hopton.)* Miss Hopton, bring me that letter from Atlantic Seabord Estates.

Miss Hopton *(proudly)*
I've got it here, Sir Charles.

Sir Charles
Well done! *(taking the letter)* Get on to their London Manager in two minutes' time, will you—not before. The *Holding* Company, you know! *(Exit Miss Hopton. Sir Charles reads the letter, drumming his fingers as he does so. The telephone rings – into the telephone)*: London Manager? Good morning. Your letter. You're asking half a million too much. Thanks! I know just how badly I want those shares and just how much I'm willing to pay. . . . That's not the point! I don't want them for investment. I simply want the controlling interest. . . . No. I can't possibly do with less than 500 square miles. You say the trees replace themselves in 25 years—by the way, I've still got to check up on that—Ritson Mills say they're buying 2,000 tons of pulp—say 15,000 trees—for each edition—that's at the present circulation level. Don't be pigheaded, man! Half a million

off . . . What? Hey, wait a minute! What about talking it over at lunch? Can you meet me at my Club in 20 minutes' time? . . . *The Feudal*, St. James's . . . Right, right. Good-bye. *(replacing the receiver)*: Blast the man! *(He rings the bell. Enter Miss Hopton.)* Miss Hopton, what's the name of the man who does religion?

MISS HOPTON

Mr. Nailsworth, Sir Charles.

SIR CHARLES

Make a note, I want to see him on his cross-headings. Dull. Better have the Sub-editor in with him. No, not this morning. Next time I'm here.

MISS HOPTON

When will that be, Sir Charles?

SIR CHARLES

How do I know? I'm off now. *(She gets his coat and begins helping him on with it.)* Thanks! And tell Make-up he's got to find two extra columns for Dog-racing and three for Football Pools. There'll be an extra page. Additional Ads for the rest of the space. He'll hear from Ads about that. *(He moves towards the door.)*

MISS HOPTON *(calling after him)*

Good morning, Sir Charles.

(Exit Sir Charles. Miss Hopton crosses to the window and opens it, letting in the noise of the traffic. Enter Ernest, crosses to the window and stands beside her.)

MISS HOPTON

Hulloa! What have *you* come back for?

ERNEST

I like to watch him getting into his 400 hp Super Super.

Miss Hopton

It's absurd, the Police not letting it wait on this side of the road for the short time he's here! There he goes, striding across the road with his big head down as usual—full of his creative plans! *(screaming)* Oh! *(She turns away from the window through which there is heard a smashing, tearing noise, followed by shouting and what sounds like wild abuse.)* He walked right under it.

Ernest *(still looking out of window)*

Gor!

Miss Hopton

What's happened? Oh, where is he?

Ernest

Just getting into the Super Super. *(turning from the window)* Gor! Did you see that? Walks slap in front of an oncoming car—and if a 'bus going the other way doesn't skid out and stop it just as it's going to get him! I believe he hardly knows anything's happened. Some people have the luck! Gor!

(Curtain falls)

(Music)

Scene 2

(The curtain rises again, disclosing a scene suggesting an irregular plateau surrounded by rocks with waterfalls visible in the distance through clouds. The whole, including the foreground, is enveloped in a light mist. In the centre a large, low rock, roughly rectangular in shape, makes a sort of natural table with its end towards the audience. On either side of the table, facing each other, stand Shezef and Raquel; at the head, farthest from the audience and facing it, Remiel.)

Remiel

The fresh-flowing love springs in my breast, Angels: we greet again,
As it floods back from your faces—

Raquel

                    I love, Master!

Shezef

                              I burn, I burn!
Let us pass swiftly to hand-clasping and name-speaking—

Remiel

                            Impart them, then,
The new Angels, who become members!
(Enter, ceremonially, Armaros, Anpiel, Khif, Chemalion, and Serakel.)

Shezef

Let each utter his own name and the time-name of the Soul he guides!
(Shezef, Raquel, and Armaros clasp hands.)

Armaros

My name Armaros: Charles Ritson's Soul's guardian, servant, guide.
(Shezef, Raquel, and Anpiel clasp hands.)

Anpiel

My name Anpiel: my Soul I name duly Robert Noakes.

(Shezef, Raquel, and Khif clasp hands.)

KHIF

I am called Khif: and guard Ernest Pratt's Soul.

(Shezef, Raquel, and Chemalion clasp hands.)

CHEMALION

            Chemalion
Stands here, not himself only but oh, numberless angels, more,
Whose souls suffer as mine suffers! Soon, Brothers, you will hear
Their word sounding in my word.
(Shezef, Raquel, and Serakel clasp hands.)

RAQUEL *(to Serakel)*

     And thou, Brother?

SERAKEL

            Serakel!
I, too, am not I only: Aspected in me behold
Angels of the cone-bearing trees spread over all the Earth.

REMIEL

We greet all of you. So, Serakel, speak!

SERAKEL

         Once there was a time,
When *we* uttered the Word, sent the sap thrilling through the trees
With our thinking and ours only: wild woodland flourished free
With the rain slanting, the light shining, the birds chanting through
their leaves.
As the wind blows, the sap rose in them. All that is changing now!
Those vast columns, man-planted, where the sun sets beyond Atlantis,
Are ghosts torn from us.

RAQUEL

     How torn? They *live*; therefore, the procreant Word
Informs each of them.

THE HUMAN DYNAMO

SERAKEL

   Ah, Raquel, today, partly, the procreant Word
Is man-syllabled: Man's planning, man's calculating thought
Of vat, pulping-machine, paper-mill, works—renders the life of trees
A life lifeless, a sad substance that sends nothing back to earth.

RAQUEL

Can this be?

REMIEL

   He speaks truth.

SHEZEF

      Is man ware of it?

REMIEL

         Hardly, yet.
Two thousand years ago Earth suddenly found herself;
The Word working in wild Nature became flesh—became his own.
From that moment our influence fades slowly from land and sea,
  And man, wielding the Word, knows it not.

RAQUEL

  We grudge not his great glory.

SERAKEL

      His great danger—he knows it not!
Wise angels, Word-wielders themselves formerly, watched him grasp
With will tainted his proud prize, the fresh power to work on Nature:
Witchcraft he found first—and then Science, snatched from sense—
  Adroit intellect, guessing for gain.

REMIEL

Your word, Serakel, bites deep. We are moved much . . . Chemalion?

CHEMALION

I fear chiefly Semjaya's campaign of mental clamour:

With old strategy made modern he blots out from human life
All silences, each fruitful pause, whereby *we* of old
Gained entry to still souls, and grew downward, until at last
    We looked out of their eyes onto their Earth.

SHEZEF

What has brought home to you this danger?

CHEMALION

                One day, in all their seven,
Is my Soul a dream-dreamer, a thought-thinker—freed from work
To grow quietly: Ask Armaros! He knows how it spends the time
Pinned down by long columns of vapid print to a flickering brain,
Gorged fat on the newspaper, the newspaper all day long!
My poor Soul! What can *I* do?

SHEZEF

       Alone, nothing: together, much,
When we all join and attack shrewdly.

ARMAROS

                Attack whom?

SHEZEF

                    Semjaya's hosts.

REMIEL

At the right hour!

SHEZEF

     Not his broad front! We must choose heedfully focal points
At his base, mark them and make plans—And then . . . forward
into battle!

REMIEL

Shezef! O Shezef! You are all fire! Steady your flame!
Let us hear Anpiel!

ANPIEL

    My Soul is a bond-slave in a harder way
To the newspaper; a mild Soul, whose heart dwelleth far removed
From his task: daily his bright fancy floats gaily among the flowers
    Of the small garden he keeps tidy and clean.
Rich humus he feels like to his own blood alive within
His dear body—feels dimly the seeds work in the winter months
Deep under the dark soil, as he looks forward to next spring.
But O Remiel, O Master, I know well that the souls of men
Are shaped, not by their own choices, their own passions and thoughts alone.
    If it *were* so, my work surely were light!
But I know, too, that the lost stream of the unremembered repeated acts
Is poured into the life-substance—deep under and out of those
His life gathers its time-shape—the wrong shape—the solid thing
That one day he will look back and see sadly that he has made!
One day—from this world—he must gaze backward and see himself,
His leal service, his hale strength, and the long tale of his labour-days
    Used only to make monkeys of men!
This *I* know. It is my burden. But O me! what I say is true,
Not of mine only—alas, how many souls like it we seem to see
In the place . . . place . . . but my word falters . . . we see *souls!* . . . in the part of Earth . . .
Am I right, Raquel? I crave help—do we all feel—is it taking shape
    Ever less vaguely in our knowing today?

REMIEL

Dark forces of Semjaya, above, binding souls to earth,
Are pin-pointed below. Well for our war! Shezef prophesied.
We seek sharply an earth-focus. Where Brothers?

RAQUEL

Armaros, Reply! Remiel, ask Armaros!

REMIEL *(raising his hand in checking gesture)*
                  First, Khif, we shall hear your word.

KHIF

The limbs growing . . . the boy's body . . . the soul opening like a bud
To Earth-influence, man's influence, sights, sounds and the world of thought . . .
Men's faces and girls' graces . . . brief wonder, before it died,
As he breathed into his up-growing the soul-hollowing Prince of Air,
As he breathed, over his world droning, Semjaya, the Prince of Air . . .
He is caught now, where work's dignity, full force of creative thought
Are all aimed to increase emptiness!
                How recently he and I—
He running and I round him—see! there! on the way to school!
The smooth, innocent face—voice of a boy seeming from far away,
The long, wondering thoughts, fluttering high, seeking in vain for me—
Shot—dragged to the ground—turned into mean greeds . . .

(He drops his head and rests it on his hand in a gesture of grief.)

RAQUEL

O Khif, mercy should steel courage! Shall yours only weaken will?
Look up! Lean on us all! Numberless Hosts, Ministers of Grace,
Await eager the hour even now! We—are—not—alone.

REMIEL

    And above, far, where the sight falters, Cherubim and Seraphim
Conspire, subtler than Semjaya himself, warping his anger-deed
To serve, mocking its own plan, the Throne fanned by their tireless wings.

KHIF

I find strength in your love, Brothers—but O Master, I burn! What aid
Can we bring *now* to our Souls caught in a knot? *(A pause)* Answer!

REMIEL

                                      Armaros!

(A pause. All turn to Armaros.)

ARMAROS

You all turned to me, all burned at me, then, too, with eager eyes,
When Shezef, with his fire, spoke of 'attack', hinted at 'focal points'
In the Base. Wherefore, I Pray? What can I do?

SHEZEF
> Angel! . . . Cut the knot!

ARMAROS *(after a pause)*
You know well I may shoot only at one mark—you know my task
Is the well-being of my Soul!

REMIEL
> It is true. Ponder, Armaros,
On its now need! Have you seen dimly the dark gulf that yawns before?
Have you thought well where the work lies?

ARMAROS
> I have tried often so to think,
But failed ever to find. I despair, Brothers. I need your aid.
Be near—love me and oh, counsel me!

REMIEL
> Tell truly what you see,
When you peer deep in his heart, Guardian!

ARMAROS
> Wheels, Master, whirring wheels
Smooth, unctuous, dead, frightening . . . swift, swifter . . . and O my Soul!
As the years pass, they are self-moved, are impulsed by a will not thine,
Till the door closes in this face, and I seek entry again in vain!

RAQUEL
What drives onward the wheels, Armaros?

ARMAROS
> Sights, sounds, and the empty thoughts
That are twined round them—the brain dancing without ceasing!
> > A tale I heard
Of a poor queen who was kept dancing—swift, swifter—in scorching shoes . . .

SHEZEF
Your own words—not ours, Armaros! Say, how shall the whirring cease

And the queen rest, till the sights darken, the sounds fade, and the brain
. . .

Remiel

                                        Alas!
It is less simple! A time comes, when the swift spinning drops the need
For the crude thrust from the blood's lust and the nerves' impetus. Souls at death,
From the weight freed, ascend smoothly—not *here!* Rising unpurified,
They slip deftly to Semjaya's realm, minded to work his will.

Shezef *(to Armaros)*

The time, Angel, is short—maybe is past—graver the burden, then
On you, surely!

Armaros *(who has been plunged deep in thought)*

                         You speak truly. *(to Remiel)*
I ask leave to recall my Soul.

Remiel

The sealed hour! I feel power from Above fill me to grant it. Go!

(Exit Armaros: a general murmur of approval, which Remiel checks with raised hand.)

Remiel

It is less simple. Be high hopers, but strong bearers!
                                   Armaros,
We doubt nothing, will act featly. But oh, Angels, have you forgot
What was here spoken—their unbroken strength, our precarious hold?
With leave granted from Gods higher, on grounds past our gree to know,
They may act also—Semjaya's hosts—instant to cross our aim!
I warn only . . . we bless Armaros . . . wait patiently . . . Come
      And let us seal our union as before!

(A pause, while the angels group themselves.)

Now cast we all our burdens in the lap
Of those Intelligences high, for whom
Our failures are success, and all our jars
Are harmony: Dominions, Virtues, Powers,

And those high Lords of Wisdom, Will and Love,
Who fill us and we them. And now not less
We meekly bow our heads to those below
Through whom we rise, remembering thankfully
That Man, who labours through his cold and dark,
Labours for us too, who are filled with light
And move always in music—

(Re-enter Armaros. All turn to him with gestures of eager enquiry, but he opens his arms in a gesture of emptiness and shakes his head with downcast looks. He takes his place among them.)

REMIEL *(continuing)*

                                          in such sort
That joy is mingled with our fiercest pain.

(Each angel places one hand on the shoulder of the angel next to him and with the other clasps the hand of the one opposite to him.)

ALL
        Members one of another
           Filled with the Spheres above,
      We bind us, brother to brother,
          To lift Mansoul in Love.

(Music, while the Angels move, passing in and out of one another, about the stage and eventually return to their places. Towards the close of this movement the music fades, and they recite)—

ALL
        Winged with the Will of God,
          I will carry His making Word
      To Man building a body
          For my Lover and Lord.

(All the Angels kneel round the rock; Remiel turns his back and raises both his arms.)

REMIEL
> *Quoniam apud Te est fons vitae.*

(Light shines down from above on the surface of the rock.)

ALL
> *Et in lumine Tuo videbunt lucem!*

CURTAIN

III. THE PARANOIA WING

Characters

Professor Paul Tallis	*A Doctor of Science*
Dr. Hugh Sedlescombe	*A Doctor of Medicine*
Homer Nasmith	*An American Citizen*
Derek Hooson	*An Industrialist*
Maxim Streeter	*A Press and Television Tycoon*
Joan Holdsworth	*A Welfare Worker*
Sebastian Minch	*A Civil Servant*
Tom Green	*A Trade Union Leader*
Remiel	*An Archangel*
Shezef	*An Angel*
Raquel	*An Angel*

Time: *Early in the twenty-first century.*

(A Drawing-room. All the male characters are seated round the room in armchairs, except Streeter who is in a heavy upright chair behind a small table, which has a telephone on it.)

TALLIS

Yes, but that is the whole difficulty. It is because so many of them are *not* obviously lunatics that this lodge was founded.

SEDLESCOMBE

They are very far from lunatics—apart from this one fixed idea, and all that follows from it. That's why we never argue with them, if it can possibly be avoided.

NASMITH

But surely we must answer reason with some show of reason?

TALLIS

Oh, if you start treating reason as anything more than a tool of science—a means to further experiment—it may land you anywhere.

NASMITH

Yes, but—

HOOSON

If you are bothered by sympathy, Homer, you can always resign, you know. The oath doesn't bind you to take any *action* with us.

STREETER

That's the only point. We are essentially an executive, not a debating unit. We are not concerned to persuade. Our aim is practical: to protect the fundamental sanity on which the Western way of life is based.

NASMITH

Very well.

STREETER

Very well. We happen to be a little more far-sighted than most people. And we are all agreed that this new disease should be tackled quickly, before it has time to spread. We want to scotch it in its infancy. Right?

NASMITH

I don't dispute that.

STREETER

Then for God's sake let's proceed to business. The next item is Dr. Sedlescombe's Report on the treatment of necro-neurosis.

NASMITH

Necro-neurosis?

STREETER

Weren't you at the last Meeting, Homer?

NASMITH

No, Mr. Chairman. I haven't been at the last three Meetings. I was way back in Massachusetts.

STREETER

Oh, that's *always* the difficulty with us—and we daren't circulate minutes—or even take them! But damn it, man—we've only just this moment been talking about a "fixed idea" and a "new disease". What did you *think* we were referring to?

NASMITH

I thought you meant the main delusion—that thought is substantial; that there is a so-called spiritual world, which is the source of the physical one; and that they have some kind of mental access to it.

STREETER (*testily*)

You'd call that *new*, would you?

Hooson

Mr. Chairman, I do not think our brother is being quite as obtuse as your tone suggests. He has not had the opportunity of hearing the preliminary Report on the growth of necro-neurosis; and, after all, what he has described *was* the threat we were originally founded to meet.

Nasmith

Thank you, Derek. I certainly wouldn't want us to waste our time discussing whether or not that threat can properly be described as "new"—which is a relative term anyway. In my Country what they called Transcendentalism began giving some trouble nearly two centuries ago. But they kept it vague in those days. Yes, sir. And the wise guys who took it up tended to retire from the world and become recluses. But the way their successors *participate*—poke their noses into practical affairs—undermine public confidence in the proper philosophy of science—isn't *that* new? If not, why is it that this lodge has only been in existence for ten years?

Tallis

I should be inclined to date it back myself to the time when Homoeopathy first became respectable.

Sedlescombe

Is it respectable?

Tallis

In the sense that it is taken seriously by a substantial number of educated people—yes.

Streeter

All right. Order please. I'm sorry, Homer. I was very anxious to get on. *(looking round)* Do you feel we must go briefly over the ground covered in our last Meetings for Nasmith's benefit?

Sedlescombe

I think it may be unnecessary. I believe I can make my Report in a form which will have almost the same effect.

STREETER

Good.

SEDLESCOMBE

If you agree, then, I will begin by calling in the patient.

MINCH

The patient?

SEDLESCOMBE

The latest admission to my hospital—or at least to the Wing we are all interested in. This time I wanted the brethren to hear what she has to say before the treatment begins. Then, if they see her again later, they can form their own idea of the value of what we are doing.

STREETER

Very well. *(looking round)* Is it agreed that we ask Dr. Sedlescombe to proceed in the way he suggests? *(General assent is indicated. Sedlescombe walks to the door, opens it and calls through.)* Bring Miss Holdsworth in!

(She enters with an Attendant, and as she does so, the light dies very, very slightly.)

SEDLESCOMBE

Good evening, Joan. Sit down, will you. *(She remains standing.)* I'm sure you won't mind answering a few questions these gentlemen and I would like to put to you? *(He pauses for a reply, which is not forthcoming.)* First of all, I would like to be sure we have got our history right. You are Joan Holdsworth, the daughter of John and Marjorie Holdsworth? And I think your mother's name was Mayne?

JOAN

What right have you got to question me?

TALLIS

Oh none! None at all. You are quite free—

JOAN

Free!

TALLIS

Free to answer or not, as you please.

SEDLESCOMBE

But haven't we gone into all that? I thought, last time, you told me you had decided, after a great deal of reflection, to co-operate—at least with information.

JOAN (*very slowly*)

You are right. I did say so. But you have all the cards . . . at present . . . one has to be careful. (*sits down*) Very well. Yes. You are quite right about my parents.

SEDLESCOMBE

I thought so. *We* have to be careful too, you know. At all events we try to be. I believe your mother had a rather unusual experience—as a younger woman—before you were born?

JOAN

Well?

SEDLESCOMBE

Before she married your father, in fact. She was not a religious woman, but some years after the death of her own father, whose loss she had felt very bitterly, she became convinced of his survival. Did she ever speak of this to you?

JOAN

Of course.

SEDLESCOMBE

And say that she was in communication with him?

GREEN

Nothing so very unusual about that. Was she a medium? Or did she employ one?

JOAN

There was nothing of that sort.

SEDLESCOMBE

So you told me.

TALLIS

You mean there was nothing phenomenal? Nothing, as I expect you would put it, through the senses? Thoughts came into her mind, which she was convinced were sent by him?

JOAN

I see no objection to anything that has been said so far.

SEDLESCOMBE

Your mother died about three years ago? *(Joan nods.)* Would you like to tell us anything of what followed? . . . Shall I tell *you* something then? Far more than was the case between herself and your grandfather, she communicates with you . . .

JOAN

I should have to know what you mean by 'communicates'.

SEDLESCOMBE

I don't want to put words into your mouth. How would you like me to put it—she "inspires you from the spiritual world"?

NASMITH

On a point of order, Mr. Chairman, I fail to see what is to be gained by prying into people's family secrets in this way.

STREETER

What do you say, Doctor?

SEDLESCOMBE

I don't think it can be called 'prying' where the object is therapeutic. However, the family connection is not the point. It merely happened to be the case here. I won't pursue it farther. Miss Holdsworth, you have conversed with the other patients in the Paranoia Wing. How many of them have the benefit of experiences similar to you own?

JOAN

Nearly all of them.

SEDLESCOMBE

Mostly with deceased relatives?

JOAN

Oh no. With people they have been connected with in other ways.

SEDLESCOMBE

Adherents, for instance, of the same line of thought?

JOAN

Why do you beat about the bush? I'm quite sure you know very well that nearly everyone kept in the Wing has been actively engaged, in one walk of life or another, or in their spare time, in the pursuit of spiritual science.

SEDLESCOMBE

So that it is mainly those who were similarly engaged, and who have lately died, who are the communicators—the inspirers?

JOAN

Before I answer any more questions, I want to make my position clear, please. I protest with my whole being against the illegal detention of myself and the others there. This is a nightmare. It's unbelievable. You get us, by all manner of tricks, into the Paranoia Wing of your Mental

Hospital; you keep us incommunicado for weeks or months on end; you override or ignore all the legislative safeguards for patients, as you call us. How long do you say it can go on? I demand a statutory visit from someone at the Ministry of Health. Unless you intend to murder me, you will have to free me sooner or later. And I warn you I shall publish everything.

SEDLESCOMBE

Aren't you forgetting your resolution to co-operate? You will be free soon—and free to publish—if you still want to. And who will believe you? Accusations of that kind are a very common symptom of persecution-mania, you know—as common as, let us say, wild talk about being murdered.

JOAN

Why are we never visited under the Mental Health Act? Do you intend to give false evidence of visits that never took place?

SEDLESCOMBE

Don't be impertinent!

STREETER

And don't make a fool of yourself trying to frighten us. You forget the wide discretion in matters of this sort vested in the Joint Committee of the Ministry of Science and the Ministry of Health. It may interest you to know that one of us here is the Convener of that Committee.

JOAN

Yes; and it may interest the Ritson Press to have a full account of this very interview—even from a certified paranoiac. There will be things about it that will ring true, I fancy.

STREETER

Young woman, I *am* the Ritson Press.

SEDLESCOMBE

Why won't you make up your mind to help us, instead of striking these attitudes? You see, there really is no hope—

JOAN

No hope!

(The light dims a little further. Against the back of the stage the outlines of the landscape of Scene 2 of "The Wall" and Scene 2 of "The Human Dynamo" become faintly visible.)

JOAN *(more calmly)*

There may be two opinions about that. *(to the Chairman)* May I ask *you* a question now? Two questions?

STREETER

Oh certainly.

JOAN

First, are you really so certain that you are all right and we are all wrong? You are afraid of any slackening of confidence in—in—in the narrow mess of tampering and prurient curiosity which *you* think is all that 'science' can ever mean: are you sure it deserves all that confidence?

SEDLESCOMBE

Come, come!

JOAN

One example only, then, from all I could give: what success is your kind—your straight-waistcoated science having with the treatment of cancer? How long has the fabulously expensive research been going on? A century and a half? When I was a child, one is six were still dying of it. Now it is one in five.

SEDLESCOMBE

And the second question?

JOAN (*to Streeter*)

What are you aiming at? Why are you keeping us?

SEDLESCOMBE

Purely for the purposes of beneficent observation. That is, as long as you remain reasonably co-operative. We regard that, as I think you know, as the most reliable test of mental health. There was the case of Arthur Cornwall . . . but we should only resort again to remedial injections—

JOAN

O God, not that!

SEDLESCOMBE

I hope it will be unnecessary. (*looking hard at her*) I think it will. But of course it will depend a good deal on what *you* think.

    Well, thank you for helping us in this way. I don't think we need trouble you any farther at the moment. And Joan—cheer up! Believe me, in a few months' time all this will seem like a bad dream—and a fantastic one at that. Meanwhile if there is anything I can do to make the way straighter for you, do let me know. Good-bye!

JOAN

You haven't heard what I have to say yet. It is this: It may be that your real purpose is to make away with us—

SEDLESCOMBE (*to the others, in a lowered but clearly audible voice*)

Note the characteristic obsession with assassination!

JOAN

I have ceased trying to understand how it came about that you are able to do as you like with human beings, who I thought were supposed, in this country, to be protected by law. (*Streeter makes signs to Sedlescombe who rises and presses a bellpush.*) But if we *are* killed—whether by design or accident—we shall only help to make stronger those who remain. If it is we who are right, and not you (*the Attendant enters and places a hand on her shoulder*), that follows—doesn't it?

ALL (*genially, as she goes with the Attendant to the door*)
Thank you! Thank you! Good evening! Thank you!

JOAN (*from the door, intensely*)
Doesn't it?

MINCH

She seems to know what she is talking about.

GREEN

There was a sort of underlying confidence. . . . I say, isn't there some danger in detaining her against her will?

NASMITH

In my country her people would be suing out a Writ of *Habeas Corpus* by now.

TALLIS

Oh yes, we have had that once or twice. But we're a bit better organised over here, Homer. English judges have to accept the evidence of experts, you know. Our standard form of Affidavit was settled by Counsel, and we find—

GREEN

But suppose the judge insisted on seeing her, Professor, and asking his own awkward questions?

TALLIS

It has already happened before now. They soon get drawn into talking confidently about imponderables. And if there's one thing the Court hates, it's imponderables.

MINCH

Besides, when a Ministerial discretion has been exercised, the Court cannot go behind the scenes and enquire into the *grounds* on which it was exercised. That was settled long ago.

STREETER

You had better proceed with your Report, Hugh.

SEDLESCOMBE

It concerns the results we are having with the new drug I mentioned last time.

TALLIS

Palinkenophrenomide?

SEDLESCOMBE

Yes.

NASMITH

If I know anything of that young woman, she won't take it!

SEDLESCOMBE

She won't know she is taking it. In the few selected cases where we have been trying it out, they took it in their food. To begin with, that is. But it is quite colourless and tasteless and we have since found it more convenient to exhibit in the patient's drinking-water. The results, up to date, are striking—not to say phenomenal.

STREETER

Can you tell us in what way?

SEDLESCOMBE

I can do rather better than that. I can show you. In the case of . . . (*He consults some notes.*) Oh yes, Alexander Reid, if you had had him before you two months ago, he would have shown exactly the same attitude as Joan Holdsworth did just now—only perhaps a little more aggressively. Indeed, he is one of a small group who specifically claim to remember a previous incarnation during the twentieth century. By the way, we have found an obstinate belief in reincarnation a very common consequence—or accompaniment—of necro-neurosis. I arranged for a tape-recording of the Chaplain's last talk with him.

NASMITH

Chaplain?

SEDLESCOMBE

Yes, yes. The hospital Chaplain's been most helpful.

STREETER

The Church—or at any rate the right part of it—is as concerned as we are about all this.

SEDLESCOMBE

What I propose, Mr. Chairman, if you agree, is to play back to you—not of course the whole conversation, but just a minute or two from it.

STREETER

I think we should all be most interested.

SEDLESCOMBE *(as he walks over to the recording instrument)*

I have marked the place where it gets most relevant. *(He turns a switch and waits while the drums revolve.)* Ah—now! *(He turns a second switch.)*

1ST VOICE *(from the tape)*

Then you don't feel you were mistaken? I thought just now you said you did.

2ND VOICE

Not mistaken exactly—no. That is just what's so embarrassing. You know how you feel when you suddenly remember an obviously fatuous remark you once let drop in company? When I remember the sort of things I used to say, they strike me as absolutely meaningless. Almost as if I had never learnt how to use the English language—or any other for that matter.

1ST VOICE

And what do your friends have to say about it?

2ND VOICE

Oh, it's no use talking to them. They are stuck far too well and truly in the old rut. Mind you, I can sympathise with them, because I have been through it myself. It's as if one hadn't been really awake before. One's mind was sluggish. *Now*, when anyone speaks to me, the answers come into my mind almost as soon as they have started talking. I even *see* things in sharper outlines—though, strangely enough, colours are *not* so bright as they used to be.

1ST VOICE

And what about that business of reincarnation? You *were* mistaken about that, I suppose?

2ND VOICE

Well, no, Sir. I would hardly say 'mistaken'. It's too dignified a word. I don't feel now that I ever got as far as that. There must first be a thing to be mistaken about. Reincarnation, if it meant anything, would mean repeated incarnation; but incarnation is not a thing. It is just a word. How could anyone ever *suppose* it meant anything? What size is it? Where is it kept when not in use? How do you paraphrase it? Something like "a not-body becoming a body", I suppose! Honestly!

1ST VOICE

You are going rather too fast for me. Let us leave incarnation alone and stick to reincarnation. You say— *(Sedlescombe switches off and returns to his chair.)*

HOOSON

Hum! I don't quite see how even Palinkenophrenomide could produce all that!

SEDLESCOMBE

Oh well, of course there are books and lectures to help. But its effect *is* undoubtedly complex. It both numbs the source of phantasy, and thus obliterates the conations—the imaginary experiences, that are at the root of the trouble, *and* at the same time greatly accelerates the patient's cerebral mobility.

Mr. Chairmain, I think that really completes my Report—if you will accept it in that rather unusual form.

STREETER

Thank you, Doctor. We certainly do accept it and we are most grateful.

NASMITH

I'd like to associate myself with that sentiment. May I speak to the Report Mr. Chairman?

STREETER

Certainly.

NASMITH

Well, Gentlemen, I guess we are all crystal-clear about one thing: where Palinkenophrenomide can be applied, we are in a position to deal effectively, not only with this necro-neurosis, but also with the more epidemic bug of philosophical Immaterialism—which, as you know, I am much more concerned with, due to its wider implications. But I have these two observations to make: Firstly, I would feel very much easier in my mind if the highly successful experiment of which we have just heard had been carried out with the knowledge and consent of the patient.

TALLIS

You'd never get their consent.

NASMITH

That may well be a fact. The question still remains, what is the right conclusion to draw from the fact. My second observation is, that in any case and with or without consent, the area over which it will be possible to make use of Palinkenophrenomide must in the nature of things remain a strictly limited one. We are still left sitting with the major problem; and I would like to know if any progress has been made with it during my unfortunate absence from the country, or if any brother has brought with him today a fresh contribution towards its solution.

STREETER

Thank you. And that really brings us to the principal item in this evening's agenda. There *is* a proposal, and it is one which I intend to move from the chair. It is a serious one. But then the situation we have to meet is serious. Gentlemen, I don't need to remind you that it is our habit to look a long way below the surface and a long way beyond our noses. It is true that nothing spectacular or sensational has yet come out of what I might perhaps call the 'camp' of the Immaterialists; but each of us here has his ear laid to the ground in a different realm of the body politic, and we know, and we are all agreed, that beneath the surface Immaterialism *is* growing and spreading very rapidly.

NASMITH

Yes sir! We certainly have to take the lead out of our pants.

STREETER

There is no time to lose. It is against this background, and let me add after prolonged and very careful consultation not only with Tom and Sebastian as to the probable reactions of operative personnel (whom of course we shall select very carefully), but also with Hugh and Paul as to any risk, however slight, of incidental, physically harmful effects on our people. . . . It is against this background that I bring forward my proposal. Well, Gentlemen, *(stirring uneasily in his chair)* you heard Hugh telling us just now that Palinkenophrenomide is most conveniently administered in the patient's drinking-water. What he did not mention was the very small, the almost infinitesimal quantity of the drug which is required to produce its effect . . . also that it can be regarded to some extent as a purifying agent.

    Gentlemen! *(He pauses, and as he does so, the background again becomes faintly visible.)* Brothers! I have made certain investigations and I find that in the Central Authority which is responsible for the purity of this country's water supply the one or two personalities who count are not unsympathetic with our aims. My proposal is, therefore . . . and of course any action we took would to begin with be regarded as experimental and would be limited to a comparatively small area. Only later, and depending on results, should we expect to cover the whole country . . . my proposal is—

Nasmith

Stop!

Streeter

Really, Mr. Nasmith! I should have thought—*(The rest is drowned in murmurs of "order, order!" from round the room.)*

Nasmith

This is a point of order, Sir. It touches the issue whether you—or any man—are entitled to say what we have reason to believe you were about to say right now. Brothers, I speak to you in all humility and I believe you will forgive me. My country is younger than yours. We have many faults and much crudity. But we do still regard ourselves as appointed guardians of human liberty. Gentlemen, our ultimate aim here is a noble and benevolent one and I'm not saying we should keep those kid gloves on while we scramble for it. But there is a point at which any conviction that the end justifies the means breaks down. At least there is a point for me. And that point is right here. For any such interference with fundamental human freedom on the scale you are suggesting fills me with unspeakable horror and detestation. I will have nothing to do with it. Not one little bit. I move therefore that we pass to the next item on the agenda.

Streeter

Your motion is not accepted.

(Murmurs of "Hear, hear!" while against the background a single figure, Remiel's, is dimly seen to enter and move to the centre of the stage, where it remains motionless.)

Streeter

The proposal I am now putting to you, Gentlemen, is a simple but far-reaching one. It is—

NASMITH (*rising from his seat and raising his arms, with the hand turned palm forward*)

Pardon me! Not to me, I'm afraid. You will please count me out from now on. If my motion is not to be even put to the meeting, I tender my resignation as from this moment.

STREETER

I accept it with regret. And I remind you of the oath of secrecy you took when you joined us.

NASMITH

I shall consider carefully where my obligation lies. (*He looks round.*) Is no-one coming my way? Very well. I wish you a very good night, gentlemen. (*Exit*)

GREEN

I confess this makes me very uneasy.

STREETER

I do not think we need fear an indiscretion. Think how he himself would be compromised—if he was believed!

GREEN

He might decide to face that.

HOOSON

Would *you*?

GREEN (*uncomfortably*)

Well, no. I suppose not.

STREETER

For the third time, then: I wish formally to propose that we take all steps to adopt the drug Palinkenophrenomide for general application and, with that object, that we—(*the telephone bell rings—into the instrument*): Yes. But he can't possibly speak now. He is in the middle of an important conference . . . oh very well, if you put it that way. *(to Sedlescombe)*: For you, Doctor, and it seems to be urgent.

(Sedlescombe crosses to the table and picks up the instrument.)

SEDLESCOMBE *(into the telephone)*

The *what?* The horizontal crane! But it's enormous—you mean the great openwork steel arm—it *couldn't* collapse . . . *overturned!* Well, and what damage—my God! my God! my God! Yes. I shall come straight away of course. Good-bye. *(replaces the receiver)* I . . . hardly know . . . where I am. It was the Hospital. The Paranoia Wing. The big crane that was working on the new addition—fallen and crushed in the roof of the old building . . . they're digging, but they doubt if there will be any survivors. I can't . . . excuse me!

(He dashes out. The rest look at each other in silence. Against the background two figures, Shezef and Raquel, are seen to enter form opposite sides and approach the central figure, where they remain motionless.)

MINCH

But this is appalling!

STREETER

It will take some thinking out.

GREEN

It's ghastly! It's horrifying! There must be some—

STREETER

And what will the consequences be for our work? Headline news . . . public enquiry . . .

TALLIS

It's not that kind of consequence I'm thinking of—when I can get my mind off those poor devils enough to think of anything. It may well be the beginning of the end.

Streeter

What do you mean by that, Professor? It's bad enough without us losing our heads into the bargain.

Tallis

But think, man, think! First of all, there's the shot in the arm that martyrdom always gives to any struggling minority. But that's not all. We don't know yet what Homer is going to do; how the horror of it is going to affect him; what he may be led to say—just at this moment, with everyone's attention focused on the Wing! And even *that* is only the beginning, as I see it. Don't you remember what the Holdsworth girl said . . . "by design or accident"? Can't you feel already how each one of the dead patients will form a new centre—a nexus, a nucleus, a sort of ganglion of necro-neurosis to link up all their friends and supporters everywhere? Oh, it will take time. It will take time. But this moment may well mark the end of the world as we know it, as we have made it, and the beginning of a new dark age!

Streeter

Semjaya, help!

Green

What did you say, Streeter?

Streeter

Eh? I wasn't aware that I had said anything. Listen: We are all badly shaken, badly disconcerted. One thing is clear. We *must* have time to think, before we decide anything. Personally, I must sleep on it before I can hope to talk any sense. Look! Can you all meet here the first thing tomorrow morning? Say at nine-o-clock? Good. Paul, I rely on you to tell Hugh Sedlescombe and have him here.

(They turn and go out. While they are doing so, the curtain begins to close, but stops when it has masked the chairs and table, leaving only the background, or part of it, visible. At the same time the light fades from the foreground and brightens on the background, where Remiel is standing behind the rock-table with Shezef and Raquel a little in front of it, on either side, facing inward.)

REMIEL

Shezef, the hour you prophesied—the hour
You pointed to, exhorting us—is here.
Momently, in this region, the tall Wall
Crushes, between the living and the dead.
Across our threshold passings to and fro
Grow common. Therefore, they that are assigned,
Beings angels, to be escorts of Mansoul,
Take now no part in this Solemnity.
Half of the mystery of their energy
They must forego,
The bliss of inspiration giving way
For a time to sole expression: they must act
Unceasingly, we celebrate alone.
    We celebrate alone, not for ourselves:
We act in them, they worship and receive
In us: we lay their deeds upon this altar,
They take, through us, His Spirit. Oh, be brief—
They need Him now!
(Shezef and Raquel make ceremonial obeisance to one another.)

RAQUEL

        Members one of another
          Filled with the Spheres above—

SHEZEF

        We bind us brother to brother
          To lift Mansoul in Love.

(Music, while Shezef and Raquel again make ceremonial obeisance, first to one another, then to Remiel, who makes the like obeisance to each of them in turn.)

SHEZEF & RAQUEL

        Winged with the Will of God,
          I will carry His making Word
        To Man building a body
          For my Lover and Lord.

(Shezef and Raquel kneel. Remiel turns his back and raises both his arms.)

REMIEL

 Quoniam apud Te est fons vitae.
(Fresh light shines down from above on the surface of the rock.)

ALL

 Et in lumine Tuo videbunt lucem!

CURTAIN

Introduction to *The Unicorn*

A poem of 681 lines in four fits, *The Unicorn* is a lovely and witty piece, similar in tone to much of the short light-hearted verse Barfield delighted in writing throughout his life; one inevitably thinks of "The Milkmaid and the Unicorn" and "The Queen's Beast"—and many others, some that few have seen.[1] Yet the pithy playfulness has purpose, as always, and muses on motifs and ideas embedded in an English sensibility in general and the Inklings circle in particular. Of note in connection with this poem is a short but wonderful hand-written review by the poet Ruth Pitter attached to the Bodleian archive copy. Pitter was a part of the greater circles to which Barfield and the other Inklings were attached—she was a close friend of C. S. Lewis who admired her work and to whom she credited her faith. Pitter's work met with moderate popular acclaim but was somewhat marginalized by elite poetic circles for her delight in traditional forms and themes, though notably her admirers included W. B. Yeats and Thom Gunn. The separation from poetic inner circles was more acute for Barfield; nonetheless, Pitter seems in many respects the perfect respondent for this piece, especially from the perspective of her own poetry, which Barfield read and enjoyed.

Light-hearted though the poem may be, it too participates in a forgetive mythopoesis, though in a more common register and playful versification than *Orpehus* or *Riders on Pegasus*. Four source quotations are given as a prologue suggesting a somewhat incongruous synthesis of nursery rhyme, scripture, and legend. Yet this wink toward absurdity has a two-fold intent: to illustrate the mythopoeic form in a stylized mocking of it, but also to recall that, as Tolkien would have it, the long-cooking soup of cultural meanings has many seemingly disparate parts that clash and blend, yet even the simplest source may have deep roots and powerful resonance.[2] The lead source is the first line of the heraldic children's rhyme: "The lion and the unicorn were fighting for the crown." The scriptures, both from Psalms, reference the KJV's use of 'unicorn' is Psalm 92 and the use of 'unicorns' in the Douay-Rheims and Brenton Septuagint translations of Psalm 78 (though other translations choose more mundane philology in these passages). Ascribed only to "Thirteenth Century Legend," the final source describes how a young damsel may be used as a lure to subdue and capture a unicorn. The resulting mythopoeic vista suggested by these disparate strands is a merry tale told by the itinerant narrator who quite unexpectedly wanders into just such a ritual just beginning in a unique and troubled town as the Dog-Star sets of a summer's eve.

Much might be said of the wry humor and playful handling of image and sound—one might even plumb the imagery for more than a clever tableau of English folk-sensibility—but as with Barfield's more serious poems, the conceit or metaphor unfolds best in the experience of the art rather than in any explaining of it—especially when whatever might in some way be serious in content is yet presented in jest. At any rate, the poet Pitter's informal yet insightful review paints all that might be needed for a swift sketch of the poem's essential qualities:

> Lovely atmosphere, like W. Morris without his coldness. Emotionally delicate & tender without sentimentality. Rather decorated. Sprightly & witty, never losing pace & rigour. Opening lines wonderfully witty & compact. Technique throughout admirable, the occasional internal rhymes etc. saving the easy rhythm from monotony. Visualisation brilliant, coming right into focus. The piety is quite lovely and decent, I accept it joyfully, conscious of the portent (how impossible this poem would have been 25 years ago) and feeling enlarged by it. The rough coquetry of the Unicorn is really ravishing. (It is usually represented as a delicate beast except in its strength & wildness, but I accept this version gladly). . . . The abrupt, light, humorous end is as good as the opening in a different way. I think the length, weight, pattern of the piece well suited to the subject. Wouldn't it make a good cantata? Ruth Pitter

Notes

1. *The Unicorn* is extant in typescripts at the Bodleian archive (Dep. c. 1115) and the Wade Center (OB/MS-105/X and OB/MS-166). "The Queen's Beast" and "The Milkmaid and the Unicorn" are available in *A Barfield Sampler*, 36–37, 49.

2. The intended allusion is to J. R. R. Tolkien's seminal essay "On Fairy-Stories," in particular Tolkien's expropriation of G. W. Dasent's soup metaphor to argue that much more can be seen and known in folk traditions than Dasent would ever allow. See in particular pp. 19-20, 26–31. Verlyn Flieger has long demonstrated the strong presence of Barfield's thinking in "On Fairy-Stories" and subsequently the essential influence of Barfield on all of Tolkien's mythopoeic work. See, Verlyn Flieger, *Splintered Light: Logos and Language in Tolkien's World,* Revised Edition (Kent, OH: Kent State University Press, 2002). Flieger's central theme is to demonstrate the key Barfieldian element in Tolkien's mythopoeic fiction; see especially, vii, xxi-xxii, 33–44, 67–70.

THE UNICORN

a poem in four parts

The lion and the unicorn were fighting for the crown.

But mine horn shall be exalted like the horn of an unicorn;
for I am anointed with fresh oil. (Psalm 92)

And he built his sanctuary as of unicorns in the land which
he founded for ever. (Psalm 78)

Hunters can catch the unicorn only by placing a young
virgin in his haunts. No sooner does he see the damsel,
than he runs towards her, and lies down at her feet, and
so suffers himself to be captured by the hunters. (Thirteenth Century Legend)

I

The Procession

At evening, when the Dog-Star sank
Below the dark horizon's rim,
Lost in the light, since Ocean drank
The royal Globe along with him—
At evening, as the sun went down,
A gay procession left the Town
And danced along the deep ravine:
A crowd of rosy boys and girls
With jet-black curls or golden-brown,
In rose-red tunic and white gown;   10
And there were roses everywhere,
Bunches of roses dangling down
Or lonely blossoms stuck in curls.
Old for girls and boys they were:
Their merry mouths and shining eyes
Told how rich Fancy's foliage greened
And what blithe summer, safely screened,
Swelled in their bosoms and their loins.
And oft—as if their joy increased
Beyond a silence age enjoins   20
On youth—the rocks around them rang;
Abrupt their happy chattering ceased,
And loud those clear young voices sang:
  'Upon a lime-tree, leafy boughed,
  There swelled and glowed a Turtle-dove
  And, cooing loud, as lion proud,
  He called and bowed and billed his love:
  Take all my heart, my Love! Thou art
  My love! Thine eyes have shamed me! Wise
  I grow at last: take all my heart, my love!   30
Then I, too old to dance or sing,
And yet all-anxious, if I could,
To plumb the meaning of this thing,
Asked my good angel what to do;
And he—if I mistake not—smiled,

As though too well he understood,
And bade me 'go a pace or two
Along with them and ask, my child,
And learn!' How swiftly I obeyed,
Half glad, half laughing, half afraid! 40

"What for?"—the stripling echoed back
My words, with just that touch of scorn
Which youth, unspoiled, must needs betray,
Amazed that any man should lack
The truth it mastered yesterday—
"What for?—to fetch the Unicorn!"
   Then I, a fool, ashamed to show
Incomprehension, answered: "Oh,
I see!" with a blank look on my face,
Through which he instantly divined 50
The empty thought that lay behind:

   "A stranger here? I see, I see!"
And now he sobers down his pace,
Resigned to walk and talk with me,
And thus begins: "Our little town,
You know, has neither towers nor walls
Nor moat, nor drawbridge to let down,
Nor sharp stockade. When evening falls,
No guard is set, no sentries pace,
To check the bordering Pigmy race. 60
We sleep secure from beasts and men,
Because a Lion guards the place,
Good custom clothes his rampant will,
He issues nightly from his den
And, like a planet, circling prowls,
With frightful, friendly roars and growls
Around our Town. All throve, until
A month ago his first assault
Showed how his instinct grew at fault.
One night a bullock from the herd 70
Was missing; next he sprang and slew
A lamb, and, last, a singing bird!

Last! Would it were! Oh sir, he mauled
A man made in God's image, too!
A friendly stranger, sir! The wound
Is healing now—but not the word
That rang through all the country round,
Warning against us. We're marooned,
Or like to be—cut off from kind
Since then: and they said we must find   80
A remedy. They counselled long,
And last they held the beast must die,
The Synod, yet the beast is strong
And we—how should we not abhor
The task, who ne'er drew blood before!"
  "One had a small black dog—would fly,
Straight as an arrow, swift as thought,
Right as his mouth was stretched to roar,
Deep in his great red yawning throat—
This seemed fantastic. Next, a man   90
Told (and it seemed a likelier plan)
How, since that frightful century
When, after prying men had planned
To split the atom and unbrace
The frame of Earth, all arms were banned
(You learnt at school, how by Decree
All weapons to destruction passed,
The latest first, the earliest last)—"
  "Learnt! *I remember!*"
                      "Well, he said
That somehow, in their potting-shed,   100
Since those bad days an old Cross-bow
Had lain—and we should use it now.
  "We started, shuddered, wept, agreed.
We found the thing. We got it freed
From dust and rust. 'Twas time to go
To seek the den. At first none spoke.
We looked at one another—oh,
But in that instant something woke,
A voice within, that thundered *No!*
Then too, an outer voice was heard,   110

Silent till now, a quiet one,
Enquiring: 'Have you considered
Who guards us, when the Lion's gone?
Who keeps the wolves and jackals down?
Who frights the Pigmies from our town?
O treason! O disherison!
Tomorrow, when they broach our soil,
What do we fight with? *Belacoil?*
How they will march us all to school!
How lecture us! How make us look— 120
Ordering all our lives by rule—
To barrack-square and statute-book
For strength to keep our City clean!
Oh Brothers, ere our bolt be shot
Once and for ever, shall we not
Consult the *Burning Babe?'*
                               "'Twas seen
He counselled well. Soon, hushed before
The Eikon that old Painter swore
Would one day talk to Youth, on whom
Virtue was never thrust by rod 130
Or precept—whose heart ne'er mistook
Fear of itself for fear of God—
We stood—and I had little faith."

   "The moments passed. A sigh, a breath,
That seemed of our own tenseness born,
Went shivering through the canvas worn,
Though no man saw it shift or shake—
And then—I scarce believed I woke—
In low, clear tones the Eikon spoke:
   "Slay not the Lion, fresh young folk! 140
   Go rather, take a Unicorn
   (But lay no bridle on his neck!)
   And let your Unicorn abide
   Free, on your City's counter-side:
   So shall the twain debate the ground
   And, furiously careering round
   In oft-encountering antidrome,

> *Either shall other hold in check*
> *From frolic ploys, and bless your home,*
> *And all with joy and peace be crowned."*   150

"It ceased—and some would fain depart,
But others showed we had no art
Of taking Unicorns! Yet, when
They prayed the Eikon speak again,
Like an old man with wandering wits
It faltered and its voice grew faint:
There were awkward pauses between bits
Of old law—jargon, forced and quaint—
And these are what we caught of them:

> "His capture lieth not in prender . . .   160
> Nec vi nec fraude . . . lies in render . . .
> At tu, venator, virginem
> Pro rosa solis . . .hem, . . . hem, . . .
> At pasture may he be surprised,
> The moon then shining. . . ."

                         "Thus advised,
With blazoned hints from ancient books
And prayer and fancy, we devised
What seemed the fairest stratagem;
And thus all this—" he waved—"which looks
So strange to you, was organised."   170
    I would have answered: but just then
Their ardent carol swelled again
And my companion poured his own
Clear voice into that unison:

> '*Upon a lime-tree, leafy boughed*
> *There swelled and glowed a Turtle-dove*
> *And, cooing loud, as lion proud,*
> *He called and bowed and billed his love:*
> *Take all my heart, my Love! Thou art*
> *My Love! Thine eyes have shamed me! Wise*   180
> *I grow at last: take all my heart, my love!'*

While thus they sang, I looked about:
Pale stars winked overhead, where green
Had changed to amethyst: the rout
Had reached the mouth of the ravine.

THE UNICORN

Here, where the valley widened out
And emerald pastures lipped a stream
Meandering, the column spread
Like water-floods. A moment sped
In which the veilly gauze of dream   190
Passed in between it and my sight—
Dusk deepens; the white roses gleam
Like moons; the flitting women seem
Papery, unmaterialised—
Warm fireflies in a lacquer night . . .

   That passed. The song ceased. And I said:
"You spoke of strategy—some plan
Prepared. I find none. Are you led?
Call you this rabble 'organised'?
I see no Marshall at your head,   200
No pope, no fathering Fugleman."

   He turned and looked on me, surprised,
Then pointed, where in midst of all,
Now by the thinning of the throng
Made visible, there paced along
Compact and ceremonial,
A central knot. I saw their gait
More solemn, marked their mien sedate.
What robes were these appareled in?
Below bright albs of baldachin—   210
In chrome or glowing madder steeped,
Embroidered, gorgeous, oxlip-gold,
With tasselled bullions—shuffling hems
Of sable cassocks drily peeped.
If priests or bards, I could not say,
For round their brows bright anadems
Of twisted flowers and gleaming gems
Crowned the fantastical array.

   The youth was silent. Love and awe
Sat lightly on him. Then I saw   220
How, high uplifted, Something masked
In blossoms moved with them: I asked:
"Young man, my eyes are weakening,

What bear they, thus hid up in flowers?
What Standard? What may be that Thing,
Whence silent streams of roses fling
Themselves in waterfally showers?"
   He raised his voice: for, while I spoke,
The sounding chorus once more woke:
"Why Sir, good Sir, can you not see   230
The cross—our Cross of Ebony?"
So said, he left and danced along,
Joining his comrades in mid-song,
Just as their plain-song burst apart
In the refrain's broad harmonies,
Then turned and smiled at me, and all
The evening rang like bell-metal:
> *'Take all my heart, my Love! Thou art*
> *My Love! Thine eyes have shamed me! Wise*
> *I grow at last! Take all my heart, my love!'*   240

II

THE LADY

Placid and warm, the candid moon
Seemed hesitating in the sky
As if dismayed to see how high
Her floating self had mounted. Soon
The moving standard halted too.
The solemn, hieratic band,
In central rigol, took their stand,
While round them in a wider ring
The red-robed youths all gathering
Stood silent. Had some hovering bird 10
Looked down, he might have deemed there was
A Wild Rose open on the grass
Enormous. But at one low word
The silent concourse broke and stirred
And shifted, while a corridor
Was opened up, where he, who bore
The sober Standard all aflame
With flowers, back towards me came
And passed me, leaving clear my view
Straight to the centre.
                    One stood there, 20
White-robed she stood. I do not care
To seek to paint her. Strange! I knew
Instantly, though now still she stood,
The way she'd walked beside the Rood
Which now had left her. Have you seen
A girl *enceinte*—the pensive poise,
Self-gathered to a globe serene,
Wherein she bears her secret joys
About with her? Her eyes how wide?
How courteously preoccupied 30
Her answers? Thronged on every side,
How none the less, aloof the press,
Sealed in a hallowed selfishness
She strolls? Even so, a while before,

Enringed, unseen, I knew that she,
Pacing beside the Standard, bore
The ark of her virginity.
    The priests with final gesture sain
Her shining curls, then through the lane
They pass, the way the Standard went 40
Behind me—leaving her alone,
It seemed that many youths had on
Rich cloaks. With one accord these bent
Forward and cast them on the ground:
And so they piled a little round
Warm island in the chilly dew.
Then all bowed gravely and withdrew
Across the field, to join the rest,
I following: Youth and girl and priest
All mingled—bard and girl and youth 50
Stood waiting by the pasture's edge,
A long line glimmering in the lewth
Of an old quickset boundary hedge,
Hushed but not mute. The whispered jest
Rose here and there, half-heard, but half
Unheard—or only to be guessed
From some low, happy murmured laugh
That followed it. That restless fit
Died slowly out of the still scene
And left the waking silentness 60
Of summer dark undoubted queen.
A corncrake chirred. Full three fields off
I heard an old sheep's quiet cough.
Each moment's weight began to press.
One pointed, while another scanned
The field beneath his shading hand,
Strown to the moonlight, broad and flat.
    Inmidst, a statue with head bent,
White, on her little isle of gold,
With folded arms the lady sat. 70
And having rested there, they went,
My two eyes, travelling on beyond
And near the great field's farther side

A dear familiar sight espied,
A farm-horse standing by a pond.
I called to mind how he would look
If I should pass him close—how still!
Asleep on legs! the honest clown
Too dumb to think of lying down!
    God pardon me! What worlds mistook
My habit-coloured senses! Hark!
The hedge stirred faintly in the dark
Behind me, rustled by a breeze,
A breeze that woke and floated out
Over the field the essences
Of all those roses. Swift they sped.
I saw the lady lift her head
One moment, while they passed her by,
The next, my farm-horse shivered, woke,
Tossed up his mane like a great shout,
And stamped once. Shattered moonshine broke
    In argent sequins off his horn.
    Like landscape in a lightning-stroke,
    Bright-cut in memory, sharp and shorn,
That moment died as it was born.
Before my eyes were even aware
Of what they saw, my hearing caught
A noise being poured into the hush,
Low, threatening, swelling, drowning thought,
A gobbling thunder. One mad rush,
Across the field, of streaking fleetness
Told how the silvery monster sought
The source of all this wafted sweetness!
    We craned our necks. A straight career
Must pass that drowsing lady near!
We trembled while we watched them—Yes!
Coltish for all his lordliness,
The white gleam from the virgin's dress
Cracked like a shot at him. He shied,
Baulked at her, tripped, reared, swerved aside.
Swiftly the proud beast's prick of fright
Was past: nor any panic flight

But anger followed. He stopped short
Long ere he reached us, quite forgot
The aromatic whiff he sought
And turned and stood. We saw his back,
His flanks just quivering, in the blink
Of the bright moon. . . . Why did I think
Of Aspramont and Camelot,
Of Kaye, Rinaldo, Lamorak,   120
And breathless waitings with couched lance
Before the apparelled pursuivants
Sounded to tourney? While I thought,
Horn down, he galloped to attack!
    Was this, then, human sacrifice?
A quarter—one third—half the space
Was covered—then, in the last trice
The lady calmly raised her face.
Nay, ask me not—I was too far
To say what happened! But although   130
I could not see, I think I know:
For late one evening long ago
When driving west, where few trees are,
Too fast, I topped a gentle rise,
The sun flamed level in my eyes
Blinding—and lord! how mind, heart, will
Shouted: *For God's sake, man, stop still!*
    When next I was again aware,
The Unicorn was standing by
The lady. Patient he stood there,   140
As if he hoped to catch her eye
By stillness; while his panting breath—
It must be so, he was so near—
Stirred the loose hair above her ear.
And she—she sat as still as death,
Her graceful head again bent down;
She neither spoke nor stirred. He shook
His great horned head, and made a sound
Half snort, half neigh, then pawed the ground
Most gently, as to say: Please look!   150
But when the statue would not stir,

He waxed impatient, desperate, bold,
And lumbering down on ponderous knees,
Flickered a flame-tongue over her
And chafed her with his muzzle. Cold
His Galatea stayed, nor moved
Save as those clumsy nozzlings shoved.
    So it went on, till, all at once
Tired of evoking no response,
The lordly creature rose, let be   160
His fiery importunity
And trotted off. Not far away
He stopped again, I cannot say
Whether in umbrage or in scorn
Or which more pointed seemed—his back
Toward her—or towards the Zodiac
The index of his taper horn.
And then at last the lady rose
And, crossing over to his side,
Deliberately made much of him   170
Stroking his taut and glossy hide,
Fussing and patting—neither grudged
Her cheek against the wiry hair
Covering his withers. He stayed there,
But all the while he never budged,
Making believe he marked her not:
Or was this only what I thought
Because my sight is waxing dim?
I heard one sharp-eyed youth declare
His ears twitched while she gentled him.   180
    Yet, be that as it may, no wrong
She seemed to feel, no snub nor hurt
But, quiet as she came, ere long
She glided back to her old spot
Upon the cloaks, and spread her skirt
And bowed her head. He followed not
Only—reluctantly—turned round
And, planting forehooves on the ground,
Sat on his haunches facing her.
    It seemed the moments were embalmed   190

That followed next, and could not fade:
Both in an eldritch pause becalmed
Sat soaked in moonshine, Beast and maid.
Strange Beast! Like some majestic Sphinx
That, couchant on the desert sands,
For ever motionlessly thinks
His circling thoughts—yet with that air
Of baby in his own high chair
Pushed up to eat, observing there,
Absorbed and pleased, how fostering hands   200
Advance the spoon, that lately stirred—
Lovable, helpless and absurd!

THE UNICORN

III

The Capture

Now past the zenith, high above,
Plain through the starry sickle shining,
The wrathful patriarchal breast
Of Leo roamed, while up the East,
Close on the tail of him declining,
Virgo ascended. I well know
How, in old mythic maps of sky,
The outspread arms of that great "Y"
Express the Ear of Corn. Not so.
For me those arms are stretched in love   10
Towards the Lion. Far below
Squatted the stubborn Unicorn
And when my eyes passed up his horn
And on to heaven, travelling far,
They rested on the Northern Star.
Did something move? Once more I dreamed:
And lo! from that horn's tip it seemed
The twisting spirals tapering
Discharged the thrust of his intent
In unseen rings intelligent,   20
That spreading, rose and, rising, spread,
Turning into Overhead—
Till all the Universe swung round
A Unicorn upon the ground;
Whose coronation by the stars
Was timeless, being time's quintessence.
So spellbound in eternal presence
Seemed all below, around, above:
The trees, the air, the very stones
That strewed the turf: no grassblade stirred;   30
I saw not how this hour could pass.
God! Would the creature *never* move?
And then an unforeseen occurred
That changed and loosened everything;
For, all at once, in low, clear tones,

Softly, the lady began to sing:
    "His hand He raised, and bade them drink
    And eat, and they were all amazed:
    'What must I do? What must I think?'
    But John leaned on His breast and gazed: 40
    Take all my heart, my love! Thou art
    My Love. Thine eyes have shamed me. Wise
    I grow at last. Take all my heart, my Love!"

Now when the lady ceased to sing,
The glorious silvery cascade
Of horn and muscle, rippling, rose
Erect and, through its quivering nose,
It—(so if it be fair to say
"The burn" and mean Niagara)—
Whinnied, by way of answering.   50
Then, having edged a trifle round
To face a corner of the field,
He starts to titillate the ground
By way of walking; with his feet
He taps and dainties, back a pace
With testy tossings of his face
Next moment in his chest concealed
For coyness. Truly, if he went
The way he must, or way he meant,
I hardly know: As one who rides   60
With feeble skill, will find he goes—
Whichever way the snaffle guides—
Somehow the way his horse decides,
So, sidlings, towards their lady moves
That awkward squad of crowding hooves.
    But when he came to where she was
Throned on her island in the grass,
And meekly his proud neck inclined,
Ah, then, indeed she lifted up
Her countenance, she smashed the cup   70
Of joy, and, through his passive eyes
Gazing expressive, launched with power
Chaste lightnings of her *belamour*.

With that he yielded up the prize—
His puissant Horn, his Tower of Kind—
Surrender! No more to be said,
Save this, that when I come to die,
In my last agony, afraid,
God grant I may remember how
Demurely on that thundering brow   80
Those lips bestowed the accolade!

IV

The Feed

   I deemed the vigil ended now,
Now when this kneeling Unicorn
Laid in her lap his humbled horn
And both were still. I pondered, though,
How she could ever move, or rise,
Slip out from underneath her prize
Yet hold it: while I wondered so,
Idly, once more I heard the breeze
Come rustling faintly through the trees
Behind us, and at once there rose,   10
Fresh and delightsome in the nose,
But startling too, a stronger scent
Than roses blow—A hot, cooked smell
Of savoury potherbs, like a bell,
Over the pasture wafted went.
The Unicorn upon his side
Lay all subdued and slumbersome,
Like one bewitched: but when he sniffed it,
I saw him perk his head and lift it,
Abrupt, exclamatory: 'Hm!   20
Provender!' I could hear him say,
And he rose and snuffed the air, and tried
To edge away unseen, I thought,
But ere he broke into a trot,
Light as a tossed bird in the wrack,
The lady leaped upon his back!
That peerless back, which never bore
Rider's nor any weight before,
Flinched not a jot, as he careered
Onward, it neither plunged nor reared,   30
But like a paddock-pony—one
Safe for a child to learn upon—
Carried her in across the field
Then gently, like a camel, kneeled
While she dismounted—by good chance

So near to me, I met her glance!
I met her glance! Four words! Like rain
It blessed away old lusts and fears,
With the awful weight of vanished years . . .
And I became a boy again.   40
   The hush was lifted, and the crowd
Broke up in knots. In altered tone,
Laughing and chattering aloud,
Recalling scenes, comparing notes
And telling little anecdotes,
They strolled: I heard one eager voice
Babbling too much—it was my own!
So, when a group of girls and boys
Collected round the oaken bin
The monster's nose was buried in,   50
I joined them rather silently.
And, by good fortune, next to me
A girl was standing, who took part
In furnishing the feed contained
Within it—one that knew the art
From ABC to ampersand
And, when I asked, she took my hand
And told me fully: First, the base:
Herbs seethed in pottage, numerous kinds
Commingled (wherewith she explained   60
Virtues of petals, roots and seeds,
How plants the least in outward show
By beauty-gardeners banned as weeds,
Work with the highest potency):
Oats, for a stiffening, said she,
But first the corny brash receives
Two liberal powders: namely, leaves
Of *Lady's Mantle*, picked at morn,
Dusted with pollen of her own green flowers,
Dried in the sun, and then for hours   70
Pashed in a chalice of thin horn;
And next, *Enchanter's Nightshade*, bleached
And steeped and set on fire and burned
To carbon, whence the potash leached

In water, fixed, and coolly urned,
She said the ash was shovelled hot
In ice-cold water on the spot,
And the white-gray solution, sealed
In Carboys, on a float low-wheeled
Was drawn by four black oxen, where   80
Deep in a narrow, rocky cleft,
Through blasts of damp and sunless air,
There ran a little mountain brook;
Pleistocene waterfalls had left
Three natural basons in a row,
Stepwise, and each from other took
The purifying overflow.
Last on a sun-baked rock the lye
Was spread through the Dog days to dry.
And so the whole sweet-smelling brash,   90
Laced with this feathery leaf and ash,
Was packed, and stored in a warm shed,
Where all those herbs' pure spirits wed
Before their grosser substances
United, "And we boiled the mess
And watched the creamy liquor swish
Smooth in an alabaster dish
And, cooling, curdle brittle-flat,
Too thin to clot, too thick to stir,
Like porridge in a porringer—   100
And only needing to be warmed
To loose again the smell that charmed,
The whiff the monster snorted at".

 When she had told me all, I praised
Their subtle lore and gave her thanks,
She smiled, but answered not, because
The Unicorn's complacent jaws
Ceased champing at that moment—he
Seemed to have halted by mistake
At first, but shortly after raised   110
His noble front, and turned it round
And gave his neck a rapid shake
By way of *Benedicite*:

Then sleeked his ears and stood his ground
And made no farther move. . . . A sound—
A sigh, a mutter, a low cheer
Rose like a little wind all round
And plainly showed the end was here.
   The end was here, I need not tell
How on the turf we feasted well   120
Nor with what greedless grace all danced
And many kissed: how far advanced
The night was and the stars grew pale
Before they gathered up their gear;
Or how in azure slashed with flame
Dawn had apparelled half the sky
Before they raised their Standard high
And started back the way they came;
How, by a word, a look, a thought,
Untouched, the Unicorn was brought   130
Into their centre by a priest;
Or how beside the gentle beast
The lady walked; she rode him not.
   Enough for me that I was one
With all that passed that summer's night.
So, with the rising of the sun,
I stopped, and watched them out of sight.
Long after they no more were seen,
I heard triumphant, skirling tunes
On clarionets and bombardoons,   140
Ringing their way up the ravine,
Grow fainter. Then I turned my face
Away—and O, for many days
Carried a brave warmth in my breast
Towards those fierce mountains in the West
Where lay my path. As for the rest—
Whether the Unicorn did act
As they imagined; if in fact
He fought the Lion round the town;
Whether they gained the promised crown,   150
Those youths and maidens, and, if so
Whether 'twas guarded or let go

By treason; if the Pigmy brood
Marched in the end, and wrought their will
To strip the roses from the Rood;
Or if he flouts the Lion still,
That Unicorn; or what occurred,
I cannot say: I never heard.

FINIS

Introduction to *Riders on Pegasus*

Riders on Pegasus is a long mythopoeic narrative poem in seven parts plus a proem completed around 1950. Originally entitled *Mother of Pegasus*, this dramatic poem is undoubtedly Barfield's most ambitious venture in producing rich and powerful verse according to his philosophy of poetry and the evolution of consciousness. Its composition seems to have followed closely on the 1948 stage production of *Orpheus* and follows the mythopoeic formula developed by Barfield for that play. Typescript copies of the poem reside in the Bodleian Library archive (Dep. c. 1110) and at the Wade Center (OB/MS-186/X). Though previously unpublished, this poem has been known about and discussed by several Barfield scholars over the years, such as Ulreich, Kranidas, and Blaxland-de Lange. In 1993 Hunter and Kranidas published the last eight stanzas of the poem in *A Barfield Sampler*. The poem blends the story of Perseus and Andromeda with that of "chaste Bellerophon," mainly through Pegasus and his creation from Medusa's blood as the mythic link, and ends with a triumphant reading of the constellations that "dominate the northern heavens."

Blaxland-de Lange in the chapter titled "Poetry, Drama and Magic" desires most to discover the mythopoeic expressions of Barfield's philosophy illustrated and inherent in his major poetic and dramatic works as part of his intent to produce a scholarly biography of the philosopher of a "Romanticism Come of Age."[1] Blaxland-de Lange confesses some difficulty with *Pegasus*, but if this poem is difficult, it is a joyous difficulty. As one becomes increasingly familiar with the line and style, the poetry stands out in relief, a breath of life for those who do the work to breathe it in, and a revelation etched within the true boundaries drawn by ancient lore. As Blaxland-de Lange notes for *Orpheus*, there is a spirit of magic in this poetry (261). However, in desiring "to establish what he was seeking to express" through the poem, Blaxland-de Lange does point to two important sources of commentary directly from Barfield. The first is Barfield's introduction to the essay collection *Light on C.S.*

Lewis (Ed. Gibb, 1965) which was reprinted in the 1989 edition of *Owen Barfield on C. S. Lewis*. The other is the essay "Poetic Licence," originally composed in 1950, around the same time as *Pegasus* and intended as a Preface to the poem. This text was revised almost three decades later and used as a talk at one or more speaking engagements in North America, but it has never been published. A third source of authorial explanation for the themes and content of *Riders on Pegasus* is, of course, Barfield's Afterword on "The Characters and the Myth," a text almost indispensable to understanding Barfield's sources and mythopoeic purpose. Yet perhaps the most important source for understanding his mythopoeic program is Barfield's own poetic *apologia* and challenge issued as the three-stanza proem to the whole work.

The first two sources of authorial insight into the poem discussed by Blaxland-de Lange vary greatly. The piece published as the Introduction to *Light on C. S. Lewis* goes straight to the heart of Barfield's impulse to use Perseus and Bellerophon to explore the idea of the two Lewises he so curiously saw in his dear friend. The other, a stinging indictment of contemporary poetry originally intended as a Preface to the poem, never mentions the poem directly or any part of it but presents in typical Barfieldian analysis the descent of modern poetry into a stripped-down mockery of itself and how it might yet still be led to drink from ancient wells and awaken into new power. It is a powerful though in places problematic essay, another piece of Barfield's poetic philosophy and both a key to his own poetic desires and a bold declaration in the starkness of post-war desolation that his poetry is worthy, is powerful, is necessary, though at the time it seemed only Lewis understood that; indeed, few people other than Lewis had much opportunity to know it.

The story in Barfield's own words in "Introduction to *Light on C. S. Lewis*" of the poem's impulse arising from his increasingly doubled sense of Lewis highlights the incredible impact these two friends continued to have on each other throughout their lives. Barfield writes: "From about 1935 onward . . . I had the impression of living with, not one, but two Lewises. . . . This experience gradually became something like an obsession with me, and it must have been somewhere about 1950 (when I was still concerned to write verse) that I made it part of the emotional base for a long narrative poem."[2] Although Barfield declares that his obsessional sense of there being two Lewises was "the thread that ran most clearly through it all . . . and which most effectively determined the structure of the whole oeuvre" (23), the poem is, of course, not just about Lewis.

> There were other things I felt the need of unloading as well, and I ended by meditating at some length, and ultimately writing, a sort of extension and combination of two well-known Greek myths in such a way that the characters and events should symbolize, at different levels, a good many matters which I like to think were still at a "pre-logical" stage in my mind . . . questions to which I did not yet know the answers and knew that, for the purposes of the poem, it was better that I should not know them. (22)

Though Lewis, in the two forms Barfield perceived, serves as a driving impulse, the poem is inevitably about consciousness and human experience. The two Lewises become two archetypes when developed in mythopoesis.

> The one (Perseus), after going through a great many difficulties arising out of preference he had developed for dealing with the reflections of things rather than with the things themselves, . . . made peace with . . . his "creative eros" (Andromeda) and was ultimately constellated, along with Andromeda and Pegasus, in the heavens. The other (Bellerophon), after slaying the monster Chimera, declined an invitation to ascend to heaven on the back of Pegasus, who had been his mount in the fateful contest, on the ground of impiety. He was thrown by Pegasus and ended his days in increasing obscurity as a kind of aging, grumbling, earthbound, guilt-oppressed *laudator temporis acti*. (23)

The text continues by reminiscing on various interactions with Lewis about poetry, including teasing him about his role in the poem and remarking on Lewis's uncanny ability to recall verse many years later, including the unpublished poems of friends. Though few beyond a small circle knew *Pegasus* at the time, Barfield reflects fondly on his production of it, most specifically the "incidental fun" of the scenes, especially with the character of Pegasus, and his recollection that he "invented a new stanza for the job" (23).

The second authorial commentary, the essay "Poetic Licence," does not directly address the poem, yet it inscribes the impulse of mythopoeic rebellion against the bleak landscape of most post-war practice.

This unpublished essay has been discussed by Kranidas and Blaxland-de Lange and is referenced in the General Introduction to this volume as an important key to Barfield's theory and program of mythopoeic production. In culmination of both the indictment against most modern poetry and the defense of his own mythopoesis, Barfield considers the poet's place in the long unfolding of the human experience and bluntly asks about one's duty to the future and the past: "*Should* poets try to keep an eye on posterity as well as on the age they live in?" Recalling Charles Lamb's quip on appealing to the present, "A pox on the age: I will write for antiquity," Barfield sees three "obligations incumbent on the true poet."

> The first one is of course to produce an effective poem; and that means effective for his own age; and that again means that he must be highly sensitive to contemporary taste and linguistic habit and concerned to meet their expectations. The second is in some measure to improve and enliven and renovate the language he is writing in; which is something he can only do with his shaping spirit of imagination as it manifests itself more especially in his original handling of metaphor, but not only in that. The third is the one I have just been speaking of—and it may be that some dim idea to this effect was at the back of Lamb's mind when he made his joke. It is to preserve, or help to preserve, the life and spirit already inherent, as its heritage from the past of humanity, in language as he finds it—to obstruct and arrest the creeping sclerosis to which I have been alluding.[3]

There are many notable ways in which the four main Inklings authors differ from each other, but one salient way they coincide is in this mythopoeic rebellion of meaning against the positivist reductive banality smugly put forth as hard reality. Their various methods of mythopoesis are rich with both the resonating pursuit of the inheritance of meaning but also the unmistakable process and signature of each. Barfield's mythopoeic signature is perhaps the least known of the four, much due no doubt to the general lack of access to much of his richest work in this vein, and this poem in particular which, following the lead of *Orpheus*, takes vistas and thematic suggestions opened up by overlapping Classical myths and pulls from them authentic power of ancient meaning given form by ingenious postmodern signature.

INTRODUCTION TO *RIDERS ON PEGASUS*

The text of the poem is beautifully developed and quite readable; the flow of imagery and speech unfolds with poetic ease, especially as one becomes accustomed to the line and stanza form—and the well-used "poetic licence" that broadens the poetic voice to more fluidly "preserve the life and spirit" inherent in language of the "heritage from the past of humanity." The philosopher poet expertly satisfies the three obligations of his essay in the poem it was intended to preface, both intertwined throughout *Riders on Pegasus* and individually emphasized in salient positions—taking special care, of course, for the neglected third, a duty to the past much more intrinsic to both the present and the future than mere homage. Yet that duty is performed in rich enough array that the poet is more than justified in providing a guide to the characters and plot elements in an accompanying Afterword.

The poem's Afterword, attached as intrinsic to the text, provides short profiles for the major characters Perseus, Andromeda, and Bellerophon, and information on many others. In the process much mythic background is given in quick summation, and the interesting potential for connections yet untold uncovered. This quick mythography declines to supply any gloss on more famous immortals, in particular Aphrodite and Athene, but includes a rich texture of other foundational beings, such as Phorcys and Ceto, and their hideous offspring, the Dragon and the Gorgons, and most especially Medusa, the Mother of Pegasus by spilled blood. Much else is told of the mythic landscape, not so much to make the poetic text more visible, but to unfold the texture of deep connections that makes this intriguing tilting of the mythic lens authentically permissible, even engagingly desirable.

It follows that though the poetry may be read first, and this quick mythography is in structural relation truly an Afterword, many readers will nonetheless want to read it as a Foreword—perhaps with pencil and page in hand to map out genealogies and points of action! The story is fluidly and engagingly told in masterful verse, but the provided texture of Barfield's Afterword opens rich vistas of meaning in the work and reveals the great worth of pursuing the mythic inheritance of meaning. In whatever order one may pair the two, the Afterword is an essential part of the text in the truest sense—as is, of course, the fourth authorial guide to this deep and rich mythopoeic work, the poet's own proem.

Inevitably the philosophy of poetry most intimately attached to this grand mythopoesis is the poetic philosophy unfolded in the proem, given after the whole title, *Riders on Pegasus*, but before section I, "Andromeda." The three stanza proem to *Riders on Pegasus* amounts to one of Barfield's great statements on poetry, mythology, the figuration of conscious experience, its past and continuing evolution, and the mythopoeic path forward—a proem as bold as Milton's grasping the prophetic mantle, and a call, a challenge to poets and poetry to leap like ancient *taurokathapsia*, the Bronze Age bull jumpers, and grasp the horns of meaning to fling conscious figuration into the paths of final participation. These many decades later the poetic challenge of the philosopher of poetry rings even truer and clearer in the depths of our cultural descent into meaninglessness and social dissolution.

The maker Owen Barfield begins this poetic stance and challenge by unequivocal declaration that his creation is true to the web of Classical mythology. The opening line, "Of Perseus and Andromeda my verses," is no idle notation of a surface resemblance to these characters of Classical myth. Barfield is claiming direct identity, a creation true to the ancient mythology. This is a true tale of Perseus and Andromeda, though "this Tale has slept till now untold." Still if the reader will "delve in thine own heart—thou too shalt find" the truth of this myth, true to "the Word" that gives form to human consciousness.

Barfield's proem claims that this mythopoesis is new but also authentic, not just true to the mythos but to the truth of maker's making, for it arises from the cultural structures we have all inherited, meanings built on the web of experience arising in us from earlier mythic figurations that became foundational myth, part of the macrocosm-microcosm of Word in which the polarity of consciousness resolves. Hence, this is a new true tale, a bringing forth of meaning from deep but strong implications in form and symbol, in sense and purpose, and so partaking in the new and old, creating tableaux inherent in the meanings from which consciousness—and therefore meaning itself—emerged and yet emerges.

What follows, implicit in old forms, is authentic and yet new, "the dew's still on my rhyme." Dew is both fresh today and part of the perennial nourishment and renewal of the earth. This image links the second verse to the first to state more directly the claim of authenticity:

> The dew—this drawing up from my own earth
> How Myth, being present in the Word, began
> To sketch on time his everlasting Now
> In master tableaux—whence the soul of man
> Took form and substance—

The line then corrects, "takes it rather," for the mythic forms underlying consciousness are still vital, as one looking deep may still find "Pan / Is piping here, and chaste Bellerophon." The poet may still tap those forces, not just to *say* something new, but to *make* part of the world and to make the world anew—and this old sense of poet as maker is inscribed in the ensuing call and challenge: "Poets—deep minds—would ye be priests of Meaning?" And how is this done?

> Reach in those souls the world's prophetic soul,
> The Whole in each become particular,
> The Myth: disclose the Word: growing aware
> Of old imagination, born anew
> As young experience: withered words shall bloom then,
> And all your tales, like this new Tale of mine, be true.

Poets can be great engagers of meaning, can draw forth from human depths lived patterns unseen, with vision such as Goethe used to imagine the missing crown of Strasbourg Cathedral and discern patterns inherent in vegetable life. The poetic soul intersects with the world soul in a macrocosm-microcosm interleaved polarity of being to reveal meaning maps and paths from ancient to future worlds as the inheritance of meaning renews itself and grants us escape from the withering of the age and a blossoming anew from old epistemic power. One may learn the depths of meaning and draw from them that which is fresh revelation from powerfully true ancient roots. Indeed, this is how tales can be most true. Hence, Barfield's claim to ancient and postmodern meaning is more than mere bricolage thievery, fashion's latest mutation for current market values, but an authentic production from the Classical mythopoeic web.

Notes

1. Simon Blaxland-de Lange, *Owen Barfield: Romanticism Come of Age: A Biography* (Forest Row, England: Temple Lodge Publishing, 2006), 266-7. Further citations of this work are given in the text.

2. Owen Barfield, *Owen Barfield on C. S. Lewis*, ed. G. B. Tennyson (Middletown, CT: Wesleyan University Press, 1989), 22. Further citations of this work are given in the text.

3. Owen Barfield, "Poetic Licence" (Bodleian archive Dep. c. 1155), 19-20.

– vidi ipse materno sanguine nasci

To C. S. Lewis

An Afterword on the characters and their background will be found at the end of the poem.

RIDERS ON PEGASUS

Of Perseus and Andromeda my verses:
And yet this Tale has slept till now untold.
For delve in thine own heart—thou too shalt find
How their long reign brought in an age of gold
In Aethiopia, where they grew not old
But passed, as thou dost, listening, through time
Out to the Myth, the Word whose form is Man;
Therefore my tale is news; the dew's still on my rhyme:

The dew—this drawing up from my own earth
How Myth, being present in the Word, began
To sketch on time his everlasting Now
In master tableaux—whence the soul of man
Took form and substance—takes it rather: Pan
Is piping here, and chaste Bellerophon,
Strong arm and martial spirit, friend, in thee,
Trampling (beneath what hooves!) Chimaera, passes on.

Poets—deep minds—would ye be priests of Meaning?
Makers—or scribes? Oh, utter all ye are!
Reach in those souls the world's prophetic soul,
The Whole in each become particular,
The Myth: disclose the Word: growing aware
Of old imagination, born anew
As young experience: withered words shall bloom then,
And all your tales, like this new Tale of mine, be true.

I

ANDROMEDA

I

From oozy Congo's fecund and sweaty jungle's
Green tangle of rubber-dropping trunk and bough—
Boisterous superflux of radical moisture
Swelling her soft hot loins—bethink you how
Africa lifts a northward-facing brow,
Till the shock of the land-locked Ocean on her fringe
Bids Thought awake—the prehistoric verge,
Where, moist and dry unmingled, streams on rocks impinge.

II

Mediterranean murmured about the base,
There, of a rocky promontory, bright,
Long baked in sun-glare. Cool and mother-naked,
In her bare temple rinsed with air and light,
A Parian Aphrodite, dazzling white,
Stood, gazing down, late-born, upon her sea
(Almost you saw its bubbles of dried foam
Popping and vanishing from her), Anadyomene.

III

Gazing toward Cyprus—and half loth to gaze,
Half turned aside. To praise a mortal Queen,
The skilful carver had prolonged in marble
That moment of sweet shame, when she had been
Surprised by soaring love; and a vast, unseen
Monster's imagined jaws had not availed
To petrify virginity, which strove
To cover up her breast with fettered arms—and failed.

IV

The time—be thou less curious—since her rescue

It may be some four thousand years had passed,
Or days, or decades—well, how should I know?
Dates are a riddle for the scholiast.
But the golden age was breaking up at last
In Aethiopia: men were murmuring
Like wasps: in secret places noble youths
Were being taught by men of wrath to hate the King.

V

Popinjay sophists argued: hollow men
Listened, believed: and guilty men pretended:
And this—this was the nature of the time
Early one morning, when the young Queen wended
Her way up to the Shrine. One Slave attended,
Alone, her mistress's slow pilgrimage,
Bearing a basket filled with fresh-cut myrtle
And a turtle cooing through a wood and wicker cage.

VI

Lucifer sailed over the Ocean, paling
In faint Aurora's crocus, where she smiled.
Lady Andromeda, coming near the temple,
Spoke to the slave girl "Leave me now, my child!"
And like one to her task ill-reconciled,
Unsure if to keep silence or to tell,
She entered a cool pallor through the pillars:
"Lady, O Daughter of Sky and Light! All is not well—

VII

"All is not well. . . ." She prayed, and halted: "Perseus—"
She ceased, as though she chided her own folly
Or stooped to chafe some hope into a heart
Cramped with long unadmitted melancholy,
Knowing no Circe could undo, no moly
Prevent that gross enchantment! Unperceived
It had increased on him. It would not cease
For ever! At that 'for ever' her breast heaved.

VIII

For all her frame was one heart-shaking sob
Swollen with suppression over mounting years.
The Statue nodded. Soon the Paphian eased
The babbled prayer forth in flowing tears,
Till out they poured pell-mell, her woes and fears:
"I do not say, God knows I do not say
"He grows unkind, discourteous! Would he were!
"I could reproach him then and scold my tears away!

IX

"Rather, too kind—like—too much like a father;
"I see, as in polished shields, when our eyes meet,
"Andromeda there, become a kind of comedy . . .
"Where is my saviour with his falcon feet
"Stooping at me from heaven? Or where the beat
"Of the plumes from God assumed? If he but knew!
"Mother of Eros, how shall I reach him? Ah,
"What shall I do?" she wailed aloud "What shall I do?"

X

She sank, all bravery gone, down on the pavement:
Dumb in her bitter grief she knelt a wife,
And rose a priestess—crossed, and on the altar
Offered the gurgling dove. The copper knife
Flashed in the air—and forth the purple life
Gushed, as bright music quits a shattered harp:
The thread that, till that moment, momently
Had payed into the panting warmth was snapped off sharp.

XI

Torn from its normal channel through warm marrow,
The throb of plastic spirit sprang, released,
To cram the hungry concave. Empty space,
Numinous near the carven throat and breast,
Put on articulation, was expressed,
And love, life's meaning, floated forth as word

Made flesh in real sound. An awful Voice
The Queen adoring, caught up in the goddess, heard:

XII

"Daughter of Cepheus, Aethiopia's Queen,
"I, Aphrodite's Self about thee, hear
"Thy prayer. Take heart; have I not also heard
"The monstrous price amerced for Cassiopeia,
"Thy Mother's boast, when, mad with shame and fear,
"Chained to thy sterile rock, thou didst abide
"All fathomless Poseidon's boiling rancour
"Toward my peculiar—mortal beauty's vaunting pride?

XIII

"First I must know thy Perseus. Grows he, daughter,
"In aught unopen? Holds he aught concealed
"From love's sharp eyes?"
      After long silence answered
The Queen:—"There is a Press. The burnished shield
"Of Pallas hangs upon it. Locked and sealed
"From me, his lawful Queen, my husband keeps
"That place, O Goddess, and each night he hides
"His signet underneath his bolster when he sleeps!"

XIV

"What lies within it?"
     "Nay I cannot say!
"It is unspoken between us, I only guess
"Some tender thing, for sure, that once had life
"And warmth, and now maintains its lastingness
"Only by some machine that feeds the Press
"Through secret flues with cooling air, because
"From underneath the door, across the floor
"Always an outward cold unnatural current draws.

XV

"I get no word. Only, when I surprise him
"Alone with the close friends who form his staff,

"I have thought ere now that the wind lay in that quarter—
"Uneasy silence—warning looks—a laugh
"From one who had dropped a phrase's broken half
"Upon my entrance—talk adroitly led
"Into new channels—all these I have heard!"
"And hast thou never asked him frankly?"
        Once—"she said

XVI

And halted: "Once—" her resolution faltered.
She closed her eyes and seemed to search her mind
For strength to probe the past—"Once—once I asked him,
"And Lady, he grew all gentle and too kind!
"Said he must tell me all that lay behind,
"And spoke so softly that he seemed afraid—
"Asking me first how clearly I remembered
"The days that followed after Herpe's darting blade

XVII

"Had smashed my chains, and my poor naked body
"Sank shivering in his arms—(but I am sure
"Of nothing after my great shock: I lay
"Delirious in a raging calenture.
"I know they fought. I know that my old wooer,
"Phineus—I must not ask of it, they said—
"And all his gallants, brawling in our Palace,
"Fell, and are lying somewhere—somehow more than dead!)

XVIII

"Then he began, without a pause, of Danaë
"In her brazen prison, and vowed he must explain:
"I heard him mutter: *Zeus Meteoros!*
"*How can one flinch, whose father was that Rain?*
"Through teeth clenched, like a skull's, on scorn of pain—
"Too fierce to mark if I were pleased or vexed
"And gazing on me so, as on a maze
"His thought were groping entrance to, and he perplexed.

XIX

"Then off on some long tale how Earth and Ocean
"Mingled in love, and how Thalassa bore
"Phorcys and Ceto, who themselves, those twain
"(Mingling in love, no doubt!) had issue four—
"Not looking at me now—and more and more
"Remote—engrossed in his own thoughts, at ease,
"He chose the foulest of the four—and glozed
"About some Dragon guarding those Hesperides!

XX

"So on he droned. And soon I could not follow
"And waxed impatient, saying I was tired
"(There were so many names!) of pedigrees
"And labyrinths and lists, and who was sired
"By whom, and I stamped, and said I but enquired
"One simple thing. He broke off, and I wept
"Then, because I had hurt him; and he smiled
"And held his peace, and laughed, and kissed me till I slept.

XXI

"But when I woke near dawn, his breath was broken
"As though his sleeping soul lay unredeemed,
"And I raised my breast and touched his poor face, gazing
"To trace the flying troubles while he dreamed . . .
"All in a rush, like some lost soul, he screamed:
"Andromeda! No, darling! Look at *me!*
"Sobbing caught breaths, like death—till I, all trembling,
"Woke him (Thou know'st if I did well) invoking Thee!"

XXII

She ceased, and for a space no answer followed;
Only the hollow silence, made more dense—
Remembrance of her own voice fallen dumb.
Until once more the rustle, past all sense,
The crepitation into sentience
Of space alert, the ghostliness was there

About the Queen; and swift uprose her heart
And slowly, at the noise of that dread Voice, uprose her hair:

XXIII

"Fear not!" it said, "pray thou to Cytherea
"Again, when Hesperus winks benign the hour,
"And I will summon Hypnos from his cavern
"And come with him in plenitude of power.
"Lo, the King's blood shall blossom, like a flower,
"And Hypnos, with his calm and wing-wide gaze,
"Shall loose his *dura mater*, and sluice with water
"Of Lethe all those secret labyrinthine ways

XXIV

"Of his brisk brain, and soak the brittle walls,
"Which instantly, if challenged from outside,
"Shall crumble and collapse, and he shall grumble
"And slip back into slumber satisfied.
"So, in the dark, that Press thou shalt fling wide
"Stealing with ease his signet-ring and key,
"And thou shalt take the Thing within the press,
"Unseen of any man, and cast it in the sea."

XXV

She ceased. The Queen arose and scattered myrtle
Out of her basket all about the Shrine,
Then passed without and gazed on the vast ocean
Pondering, and scarcely saw its calm, sweet shine
Or marked the Nereids dancing in the brine,
But swift, in fear, she wheeled about and wondered,
When from the morning sky's pale shell of blue
Unblemished by one speck of brightest cloud—it thundered!

XXVI

She only heard—the goddess *saw*—the Father
Urging his chariot through his empty sky
And felt the thunder of his frown condemn
His dangerous Daughter's awful levity,

Bearing it out at first, with conscious eye
Unwinking, thinking she should not look down—
The Queen, affrighted, saw the temple quiver,
When Aphrodite's eyelids fell before that frown.

XXVII

Bright gleamed the glossy waves, to see the passing
Of Cytherea's brief discomfiture
And skipped, to feel again her lovely lips
Set in their solemn smile, self-pleased, demure.
What did she care, who, rather than endure
One morsel unpossessed—one distant look,
Unhindered by a qualm, would burn to cinders
The Golden Fleece wrapped round the last Sybilline Book?

XXVIII

The Lady struck a gong. The slave returned
Humming a ditty, while with leather thong
She strapped the trug and cage. As towards the City
They went, the Queen's heart melted into song
Outpouring—'Praise the Goddess wise and strong!
'Praise we our Lady of Cyprus, praise and bless!
'Who, if we trust her, teaches how to thrust
'Against themselves the danger of their tortuousness!

XXIX

'Oh, but this hateful thing—this Thought of theirs,
'That never strikes you squarely on the face
'But, meeting with itself behind your feet,
'Includes you in some passionless embrace,
'That softly eats away the very base
'Whereon you stand, like the incoming tide—
'How sweet a thing it is! How simple and neat!
'How economically it may be applied!

XXX

'One simple plan! And all shall soon be well,
'And well, and well! Once more upon this breast,

'Uncrowned, his orbèd gravity profound,
'God's wisdom in its box apart, shall rest,
'My little one, hushed quiet and possessed,
'Content (and smiling in his private way)
'As Uranus—Himself containing all
'Was pleased with Gaia—pleased to be contained till day!'

XXXI

Sighing, she glanced ahead. How sweetly sang,
How couthly, debonairly, paced the slave!
And, when they reached the little white-walled town,
How cool a gloom how quietly it gave!
How fresh and clear the morning! Ah, how brave
The world was! And the Queen thought, as she smiled:
'A grand, cool closet will be splendid too,
'To save the milk—I mean to have it paved and tiled!'

XXXII

That very night she prayed to Aphrodite
Devout, when Hesperus winked benign the hour,
Who summoned Hypnos from his shady cavern
And came with him in plenitude of power,
And all the King's blood blossomed like a flower,
Till Hypnos, with his calm and wing-wide gaze,
Unloosed his dura mater and sluiced with water
Of Lethe all his thinking's labyrinthine ways.

XXXIII

So, soon, Andromeda has ring and keys
With ease and, as she glides, with hand half-closed
Warding her taper, down wide corridors,
Nocturnal panics filch her breath—and, most,
Dread of her white self, moving like a ghost,
The pale home-stalking spectre of Medea
With lurid torch, or chamber-haunting Fury
Nearing the couch, where one lies staring back in fear.

XXXIV

What is the Disc that hangs up on the door
There, on the farther side of the vast chamber
Andromeda has reached? A swelling Mirror,
The shadowy gloss of whose distorting camber
Bosoms in polished gloom a star of amber
Quavering—the taper's splintered aureole—
That frames—what creature waddling down to meet her,
Dolled in the Queen's nightgown? What portly little droll?

XXXV

With that her courage failed. She strove to pray—
Aye but to whom? the Cozener of men,
The Hoodwinker of all the Gods in turn,
Desire's uncertain Self? She had fainted then,
Had not proud Cythera's subtle denizen,
She of the graceful snood, her mood inclined,
Accepting her not-prayer as a prayer
And swiftly sent an answering thought into her mind:

XXXVI

'Thou little undesirable, absurd!
'Not all the gods are feebler than desire.
'Look now, where hangs before thee Her bright Shield,
'Whose steadfastness prevailed—nay, look higher
'To the Mother of us all, whose sacred fire
'Tall on her altar burneth, night and day,
'Deep in thy central chapel's holy quiet,
'Thy Home's eternal Focus—turn to Hestia!'

XXXVII

She prayed—she thought she heard a rush of plumes
Invisible, such as once she had heard before—
Once only, bearing love and banning horror—
For Hestia sent the Carrier, who wore
Talaria on his god-like feet, and bore
A daydream, wherein she saw Perseus rise

From table, saw him resting, laughing, jesting
With sunny little puckers round his faithful eyes . . .

XXXVIII

When Perseus' life was threatened in Seriphos
By envious Polydectes' craft malign,
The gray-eyed Goddess and swift Hermes gave him
His wingèd sandals and her Shield divine;
The first he had laid back in the Giver's shrine
Long, long ago. The Shield he guarded still,
As a magic mirror for the stony Terror,
Medusa, whom Athene taught him how to kill

XXXIX

With backward cut, not looking in her eyes.
For when the time for render came, he had pleaded
Extension, since he owned the Gorgon still
And those dead eyes, he said, were sorely needed
To keep the peace and crush the passion seeded
Deep in the hearts of the Queen's rebellious folk,
Which sprouted often in disastrous floutings
Of the edicts of his just and reasonable yoke.

XL

This was the Shield that hung now on the door
Far, in the end wall, where a deep recess
Tomb-like and cyclopean, hollowed out
By the masons in the ashlar, was the Press:
All down the room's unfurnished eeriness—
Her head most carefully, while she drew near,
Averted, lest she catch the distant gleam
And see herself again, the Queen approached in fear.

XLI

O Heart? She questioned, and her heart replied:
Ah, tush! What so it be, it is unreal,
So it presume to part us! Without more:
'Husband, I come!' she thought, and broke his seal.

The door swung back with loud, long, sobbing squeal—
Look, there was nothing there—save slips of rag
Lying about, the sort that soldiers use
For scouring shields to make them bright, and one old bag,

XLII

A goatskin bag—these and the rush of cold
Expected—round her belly like a pall,
An icy hauberk clasping it. She passed,
Breathless, the threshold of man's arsenal,
Stooped, where the bag leaned up against the wall,
And peered into its top—with criss-cross thread,
Roughly, except one corner, caught together . . .
One glance . . . the gloom was merciful . . . she glimpsed the Head . . .

XLIII

She shut the door; was sick; with stiffening tendons
And jerking taper sealed the dropping wax.
Then, slowly as the Earth, she turned, and slowly,
With taper, ring and key, retraced her tracks,
Gray-faced and Saturn-shouldered, seedy, lax,
Creeping over the floor like some old crone
With sagging knees and dragging heels, who feels
She must sit down, and cannot while her work's half done.

XLIV

Not loathing any more, desiring nothing—
So, back the way she came, uncrowned, unblest,
Poseidon's prey and Perseus' glory shuffled.
At last, the ring and key restored, she pressed
The couch: one hand fell lightly on her breast,
Feeling the frore mist roll up from the plains
Beneath, and swirl around the rosy tips
Of those responsive, milky hills of rilling veins.

XLV

Slow, as she lay beside the King, alone,
Through all those veins the deadly marmor ran

Inward. The stream of life-with-memory
That maketh woman woman, and man man,
Shuddered and changed. Her curdled mind began
To turn its sourness backward. Hate and doubt
Crawled in the bud unseen, as outward sheen
Of warmth and health returned. She flung her arms about

XLVI

Each time the venom touched, with severing power,
Remembered hours when they had seemed most near,
Or striven all-utterly together, given
Either to other; or when she felt it smear
Ineffable caresses with what sneer
Of vile reserve—oh, knocking, bruising, blotching
What tenderest quick of candour! All the while
She dreamed the curious eyes of Perseus watching, watching.

XLVII

The morning came—the day passed—and more days:
She showed not all at once how she was changed,
Only, forlorn, she dared not be alone;
She must be with him now, where'er he ranged
On foray or assize—but worst estranged
They grew, when she would not be left behind,
The Royal Consort—or as such acclaimed—
Even on those inward journeys of his questing mind.

XLVIII

The less she stayed the pace, the more she claimed
A vain pretence of it, as courtesy due,
The which receiving, still the more incensed
By that pretence's mockery, she grew
A feverish, iridescent assidue
Of passion crude—alloy of shame and pride—
A brassy flower, a thin Danaë's Tower,
Barked her about, and Perseus watched it, anxious-eyed.

XLIX

And he, God knows, had weighty care enough
Abating this last straw, unhappy King,
To save the realm, because, clear-eyed, he saw
The way the tide was flowing, how the thing
He loved, his god-machine for governing—
The Head inside the bag there in the Press—
(Such singular reports were coming in)
Would stem no longer, soon, for all its lordliness.

II

PERSEUS

I

There was a time, before Deucalion's flood,
A man whose sacrifice with herbs was clean
And smoked aright, would smoothly sleep at nights
Though fortune spat upon his gabardine;
But I am old—too often have I seen
The gentler virtues work their proper woe
And sweet forbearance fortify misprisions
One flash of passion might have scattered long ago.

II

So—when his Aethiop queen was crossly charmed—
Was Danaë's child disarmed by chivalry.
He was Athene's Knight, her perfect Knight,
Who willed all men and women to be free.
Even his enemies he loved to see
Unhampered, strong to strike, with room at least
As ample as his own; as he had shown
Often in ambuscade—once at his wedding feast.

III

(Not till the blood of Phineus and his brood
Had flowed, till the dead and dying choked the hall.
Not till his vaunting victims taunted him
Weakening, with his back against the wall,
On the Gorgon's vantage had he deigned to call,
Crying with a loud voice:—"Ye mock me, hey?—
"Would toast this boasted mistress with me?—So!
"Meet her! *now let all friendly eyes be turned away!*"

IV

And raised aloft the Selfless soul's Imago,
The lapidary Hate, with seething hair!
The shrill Virago—chanticleer of death—
Crowed through their brains the venom of her stare . . .)
The horror of that victory made him swear
By Styx himself, by Cerberus' three faces,
Never, never to rip the sack again,
Unless disaster threatened the last holy places.

V

And he kept his vow with ease, because for years
Through the Queen's native heart at once he heard
If any man were nursing fretful dreams
Or in their bosoms infant treason stirred.
For, as some solitary migrant bird
Strains in its cage, agog, with vibrant wings,
When myriads of small blood-brothers at large
Assemble flockmeal, ripe for journeyings,

VI

Her lissome breast in secret sympathy
Thrilled with her people's humours—a live sense
Of currents stirring. So, his Queen preferring,
With the old intrigue of spies he could dispense.
Andromeda was his intelligence.
It was enough. Before the imposthume swelled,
He would ride forth, and Herpe's glancing blade
Lanced it, and so rebellion at its source was quelled.

VII

But the trickle of intransigeance increased
And swelled into a flood, as that distress
Throve in the Queen, which drove her to the Temple,
And she began to spoil their singleness
By probing to improve it. Scot and Cess
Mysteriously decreased; and here a town

Proclaimed democracy and built a wall,
And there Athene's hateful statue was pulled down.

VIII

Disorder, hydra-headed, sprang and spread
More vigorously, it seemed, the more he lopped.
Foray on foray now and raid on raid
Followed; he never rested, never stopped
Quelling their riots; closer though it cropped,
Herpe but shaved the haulm, and left still sound,
Supple and intertwined, as stubborn bindweed,
The roots of insurrection shooting underground.

IX

And so, about the time the Queen set forth
On that nocturnal quest, their plight grew worse;
For Phineus' son had roused a flighty nation
In freedom's name to wreak his father's curse;
Whose marble eyes (dead hate's executors)
Converted random raids to planned guerilla
First, and then open war. The Soothsayers
Spoke, and the King, to save the realm, invoked the Killer . . .

X

What weary years the civil strife dragged on!
Begetting all things vile—vendettas, vices,
Garottings, tortures, treachery, young souls rotting,
The gods despised and starved of sacrifices—
Countering the Gorgon-ray with fresh devices,
Which, following its shape, the Myth will tell,
But, following its shape, must first relate
What thing, what strange and doubtful change, the King befell.

XI

He in a thought-well of divine reflection
Saw truths, so mere they make mere glancers blind:
So, when men wrangled fruitlessly, entangled
In secondary thoughts, his sovran mind

Dropped blessing on them, dancing round behind
The parrot phrase, or pricking vested error
With its own point—the little spot of light
The everywhere at once, the Sun's—his mind a mirror

XII

So slightly turned, it never lost the light,
And with what ease! and not as having striven,
But laughing, like a boy—yet afterwards
Men marveled at the strength they had been given,
And told each other: 'He came down from heaven!
'Those Shoes his youth had on, they left this knack
'Of charming wingèd Thought from lucid Aether
'To split the region cloud in rescue or attack!'

XIII

But on the cold Press hung a different Mirror:
No joy consoles like easy action, reft
Of effort by past efforts—weary Will
Leans on his spade and nods, to see how deft
Are mind and muscle grown—young lords enfeoffed
Of lands he tilled with sweat for them; so nods
Approvingly a father in old age
To hear his grown sons of their own accord revere the gods!

XIV

Men love reminders of ability,
No matter if necessity or choice
Pricked its acquiring (every speech he made,
I think, would old Demosthenes rejoice
To hear his own suave, unimpeded voice—
Recalling pebbles): and since it took much knack
To strike a foe reflected in a Shield
And wield a sword in cut and thrust, with head turned back,

XV

Perseus began to love the sacred Shield
Itself, its rimmed horizon; before long

He needed it beside him everywhere.
To use it made him feel so firm and strong;
For in those depths he judged of right and wrong
Aloofly, saw the Whole without infection
Of contact with the part—his darting mind
Pierced all things, insulated from them by reflection.

XVI

He had the Shield hung in the Place of Dooms
And gazed upon it while he heard the pleas,
Disseisins, ousters, writs to curb the laws,
Arsons and piracies on the high seas.
The doers and their knots of witnesses
Whispered, the advocates declaimed and fought
Low on the floor: high on his throne the King
Sat looking at them with his back turned to the Court!

XVII

Or on the round wall of the Council Hall—
There, in the high hush, through the mumbled drama
Of Acts of State, Impeachments, grand Debate,
He faced the Bronze, himself ensconced in armour,
His privy councilors a cyclorama
Of dwarfish images—with friendly greeting
Passing from eyes to eyes, and sound advice
From mouth to mouth: truth meeting truth—and no true meeting!

XVIII

Framed, like a toy, to please, he deigned to sample
The city hum, where raucous men compete.
He had the Mirror fitted in his litter
And let himself be carried through the street,
Whose brouhaha, in bioscope, was sweet!
To view all men, himself, too, very small
And quaint, relaxed his fighting Spirit, faint
With mightiness—to seem a child among them all!

XIX

Till once, from such amusement he returned
And came to where Andromeda sat, wan,
Plying her listless loom—the Shield beside him
Borne by a slave, a captured Nubian;
His mind still on his toy, the King began
To meet the Queen's reflected eyes, and speak,
Nor saw (they were so small) their glance of horror,
But heard, half-choked, behind his back, her actual shriek.

XX

He turned, amazed, but ere he met her eyes,
She had expressed from them all trace of pain
For fear of paining him—so haply scaring
What spectre of their Hymen might remain.
And he—he thought: 'Who knows? Would she explain
'That shriek . . . well, I will try! . . .' How gently lay
His hand upon her hair, as he began:—
"Andromeda . . . thou dear! . . . look up! . . . Andromeda . . ."

XXI

But while he paused, a runner was brought in
Unheralded, all damp with sweat; who kneeled
Craving an audience. Perseus turned his head
And signed to him to talk into the Shield;
And he gasped out news of forces in the field
In strength unheard of, ragged rabbles merging
To disciplined detachments, openly,
And from all quarters on the little town converging.

XXII

Then the King turned and faced him stern:—
                              "My army?"
"Cut down! Surprised in leaguer! Our vedettes
"Drugged with new devilries—this hour to-morrow
"That sun that in the sea so calmly sets
"Will gleam upon their barbarous burgonets

"Advancing!"
                For a space the King, astounded,
Stood, then a third time turned, and strode away,
Struggling to feel the true was real—his base surrounded!

XXIII

Alone, his thought mounted those snowy peaks
Of cold Olympus, where the high gods rule,
As oftentimes in those old fervid days
Back in Seriphos, where men called him fool
And tossed him with their taunts and threats. How cool
Came floating from on high the Wreath that crowns
With earnest olive-leaves her countenance,
Athene's, tall Protectress of invested towns!

XXIV

Within the Palace grounds there rose a Temple
Used by the King alone; and there men called her
Athene Basileia. Thither now
Went Perseus, there his priest led by a halter,
Lowing forlorn reproach, and on the altar
Slew, at his Lord's command, a milk-white cow.
And lo! the Sacker of Cities—the unborn
Crackle of harnessed Levin, darted from God's brow—

XXV

Pallas Athene, through sharp, thin-walled nostrils,
Savoured fat of soul in the steaming blood.
Broad gazes of surprise, important grazings,
The slow, phlegmatic sacrament of cud
And the softness of fresh dung on trampled mud
Uncurled into the smoke of the sacrifice
And censed her brainy truculence—there crept
A lazy gleam of hazel over those Gray Eyes

XXVI

Responsive, as he bent his brows and thought
Of all he knew of feeble and innocent

Leaning on him—Andromeda's white face
And, what more touched him, her bewilderment;
He called up all that sack of cities meant—
Faces of children waiting to be killed,
Shrill panic, blank despair, stark violence—,
Then, with one grisly wrench, renouncing all, he willed . . .

XXVII

As once, behind the walls of Ilium
Great Hector, his stern mood to war addressed,
Lifted his child to kiss, and back the boy
Started from helmet and swart, nodding crest
Looming too close, and towards his mother's breast
Stretched little arms, wailing to be let go
Back to his wooden toys, bad Greeks, good Trojans,
And the goddesses and gods in his galanty-show,

XXVIII

So now a huge Casque overgloomed the King,
As stooping Pallas caught him to her Place
High in the heavens, to make him of her mind;
So, while his Spirit met her face to face,
His body's arrogance—which deemed it base
To have been so invaded—gave a groan
And sank to earth indignant, hankering
After the Shield—still, still to call his mind its own!

XXIX

"Thou hadst the Gorgon's Head!" Athene said,
"That, and my saving Shield—how hast thou failed?"
To her his naked reason, undismayed,
Answered:—"O Goddess, thy fair gifts prevailed
"How nearly! If Medusa's eyes unveiled
"Grow impotent, and I must know defeat,
"It is because this clever Aethiop race
"Evolves new engines in the womb of its conceit."

XXX

And so went on to tell (for there are news
Which even the gods can learn from men alone)
Of their new man-made ore—which ash and air
And flame, compounding, bound more hard than stone,
Yet light and structural withal, as bone,
And missile unbelievably; and more:
For by their skill, disposed throughout the mass,
Their smiths could parcel hard and soft. About a core

XXXI

Soft and disgustful, mashy, like a brain,
And irritably active, they could case
Impermeable cortexes, protective—
The gelatine kissing the carapace
In cockroach-union—soft in hard's embrace.
Nor was this all: the kiss was consummated,
When very essence in their crucibles
Was broken down, and counter qualities equated

XXXII

Of soft and hard, to breed some substance new;
For truly soft are things that men may mould,
As lead or potter's clay: if pressed askew,
They keep the new shape and forget the old;
But smitten bronze, alert with instant, bold
Elastic will, regains its old extension
It scarcely ceded; soft is like a child,
Hard like a soldier, drilled to start back to attention.

XXXIII

But this new stuff of theirs, he told, combined
Hard's elasticity with soft's compliance,
A bladder-stuff, membranous, tough like gut:
Dead matter aped, through their unholy science,
Resilient Woman, who, without defiance,
Her meek heart by him from her purpose blended,

Obeys her lord—and then, the dawdling way,
Does what her slumbering Will has all the while intended.

XXXIV

Tersely, his girt intelligence reviewed
The gear constructed from it—young Phineus's
Silky translucencies that gloved the face,
Impregnable—its more ingenious uses:
Lithe tubes, in which, through copper, subtle juices,
Swift, and with speech suspended in them, sped,
So that his forces met, reported, planned
Snug, without faring forth to risk the Gorgon's Head.

XXXV

But when at last he ceased, Athene frowned:—
"Thou know'st I have been ever at thy side.
"Thou speakest much of cleverness. Art thou
"So dull?" she questioned. And Perseus replied
Heavily:—"O high Goddess, I have tried
"All, never wearying, all deeds the foe did
"Myself have done. This war may not be won
"By workings of men's wits alone: the dice are loaded!

XXXVI

"Always their fantasy anticipates:
"Some Influence, whether of Earth or Sky or Ocean
"Works to advantage them; it dreams behind
"The Thought beneath their thought, and speeds the motion
"Of keen invention's wings. As idle notion
"I scorned the tale at first; but now concur,
"Since mine own ears have heard their renegade
"Talk in his wine-cups. He was their philosopher;

XXXVII

"And told of Gordian problems, one by one,
"Solved in a twinkling by some happy guess,
"Which men had thought a task for years; of glances
"On faces startled by their own success;

"Of mushroom sproutings of ingeniousness
"Beyond belief; and how there seemed some flux
"That let, like molten tin, dexterity
"Run in their minds and muscles with strange ease, like luck's.

XXXVIII

"I know not its true name, this unseen Power,
"If some new rôle of Chance-controlling Fate,
"So! If aught less, if some malignant God—
"O Thou, who didst not let inordinate
"Unboundaried Poseidon liquidate
"Wily Odysseus on his tiny prow!
"Sweet Casemate of men's little moated towns!
"Stern daughter of my Father! Sister! Aid me now!"

XXXIX

He ceased, and peered deep in her shadowy features,
Dismayed to mark the solemn look they wore.
"Thou knowest," she began, "how Earth and Ocean
"Mingled in love at first, till Ocean bore
"Phorcys and Ceto, who had issue four,
"One mortal, three immortal. One alone
"Thou hast subdued—thine enemy and friend,
"Medusa, who, being dead, turns breathing flesh to stone.

XL

"Medusa, firm of breast and soft of hair
"Beyond all mortal women—till that hour
"Of love-play in my temple with Poseidon—
"My Temple!—Much availed her Paramour
"To shield his Fondling! Yet I wield no power
"Over immortals. So those other Three,
"The Dragon of the Garden of the West
"And those vile offal, Stheno and Euryale,

XLI

"Still brood disastrous malice—hard Stheno
"And soft Euryale abominable!

"And since the two have watched Medusa's Head
"Sundered by thee and made the unwilling tool
"For fastening on impulse Reason's rule,
"Either with other cunningly conspires,
"By mingling their vile natures, to frustrate her:
"For thus what their dead Sister's deepest Self desires

XLII

"They muse to bring about. All this I saw
"Here, where the seeds of human deeds are sown—
"The outcome of that ghostly husbandry
"Now for the first time by thyself am shown.
"O Perseus, not the Gorgon-ray alone,
"Or not as thou hast used, for this last fray,
"I tell thee, shall suffice. A heavier price—
"A heavier price—a nobler deed—some other way!"

XLIII

The Goddess paused:—"There was a time," she said,
"Before thou wast entangled with thy love,
"When with thy shadow thou didst sweep the earth,
"Unconquerably swooping from above,
"Armed with the Gorgon. Atlas did not move
"After thy passing. Even so shall it be
"Again—from air—and yet more godlike, too—
"Less hampered—more controlled—wide—with a scope more free!"

XLIV

Eagerly whispered Perseus then:—"The deed
"Is mine. I came to Thee, that I might *know*.
"Oh speak!" And him the Goddess answered not
But pointed downward to where, far below,
His body sprawled, which had resisted so
Its mind's release, and shook her shady head,
And the sad olives round the temple rustled
Gently, as with her pitying smile:—"Not thou!" she said,

XLV

"That flesh is all Andromeda's, whose breast
"In sympathy (who knows if not in league?)
"Beats with the enemy! I may not chance
"My holy Targe in peril of intrigue.
"No earthly mind that turns, a whirligig
"In soft affection's breeze, shall lift this curse
"Of Stheno and Euryale—and thine?
"I saw thy soul within this hour wholly hers!"

XLVI

Then, as a tit that darts into a chamber
Filled with some company of romping boys,
Astounded in a strange, unfriendly world
Of clumsy motions, and shrill, dangerous noise,
Is very still; and naught but that poise
Disowns the ice of death—so Perseus grew
Still at those grievous words. Long moments passed
Before his whisper, hoarse and low:—"What shall I do?"

XLVII

And she, in measured tones:—"Thou shalt go forth
"And thou shalt take with thee the Goatskin Sack.
"In no wise shalt thou seem a King—disguised
"And like a beggar, by the westward track
"Thou shalt forsake my City. On thy back
"My Shield, Medusa's Head upon thy arm,
"Thou shalt go forth alone—"
                                "Alone?" he said.
"Alone. Her Kinsmen shall preserve thy Queen from harm—

XLVIII

"Because thy trumpeter shall sound surrender—"
She paused, and like near hills, her stony stare
Lay vast upon him: "Hearest thou me, Perseus?
"Hearest thou me? Thy task lies otherwhere.
"I, Pallas, am commanding thee to fare

"Forth from the Land thou savedst not, to find,
"Through endless journeyings and awful queries,
"A Prince on horseback, who shall tell thee all his mind,

XLIX

"Thinking thou art some common wayfarer.
"Thou shalt not tell him of thy heavenly birth
"Or after-traffic with the Gods, for he
"Abhors proud men, and prizes simple worth
"Beyond nobility. His mind to earth,
"His heart turned to the Gods, he pricks, demure,
"Erect, the path of duty—whom all the beauty
"Of Argos' frail, pathetic Queen could not allure;

L

"Nor yet the Gorgon's blood incarnate grown,
"Chimaera, thrice inhuman (who transgressed
"The shape of man's one figure, even as thou
"Art disincarnate now for me), could wrest
"His will unwilling from his mind's behest.
"Himself disguised, he neither shall make known
"To thee (save unawares) his true estate,
"Thereof ashamed, nor own his name—Bellerophon."

LI

Next she unfolded some undoubted signs
By which the King must recognise the Prince,
His gait and garb—but, most of all, the Steed
He rode, whose gentle fierceness made it wince
At all but loving tones; of strange hoof-prints
She spoke, and named the Fountain, springing clean,
That gushed from the hard rock the hoofs had struck,
Whose thunder trode Chimaera under—Hippocrene!

LII

"But when thou hast his name, if in discourse
"On duty or great need he shall enlarge
"Or weighty deeds, thou shalt deliver him

"Medusa's Head and my misusèd Targe,
"And bid him—nay, the rest is not thy charge.
"I will Myself—"She ceased, for like a stone,
His stunned and weakened spirit earthward plunged
And, like a meteor after, fell: "Bellerophon . . ."

LIII

Bellerophon! a sound—a name! But when
Behind its fleshly eyes it fully woke,
Because his spirit had gone out in fear
And home in haste, all else Athene spoke
Vanished aloof his memory, like smoke,
He only knew he must go forth alone,
Forsaking all his will had once defended—
Must wander o'er the earth to seek Bellerophon.

III

BELLEROPHON

I

How well for Perseus, that not weeks or days
Are granted for his exodus, but hours!
Ere dusk to dawn can change, he must be gone:
He whips his spirit up and goads his powers
To order all things well—but still it cowers
From choice to tell, or not to tell, the Queen:
Which? In the end he dared not take farewell
But left a letter lying where it must be seen.

II

The sentry, stamping to keep out the cold,
Chaffed the old scarecrow in his rags uncouth
And let him pass; behind his back arose
The sun; old warmth that warmed his heart in youth,
When Pallas urged him to wear wings for truth,
Rose like a ghost with it, as, like a ghost
Furtively quitting the dear light of day,
He made his way, unhindered, through the invading host.

III

The unchanging motion of his rangy limbs,
As Phoebus mounted, rocked asleep the ache
Of the overburdened breast. The road lay bare.
He thought:—'No more with each new dawn to wake
'To tangle of hopeless knots! No plans to make
'Or forward-look to feign! No more abiding
'The pressure of her inexpressiveness,
'Watching that mask-like face and wondering what it's hiding!

IV

'At least now I can breathe! I am alone,
'Free, unoppressed, untormented!' He drew,
Striding, deep breaths of air; and so, by night,
Came to a cool oasis, where the dew
Lingered, and water tinkled, and things grew,
And lay flat on his back and almost wept
Because he was so much at peace. Above
The shining Bears walked round Polaris, while he slept.

V

The same dawn in the Palace round the Queen
Slaves ran about like ants in some dry mound
A passing heel has brushed; and mid those shouts
And aimless hurryings back and forth and round
Andromeda in the same moment found
His letter and her purpose—but the Myth
Runs on through time and space to where, alone,
The King's prone majesty lies, like a monolith . . .

VI

He woke—or he was wide awake—alert,
Staring: on high the flaming Almagest
Of changeling constellations told the hour
Nigh dawn: one ear against the ground he pressed:
No drum of hooves! his quick experience guessed,
Some animal was near; he made no noise
As he rose and peered around: There! On the ground,
A panther's bound apart, a human shape—a boy's!

VII

Stirless, abrupt, beneath the stars he stood,
Then instantly resolved to close—to wind
The youngster in his cloak, before he woke,
Mobling his smothered captive dumb and blind,
Taking no chances: He crept up behind
And cautiously bent over the small face

Peeping above the sheepskin caked with dust,
Trustfully sleeping like a child's—Andromeda's!

VIII

Silent he stared: she had followed him, it seemed!
What! had some idiot servant failed to keep
His secret – told the Queen (intruding fool!)—
Then mounting passion ebbed to reverie deep:—
Musing, he gazed: Who can be wroth with sleep?
How shall the vertical rebuke the prone:—
This brisk vulgarity of instant self
Be angry with that far-off unresisting one?

IX

Rather the prone upbraids: the shuttered flesh
That vacant majesty of stars possesses
Chides this rank tenement, still occupied—
Then hers unlocked such famished tendernesses
(Imagination blending, once, her dress's
Light rise and fall with affluent, effluent Nile—
Watching—her Sphinx—till cautious windows opened
And revenant Psyche flashed through wonder to a smile)!

X

Who can be wroth? He could not wake her now.
He wrenched himself aside, and bowed his head:
"Pallas Athene, who art all my thought,
"Be thou my will! O let myself be dead!
"Be Thou me absolutely, Thou!" he said—
Before he slept, stern phrases, with no lack
Of tempered kindness in them, teased his mind,
With which, at first of morning, he would send her back.

XI

Dawn broke, and slowly brightened, while the spring
Tinkled unheeded into silence. Day
Shone far advanced, before the ravening wolf,
Couched in this Traveller, woke him with rough play:

Lord! He was hungry as a castaway,
Keen as a razor, empty as a drum:—
'Fit life for men!' he thought—and then remembered
What grievous tack his butler called *viaticum*.

XII

Next he recalled the night, and glanced across
To where, attired betwixt a boy and man,
Andromeda, low kneeling by a fire,
Where larder victuals in some sort of pan
Were frying into fragrance, now began,
With dainty manage and approving head,
Smoothing a little square of diaper
And chopping into dice a loaf of wastel bread.

XIII

And I—I know not which to find more strange,
The man's unnatural silence, or the woman's,
For when he rose, as all had been arranged,
Seated together both, they took their commons;
With nothing asked about the awful summons
That set a monarch flitting like a debtor
And nothing offered—where the thunderbolt
Had fallen, it lay: the escape, their journey, his brief letter.

XIV

Before they left their bivouac, they saw
Float, like a phantom from the gates of Dis,
Shadowy through the trees a wingèd shape
That flapped off back to the metropolis
Whence it had followed him unmarked; and this,
This glimpse of the white owl aflit, where no men
Dwelt and no creature tarried, pleased the Queen
As boding some good hap—but Perseus read the omen,

XV

Vexed with himself, and quibbling with the gods,
Perplexed to find he could not turn her back,

Answering his heart:—'I did go forth alone!
'Was it my fault she followed? Eh? Alack!'
So these two travellers, with no almanac,
Save the bright stars at night, to tell their days,
Wandered together through the desert sands
And came at last again to tilth and trodden ways.

XVI

The Myth despises daily accidents,
The dry and the damp sirocco—passes closed
Fevers and sores and rotting sandals—West
They wandered, and then North up to the coast
And, thence embarking, in a small ship crossed,
By night, the waters flowing through the Gates
Of Heracles, and reached this later world,
Whose shores a vaster sea indents and inundates,

XVII

And, crossing longshore between moist and dry,
Incessantly retires and advances . . .
But always Perseus marked, through dust and storm,
In shelter or no-shelter—travellers' chances—
What sulphurous (or were they timorous?) glances
She cast upon the Sack—and he would steal
Furtively then, like one who hopes he dreams,
A finger towards the finger which still wore his seal,

XVIII

Wondering how much she knew, and how—what caused
That stare—And once he paused before a choice
Of forking ways and said:—
                          "Well, Lady, which?
"Choose thou! We are the gods' and Fortune's toys.
"It matters not." And she, in toneless voice:—
"My Lord, my thanks; but this I think is clear,
"I cannot make the choice, who do not know
"Where thou and I are going, or why we are here!"

XIX

Pricked, he began to teach her in low tones
How to Another soon the Shield must be
Yielded, because—"the gifts the gods bestow
"The gods require"—with conscious majesty
And calm Hellenic poise, looking to see
Respect and wonder light up in her face
Even as he spoke, and, after, to receive
Perhaps her gentle pity, certainly some praise.

XX

She waited patiently till he moved on,
Then moved along with him. She did not speak:
Her silence did. It cried: 'Remember, Man,
'The cause of all my woe is still to seek!
'Once, in the Palace, when thou heard'st the shriek,
'Thou didst remember—why hast thou not tried
'Again?' And even as he drew breath to speak,
A horseman overtook them and fell in beside,

XXI

Fell in beside and slowed to walking pace:
Strange rider on a strange mount—square, the man,
Huge, glooming with bowed head; his tattered garb—
A sort of dull and angry fustian—
Hung from his shoulders without shape or plan
As from a rail; as for his horse, a hood
Covered it wholly, trailing cap-a-pie;
Alone the dusty tail, the pasterns caked with mud

XXII

Showed plain to view—then, caverned in cloth holes,
Two lustrous, conscious, heaven-absorbing eyes!
The woolen cloak that mocked his noble pace
Itself was mocked by such unsuiting toys
As purfled earcaps, fitted point-device,
Stirrup and bit that flashed like miracles,

Two spurs in gleaming gold, a surcingle
Tasselled or tied adroitly with small, jingling bells.

XXIII

He rarely smiled, this monumental man,
Save as he, glancing, caught from time to time
Bright knurl or glistening loop, or stooped to listen
To the tinkle of those bells, whose daedal chime
Brought joy into his face, as though sublime
Auloi were softly breathing Doric airs.
Courteous he was, and ready of fair speech,
But quick to parry trespass on his own affairs.

XXIV

Perseus was careful to accost all strangers
And, after fair exchange of talk and jest,
To draw from each of them (thereto impelled
By some dim memory of the gods' behest)
The story of his life; and this request
Had never been denied him yet—in truth
I never met a man in all my days
Who needed much cajoling to recall his youth.

XXV

So, while the vanished sun suffused with rose
A fleecy canopy of cloud, content,
They talked of ways and weathers, men and gods,
Until, as they toiled up some slow ascent
That lay before them, crime and punishment
Were spoken of by Perseus, when such zest
Rang in the Stranger's voice as made the King
Resolve to work upon that wakened interest.

XXVI

He, who knew how to win men's confidence
By slipping in his own, recalled the fate
Of Proetus, Argos' King, who bilked his brother,
Acrisius; the just gods, he said, though late,

Visited the usurper's hate with hate
Most terrible, hate solid, hate's dark flame
Frozen to marble everlastingness,
When he, Acrisius' seed, the Gorgon-bearer, came.

XXVII

"Proetus?" the Stranger cried, "He was my friend!
"I may not think he was a wicked man,
"Save only as all hearts are wicked! Lonely
"My youth was, outlawed, cowed beneath the ban
"Of the stern gods, and wandering with no plan
"Over the earth, when Proetus took me in
"And friendship healed my sore, and priestly lore
"With sacrifice and intercession purged my sin.

XXVIII

"Those were my best years, while I shared his board
"And the liberty of Argos, while—"
                                "What sin?"
Andromeda had spoken. Perseus frowned,
Hearing her so discourteously break in;
To whom the Traveller, armed against chagrin
In fierce humility—more self-reliant
Than innocence or pride—forthwith replied
In a calm voice, not more submissive than defiant:—

XXIX

"Boy, in Ephyrae, when we both were boys,
"I slew my brother!" So, a little space
They all were silent. Both from time to time
Shot sidelong glances at the Horseman's face
That searched in vain for tracks of weak or base.
The Stranger said:—"So swift year followed year,
"Until the Queen wrecked all. The restless will
"That ever fills their busy minds provoked Antea

XXX

"To dream she loved me! Who, when tears and wiles
"Nor all her wanton wanderings in the night
"Nor shameful gifts depraved me—tore her shift
"And hissed: *Thou miserable anchorite!*
"Then shrieked to her sweet lord to do her right
"Ere he be cuckolded. To see me slain
"Before her silly eyes was Madam's will—
"But Proetus only packed me wandering again."

XXXI

He ceased. And from the excitement of the Queen
A gloaming impulse, neither thought nor dream,
Sped Eastward, mothlike, to the Cyprian's throne,
Who, mounting swift behind her feathery team,
Flashed back over the momentary gleam
Of Ocean, thence across the northern lands
And, lost in twilight, stayed her car unseen,
Hovering lightly over where the lady stands,

XXXII

Bidding her murmur, half against her will:—
"Not all men, Stranger, would have wrought like this!
"Not all men would have strained bright honour so
"To spurn in dismal night the cup of bliss
"Freely bestowed on them—"
                          "By Artemis!"
The Stranger laughed, "Not all men would have seen,
"Boy, in the crutch of those seductive arms
"There, where a moment since, a pretty breast had been,

XXXIII

"Mantling, unbodied, pitiless, aghast
"With blank, horrific stare, the Old—"
                                      Abrupt
He ceased, because his sober-pacing beast
Had halted, whinnying wild and shrill, and upped,

Staggering with forehooves high in air: he cupped
With hand possessive the taut, straining neck
Nor cursed, but rather, chiding like a nurse,
Whispered: "Ground, Ground, my Fury! What? Check, hinny, check!"

XXXIV

Meekly the creature sank on all four feet,
Heeding his voice, but ere it deigned to walk,
The dallying Goddess grasped her silken reins
And stayed no more to listen to such talk:
She sprang aloft, her bright hair's orichale
Streaming to mingle with the sunset's flame,
And, darkling, piloted indignant doves,
Through flocks of blushing cirrus, home the way she came.

XXXV

All day they had been climbing. Now the way
Led between flanking walls, cut through a mass
Of rock, and now began to drop—and now,
Turning his head to glance back at the pass:—
"So," said the Traveller softly, "so it was!
"In such a spot! I had plodded up the strath
"Thirsting all day, and so at shut of eve
"I came upon Her swiftly, sprawled across my path,

XXXVI

"Seeming at first to be an old She-goat
"Squatting inert: I cursed the noisome stench
"And halted as it smote on me, then spat
"And started on again—ashamed to blench
"Before the plague that any farming wench
"Encounters daily. Only her vast size
"And squalid shapelessness, I know not how,
"That, and her foolish mouth and mean, sardonic eyes,

XXXVII

"I know not how, enthralled me as I neared,
"Till a most hideous hate began to freeze

"My blood: how politic, how old in sin
"The tufted chin! Ye smile, but thoughts like these,
"The greedy simper of her cold caprice,
"The impudent streamline of the backward sweep
"Of her delicate, thin horn were horrible:
"I drew my sword . . . And friends, I saw her melt, like sleep,

XXXVIII

"Into all-otherness! My hatred died:—
"A ghastly Lioness's counterfeit
"Sheathed and unsheathed her claws, and stretched and yawned,
"Purring unholy puissance:—Oh, most sweet
"It seemed to me that 'twixt those velvet feet
"The strength of all my limbs must be outpoured,
"That, while she arched in ecstasies of ease,
"I must be teased and mauled and languidly devoured!

XXXIX

"Round either haunch appeared and disappeared
"Obscenely pilled, provocatively slow,
"A sinuous lean tail, whose felted tip,
"Continuously hovering to and fro,
"Slid like a living Serpent's head! And so—
"And so—"
          The Stranger halted; his square jaw
Dropped with recalled dismay, and now he said,
Patting his Horse: "If once the creature rips the Law

XL

"Fixed in its Form, old Chaos shoulders through
"And monster buds from monster—as Despair
"Breeds fantasies . . . The Hooded Horror grew:
"And still I stood and stared into the stare
"Above that flickering fork—how every hair
"Stood out upon my skin! Enamelled coils,
"Compact of buxom rondure, glistered bright
"With copper-slippery colours, like a witch's oils—

XLI

"Oh long, long afterwards—and even now,
"May be—when young Aurora laughs serene,
"And horns are blowing, all the freshness fades
"From her fair hues, and that too beauteous sheen
"Slips, like a stealthy lacquer, in between
"Creation and my eyes—a scaly crust
"That brightens, first, the visionary gleam,
"Then leaves me chewing bitter ashes of disgust—

XLII

"Faugh!— let us talk now of some other thing!
"There is no mystery here. Let others yield
"To their Antea, Boy, for whom the gods
"Never ordained their memories should wield
"The spectre of Chimaera for a shield—
"Not I!"
        "But is she—lies Chimaera dead?
"Thou hast not told us how thou didst prevail
"Over the Beast at last!" the Gorgon-slayer said.

XLIII

"And were it *now*—and had I prayed the gods
"For strength to flee," the Traveller replied,
"And they had heard my prayer—but I was young
"And honour was the name I gave to pride:
"So I returned to Her—this time astride
"My Beautiful! We rode for death or glory,
"My Beautiful and I—" so, making much
Of his great Beast—"and—well—here was another story!"

XLIV

Now, while Andromeda kept in her heart
His history, and was silent, there began
Between the twain a rapid interchange
Of argument, debating man with man
The mystery of craft equestrian,

Of stud and manage and the Trojan art
Of taming steeds—from which, having heard enough,
The Queen withdrew herself a little space apart,

XLV

And lapsed into a reverie, whereat,
Seeing her lagged beyond their voices' range,
The King spoke out—because he loved the man,
And purposing in no wise to estrange
Fair candour by withholding fair exchange
(For always he recalled his temple-trance
Wherein Athene named Bellerophon
And warned him he must find in words let fall by chance

XLVI

Signs that would privately reveal the Prince
To whom the Head and Shield must be resigned)—
Therefore he told him of the Queen's disguise
And hurriedly disclosed her womankind,
Passing to other theme, as from behind
With hastening steps, she drew once more abreast
And, silent still and smiling to herself,
Walked now upon the far side of the Stranger's beast.

XLVII

She smiled because her practised eye had seen
There, in the shabby cloth, what guileless art hid,
Or failed to hide, with stitches, a long rent,
Which, as she guessed, the golden spur had started,
A grievous gash that zig-zagged up and parted
Over the rippling shoulder in a tear
Hard by her cheek, wherethrough she slipped a hand
To feel his friendly hide and sleek and pat him there.

XLVIII

In early Spring, when slivers of blue sky
Upon the meadows lie, in shallow floods,
Ere any shiver, any cuckoo cry

Has shaken the bare boughs of the wet woods,
The sallow-branches, trim with sallow-buds,
Are broken by the children off the trees,
Who hardly fancy little button-flowers
Could be so silky-soft to touch, so hard to squeeze:

XLIX

So hard, so soft was this whereon her palm
So lightly rested—once, and years ago
(Her startled heart stood still as she remembered),
This pleasured palm had rested even so
Even upon such feathers; when great woe
Smote her because they quarreled, and all day,
After he left, she stayed in Hermes' temple,
Stroking the god-like plumes of his Talaria.

L

Now she withdrew her hand and laid her cheek
An instant there, where through the narrow rent
The pinion gleamed, and closed her eyes and whispered:—
"Thou darling!" Now she prayed, now round she went
And walked beside the wordy two, intent
Still on the thing they loved, as men will be,
Impersonal, exact about the facts
Of the clever, beautiful technique of Chivalry.

LI

Soon, following the mountain's downward slope,
The track had reached a turfy, smooth plateau
Whence, like a lingering hawk, the rested eye
Could hover over all the plains below
Exulting; but delaying afterglow
Was dying Westward now; two planets bright
Showed in the East, and overhead the stars
Were winking faintly. Here they halted for the night.

LII

The Stranger's horse, loose-tethered, cropped the thyme

Through tender lips with dainty appetite;
The three on the smooth turf reclined together,
Savouring the warm wonder of the night;
The moon set; the cigalas chirred; a slight
Rustle of beechen foliage round shed deep
Contentment, while a great fatigue possessed
Their resting limbs, that seemed a substitute for sleep.

LIII

Soon for the full tale of Chimaera's death
The Queen, who had pondered much, began to press
The Stranger; but the Stranger had put on
Some creaking panoply of courtliness,
Because he knew her sex, an arch address
Larded with *Madam*'s and Arcadian bows,
Turning her serious questions with a smile
That met no answering smile upon the lady's brows.

LIV

There was a time, when she must have responded,
And gaily—stepping out the double dance
Of gallantry together; but not now,
Not since the night of that fell, fleeting glance
Within the Sack! What hateful arrogance
Grinned through his mask of homage, what contempt
Too deep for words! She heard, or thought she heard,
What biting irony behind a compliment!

LV

At last, as one confused:—"Madam," he prosed,
"So just, and so"—he bowed—"so fair a Court
"To faulty recollection, halting testimony
"Will grant indulgence"—here she cut him short
And told him briefly to describe the mort,
Asked if his horse had panicked (her two eyes
Were needles while he answered) and then said:—
"I hardly think, O stranger, all was in this wise.

LVI

"Thou hast not let us hear of the grapple yet!
"How did thy destrier support her gaze?
"Or rode ye round? But if she blocked the road
"Between the rocks, ye met her face to face!
"How then escape the all-smothering embrace,
"The stare, the sting? Or was, perchance, thy blow
"(Dost thou remember now?) not rather struck
"Sir Stranger—I am guessing—from above, below?"

LVII

Thus boldly she. But Perseus grew abashed
And yearned to make amends on her behalf,
Hearing her rattle; so he sharply turned
And cried out to the Stranger, with a laugh:—
"I think the Trojans never bred, Sir, half
"So leapable or so sweet-mouthed a foal
"As this, the lady's Fancy—by my troth,
"A capital curvet—a topping capriole!"

LVIII

But when he ceased, the Stranger into the fire
Stared more intently, seeming not to hear,
Then towards the Queen a little turned his face
Saying—his voice now solemn and severe:—
"Not over-courteously thou comest near,
"Unbidden, Lady—well, it shall be so!
"The mark at which these pointed shafts are aimed,
"The mystery of my Courser's breed ye both shall know!"

IV

PEGASUS

I

"There is a pool men call 'The Fountain Tarn,'
"A windless mirror of aetheric light—
"Nay, but I ride too fast; I first must tell
"How, in my budding manhood, to requite
"That old iniquity, the gods my sight
"Forsook, their ghostly breath from Earth withdrew,
"Which gradually, like the morning haze,
"Vanished away beyond the overarching blue.

II

"Praise ye the living gods, who have not known
"A world forlorn of god—her oceans dry
"Of all save water, her soft heaven of night
"Hard as if hollowed out of porphyry—
"Who never watched the nymphs and naiads die,
"Like wintry birds, or heard from some stark tree
"Not Philomela but a nightingale
"Mocking with trills deaf dark that is not now Procne.

III

"And worse than a world forsaken, worse than all
"That mausoleum of mere earth and sky,
"The charnel stillness of the world within;
"Where impulse checks at reason's bantering *Why*;
"Till will has put on mind's infirmity,
"And old man's languor settles unperceived,
"And lotus-rotted are the lips that mutter:—
"'Nought can be felt or done, since naught can be believed.'

IV

"Alas, how desolate young men may be
"That look so brisk! What listless days, what days

"I lolled beside the Fountain Tarn, assoiling
"In the quiet water my unquiet gaze!
"(Dear dimple on Acrocorinthia's
"Rock-wrathful countenance!) Till there befell,
"After my first encounter with Chimaera
"Not many days, this thing I scarce know how to tell.

V

"Often I mused if there might come a time
"When youth, all youth, were ill, as I was ill—
"How if the god—enough! One Autumn day
"When the surface of the water spread so still,
"Its turfy edge was like a window-sill
"Opening upon Antipodean sky,
"Where now and then, from unreflected trees,
"A falling leaf came fluttering up reluctantly,

VI

"I, as my wont was, lay beside the brink—
"When nothing signifies, when we despair,
"Then most to silly trifles we attend;
"So I at one dead leaf began to stare—
"Followed it planing through that mirrored air
"Some less meandering error than the rest—
"Courting absorption for absorption's sake,
"Because it seemed to slack tight bands about my breast.

VII

"Friends, have ye ever stared upon a word,
"Some common word men utter every day,
"So hard that, on the parchment or the wax,
"Somehow the little syllable looks *fey*?
"Seen all the pith of meaning drain away
"That made its face familiar—stood spellbound,
"A barbarous man that never learned to speak,
"Gaping upon that slab of unrelated sound?

VIII

"So went it with me now, beside the Pool,
"Lying so tranquil in that mountain air,
"So blank and so familiar—suddenly
"There was no reason why it should be there . . .
"And in that instant I became aware
"Of goings-on—some older tale than Reason's—
"Pirene's fountain streaming far above,
"And the lift and lapse of vapours in Earth's dance of seasons.

IX

"Then, in that instant, shaken, I beheld
"Most clear the shape my mind miscalled a leaf
"Alter to some thing, large and far away,
"That moved with purpose: Eager sprang belief
"In the unbelievable—a sky-born Skiff
"With spreading sails, a Dragon, some great Fish
"Oaring the air with wings . . .
                              'Imaginings!'
"Said dull experience drily, 'You see what you wish.

X

"'This is that gleam the thirsting Arab sees,
"'Mariner-mirage in the barren main!'
"And I looked up from the water, swift as thought:
"And found it was a phantom of my brain! . . .
"But when, after some days, it gleamed again,
"I held the image, while its questioned source
"Dropped earthward, like a blessing, and this time
"Glassed in the Fountain Tarn beheld a Flying Horse!

XI

"Trembling I gazed—remember, I had seen,
"Save for Chimaera, now, for long long years,
"No numen fair or foul—river and cloud,
"But never a glimpse of Arethusa's tears;
"Odorous gums I smelt, not Leucothea's
"Warm body perfumed for Apollo's kiss;

"To my dull sight no beastly form was bright
"Or passionate with a recent metamorphosis—

XII

"Trembling I gazed and trembling misbelieved
"The orient shape I met reflected there,
"Then raised again—poor cautious dupe—my eyes
"To rake with killing custom's pursy stare
"The iron crags and all the empty air,
"Where dead leaves loitered, where an eagle screamed
"Angrily—ah, but, friends, the third time, when
"Deep in the sleeping waters argent plumage gleamed,

XIII

"I was prepared, and lifted not my eyes . . .
"The travelled helix, which he left behind,
"As nearer earth in narrowing sweeps he planed
"Scooped, as if some enchanter's wand defined,
"A giant funnel, in whose heel reclined
"My breathing self—in-tapering from a rim
"Wide as the infinite embrace of Heaven,
"Whose breaths are moist and dry, hot, cold, and bright and dim.

XIV

"This time I never stirred, till I was sure
"His feet were on the turf. How shall I say
"What then I saw, how paint the gentle joy
"When hippogriffs on earth make holiday?
"It was like looking at a gusty day
"Made of a horse, tough trees and restless ocean
"Tossing, rip-tearing, scampering, scudding, skimming,
"Each twig and every shivering wave alive with motion.

XV

"Then there would follow calm, and he would stand
"Grave as a priest—except one jolly whisk
"Of his bushy tail—to crop some asphodel
"(Look at him now, beside the tamarisk!)

"Then up again his mane, and oh, his brisk
"Melodious neigh! slow nostrilfall of sound,
"Whose multitudinous neesings seemed to say:—
"*Never heed a penny any heaven—Ohé the Ground!*

XVI

"At last he trotted to the Tarn and drank
"And shook himself and neighed. I watched him fold
"Closer about his flanks his silver wings
"And lapse into the flowers, where he rolled
"Savouring who knows what potable gold,
"What ecstasies! whereof having drunk his fill,
"On Gaia's breast he, staring at the sky,
"Wise like a baby, four stiff legs in air, lay still.

XVII

"Here was my chance: I rose: but, when I stirred,
"He, with a cat's quick back trick, on all fours,
"Twisting his torse, had landed. As I neared,
"For one bright trice remembrance racks to hours
"He rested on me two soft eyes like flowers,
"Then, like the morning cock in act to crow,
"Clapped his great wings and off into deep heaven
"Streaked, like a silver arrow clanged from Phoebus' bow.

XVIII

"Now, Lady," smiled the Stranger, "art thou pleased?
"Will those death-darting eyes leave off to scold
"Their humble serjeant? Shriven am I? Not therefor,
"I swear it, shall I leave my tale half-told—
"Yet ask not of what Sire he was foaled.
"I only know that he was born in heaven
"And flew to earth."
                    But Perseus thundered "No!
"By Zeus the cloud of my forgetfulness is riven!

XIX

"All that Athene showed me in my trance
"Comes whelming back—Chimaera—the Winged Horse"
(And then, half-fallen into a trance again,
Moulding each sound with hieratic force—)
"While through the sky (she said) I steered a course
"Towards Aethiopia, from Medusa's neck
"Drops of arterial blood, too fierce to clot,
"Dripped on the Libyan Desert, fleck by fleck by fleck:

XX

"And where they landed, drank them the hot sand,
"Till soaked in blood and sun, the barren grains
"Grew seminal, and soon you might have seen
"An alteration in the sullen stains,
"A bloom, a ferment, struggles, growing pains
"Of Anger crowding into space, a smother
"Of fiery serpents, dragonish, and some
"With wings, the loathly bantlings of that lawless Mother.

XXI

"Not all engendered so: when one drop dripped,
"A tiny cloud was sailing past the sun,
"Softening his glare: it spattered on a rock
"And, ere the shadow lifted, from that one
"Gout of the Gorgon-blood a Stallion
"Started up lordly, snorting, plumed, aglow,
"Which straight (her own words) *off into deep heaven*
"*Streaked, like a silver arrow clanged from Phoebus' bow.*

XXII

"So sprang from Earth thy Pegasus—whom so
"She named—and soon on Earth again was known,
"Was often seen among the chaste Novena
"Of Lady Sisters, who trip naked on
"The smooth slopes of Cadmeian Helicon:
"Who danced, and decked his flanks with garlands bright

"And musically groomed his wilting plumes
"And crowned his Horseship their sweet, masculine Delight.

XXIII

"But, as the world grew old and weatherworn,
"His feathers clogged with particles of dust
"For all their grooming; so he neighed adieu
"And flew off up to heaven in disgust:
"'Lest Pegasus should be dis-Pegasus'd,'
"He thought and, in the thought, the barren rock
"Spurned with his glancing hoof . . .
"A gushing Fountain rushed to answer that sharp knock!

XXIV

"This was the Horse's Fountain—Hippocrene—
"And, O sweet Prince Bellerophon, and thou,
"Dearest Andromeda, that happy stream
"Ceased not to gurgle—hark! tis gurgling now!
"Yea, wheresoever there is earth to plough
"Or plant with corn and vine (she said) redound
"The voices of its waterbrooks inaudible;
"Asleep, mysterious, wilful, purling underground.

XXV

"Even in the far North, where thick, smarting mists
"Have blotted all our Muses, all our gods
"From humorous eyes, in melancholy Thule,
"Mad poets wander with divining rods,
"And now and then the pithy hazel nods,
"Cramping their fingers, while it stirs the spleen,
"They dig, and from below a slip and crumble
"It dashes out again, undoubted Hippocrene.

XXVI

"Few (said the Goddess) hear the sound, few listen;
"For out of patience their sad sense is deaved
"By harsh banausic dins, but, once they take it—
"Mark now the marvel!—once they have received

"The local chuckle, ears grow unbereaved
"And drink the whole great Fountain of the Horse,
"The general noise commingled or, at choice,
"Each babble, cluck, roar, gurgle, far back to the source.

XXVII

"Each fancy chooses where to tune her ear,
"And, if she will, in turn may hear them all:
"Soft Scythian burr; Danubian rustle-rush;
"Diamond drip drip on worn stones in Gaul;
"The clean, abrupt Castilian waterfall;
"Ausonia's bell-mouthed clangour; last she wins
"To where the water pounds, in Thessaly,
"With boom and crash and thunder, on those cauldron lynns."

XXVIII

He paused: the Graces morris'd in his eyes:
Now, while the word had hovered by the Beast,
The Queen had hung upon the Prince's tongue
Entranced, and her intensity increased,
When Perseus followed on and, like a priest,
Sang of the true nativity; she heard,
She saw—and once he looked at her and caught
Her half forgotten dazzling smile—but when the word

XXIX

Checked at the Fountain, her attention strayed—
No King can mount, no Prince back Hippocrene:—
"But what now of the wondrous Horse?" she said.
"Why, Pegasus no more on Earth was seen,"
Perseus replied, "save when, Belovèd Queen,
"He visited the Fountain Pool for sport,
"Or some light reek or rumour of Chimaera
"Reverberated up in some man's soaring thought,

XXX

"And overbore his natural buoyancy
"That lifts him swiftly back to his abode

"In the moment of forsaking it—as mass
"Darts oppositely down to that dense lode
"That nestles at Earth's core. Athene showed
"How the great sides can scarcely hold it in,
"The greater heart, that swells with rage to trample
"His arch, hereditary, soft, detested kin."

XXXI

"Kin!" cried the Horseman (stranger now no more,
But named by his true name, Bellerophon)
"How oddly tripped thy tongue, intending 'foe'!"
And all his guileless face with anger shone.
But Perseus gravely laid a hand upon
The Prince's arm:—"The gods must be believed!
"Chimaera was, no less than Pegasus,
"Through that same 'odd' Medusa, whom I slew, conceived.

XXXII

"Pallas discovered all their pedigree,
"But all as at this time I do not tell,
"Lest I ungently maze my gentle Queen—
"There are so many names!—More fierce and fell
"Than slain Medusa those twin slips of Hell,
"Her deathless Sisters, leagues beyond the sea,
"Seethe with astute intrigues, and loathe the gods,
"And plot my overthrow—Stheno—Euryale;

XXXIII

"Who saw their ghostly Sister by me forced
"To baffle their own lawless will, and dreamed
"A plot to baffle mine; but when they heard
"That Pegasus was born, they clanged and screamed
"Horribly:—*Gorgon! Gorgon!* Since it seemed
"Almost as if Reason herself had wings,
"Whom, bound to earth, they could have scotched, but now
"Beheld the wreck of all their gloomy purposings.

XXXIV

"Those are not lightly to be overthrown,
"Who work through generation: deeply laid
"Their plans, and ripen late: Medusa's Son
"(Begotten when she, still a candid maid,
"With huge Poseidon in the Temple played),
"Chrysaor, lives; from whom a monstrous birth,
"To counter Pegasus, the twain procured
"With cantrips foul, and so Chimaera came on Earth.

XXXV

"But now"—he smiled—"but now it seems Chimaera
"Herself is countered—happy, happy day!
"Far-sighted Gorgons, who might not foresee
"Bellerophon! How far ye planned astray!
"Then praise—"
               "I wonder," said Andromeda
Softly, and held her peace. When the two turned
Uplifted brows on her, she smiled, and said:
"Finish thy story, Prince! As yet we have not heard

XXXVI

"How he was captured at the last, and tamed,
"This hooded jennet here, that was so shy,
"And now he only jingles little bells
"And stalks sedately with that conscious eye!
"When will he disappear into the sky?"
"Madam, be sure that he would dwell there still
"For any skill of mine! What use to tell
"My baby ruses? He was bridled by God's will.

XXXVII

"Many more times I waited near the Tarn,
"Patient till he alit. All calls I tried,
"All cozenings. (Gods! I nearly danced and sang,
"Hoping the creature would be mystified
"And take me for a Muse!) I learned to hide

"Behind the very bush he grazed upon,
"But always, when I sprang up with my bridle
"And thought to fling it—like forked lightning, he was gone!

XXXVIII

"Almost I yielded to despair: at last,
"One night, when in deep sleep my sense was sealed,
"A tall, still Goddess, whom I knew to be
"Pallas Athene, though she bore no shield,
"Stood by my bed, to whom I humbly kneeled,
"Because she was so huge and I so small,
"And many secrets she made plain to me,
"Which, waking, I was never able to recall.

XXXIX

"At last she pointed to my heart, and looped
"A golden curb and bridle on a tree,
"Then turned, once more admonishing, and vanished,
"And I woke—and thought at first my fantasy
"Had painted all, the Goddess, ay, maybe
"The Horse himself: to think at all seemed idle,
"If dreams were about dreams—and then I knew
"Gods do not mock men—on the tree still swung the Bridle!

XL

"What followed, Lady, thou at least, I fancy,
"Knowest untaught. To bring my barque to land
"In few: upon the next day, by the Pool,
"The heavenly Horse that never yet was manned
"Came trotting meekly to a murderer's hand
"And sniffed his Bridle—no need to recount
"What followed next: Suffice that, even willing,
"A hippogriff is not an easy beast to mount!

XLI

"It cost me, who am rated to excel
"All men on horseback, countless desperate tries,
"But, seated once, all effort lay behind:

"To tread, with Pegasus between his thighs,
"Chimaera, seemed man's natural exercise!
"And Oh, I would I could forget that hour—
"Holding the divine Ire—upheld—white wings
"Threshing—tiny Aegean Isles—Ah, god-like Power!"

XLII

He had risen, and now was pacing to and fro;
A faggot smashed, a flame leaped in the fire,
And all the dancing shadows, born of night,
Bowed to the huge shape of the stooping Flyer
Sublime against the dark; and ever higher
His stature grew in the King's eyes, who scanned
Him marvelling, till at last he dreamed he saw
Indolent in the sky, a spent bow in one hand

XLIII

Dangling, the other raised to his broad brow
To shade his gaze against the target Sun,
Smiling, at ease, a shagged and mighty Centaur;
And the King said:—"O thou Bellerophon
"And thou Andromeda, what was begun—
"In Pallas' fane is now accomplishèd.
"I had thought to break my heart, when I must part
"With these so dearly bought, the Shield, the Gorgon's Head.

XLIV

"I find it is not so." And all his soul
Flamed with devotion swift and rosy love,
As he got upon his feet, half shy, half smiling,
And towards Bellerophon began to move:
Suddenly he threw up one arm above
His head, and cried in a loud voice:—"Receive
"The Hallows!" And forthwith Andromeda
Breathed in an urgent whisper, while she plucked his sleeve:—

XLV

"Ask him, Man, ask him first how he will use them,

"Before thou giv'st our property away!"
And, when he would not speak, she cried herself:—
"What wilt thou do, Prince, with God's bounty? Say!
"Wilt thou fly over Aethiopia
"And help us?"
                    But Bellerophon stood by
The dying fire and gazed into the glow
Sadly, before he answered:—"I will never fly.

XLVI

"Never again, never, till black be white,
"Hard, soft—till frost shall burn and fire freeze,
"Never, though Pegasus were boun to spread
"His white wings over the Hesperides—
"Though Kings command and Queens upon bare knees
"Weeping implore!"
                    The Gorgon-slayer stood
Gaping, astounded:—"So! In spite of all
"Thou found'st thou could'st not manage him?"
                                        "I found I *could*,"

XLVII

The Prince replied, "Have I not bared my pride?
"Have I not answered to thy Lady free
"All her pert questions, and wilt *thou* begin?
"Nay, by the Dog, ye get no more of me—
"Alas, dear Aethiopia's Majesty
"And thou, fair Queen, I know not what I say!
"Forgive, but ask not of my flight toward Heaven.
"Enough, ye know I tried: the way is not that way!

XLVIII

"The Empyrean barely reached, I felt
"A gathering weight of cloud press on my mind
"And heard, like thunder, the Cloud-gatherer's
"Enormous Voice:—*Wilt thou, thou little blind
"Bellerophon, o'erleap the law of kind
"So easily? Great Prince! How thou wast born*

"*Hast thou forgot so soon? Down, down to earth!*
"*Lift up thy heart henceforth, O Man, and not thy horn!*

XLIX

"Friends, it shows meritorious in the creature
"To cover up such dangerous parts as lack
"Prescribed, obedient function. Quadrupeds,
"Mountant on wings, blaspheme the Zodiac.
"So, when we grounded, I flung o'er his back
"This duffle housing here, which safely tents
"His insolence of wings and holds his rage
"Harmless, and charms with these permitted ornaments."

L

He smiled and stepped up to the Horse and shook
Athene's golden bridle, making tingle
The strapped up arteries with a hearty slap
That stirred beneath the housing and surcingle,
So that they heard the tiny bells all jingle
Delicious in the dark. But Perseus cried,
Impatient now:—"What is all this to me,
"This talk of God knows what and quadrupeds and pride?

LI

"Thou art Bellerophon, I think, that Prince!
"Then know that of Bellerophon I ask
"No questions. Who am I? Divinity
"Made plain to me the rest was not my task,
"Rather declared she would herself unmask
"Her further purposes. Why then delay?
"The time is ripe now for Athene's deed.
"Leave us a little space alone, Andromeda!"

LII

But when she heard such words, Andromeda's
Deep heart grew desperate for time: and sent
Out of her mouth a tumbling stream of words,
Which buzzed them both to dumb bewilderment,

Industriously seeking her intent
In the thicket of her speech—while underneath,
Fierce in the silence she had forced, she prayed
To Aphrodite:—'Smiler under the gay wreath!

LIII

'Guardian of Paphos! If I ever pious
'(Though late apostate) have adored thy throne,
'If thou hast ever drunk within thy Temple
'The music of my sighs, my pigeon's moan,
'Now by thine azure snood, thy holy Zone,
'Let not Bellerophon have Pegasus!
'Let Perseus ride him!' while aloud she ended:—
"Therefore I say it will be wiser far for us

LIV

"To sleep till morning. Go we all to bed!
"It is so late now, Perseus, and I grow
"Sleepy. I doubt not that the Prince is tired.
"Is't not discourteous to importune so
"At all hours of the morning, when we know
"He can do nought, before Aurora leaves
"The couch of old Tithonus and the rose,
"The half-forgotten rose of Phoebus' kiss receives?"

LV

She looked towards Perseus, but Bellerophon
Pointed them to the sky with smiling mouth,
Sweeping an arm to show where westering dipped
Arcturus, where the Bowman ruled the South:—
"Say what we will, the Lady speaks the truth,"
He said, and yawned, "And I—I do consent
"Gladly for my part." Perseus nodded. So,
Scattering the ashes of their fire, to ground they went.

V

THE GODS

I

Dreams are the strangers in our gates. Today
We laugh, or else we marvel, or we go
Paying the young soul-doctor a gold fee
For his yesterday-born jargon: but not so
Shall it be always. One day we shall know
More with the morning: out of sleep will break,
Warm with melodious reverberations,
Answers to earnest questions humbly asked awake.

II

So, while the glimmering Hyads in the East
Rose from the bath of Ocean—rose to fade,
Withdrawn into dim dawn—Andromeda
Began to dream, who had so lately prayed
Asking the Cyprian so, and for such aid
As, whether or no she willed it, that appeal
Sank through the gateway of her human shape
Into the Myth-womb of man's total woe and weal.

III

Deeply she slept, and she slept deep. She saw
A vision in deep sleep, a waste of water
Extreme, and, rising far out from the land,
A marble-pale Colossus was the Daughter
Of Zeus, bold Leman of the God of Slaughter;
About the waves were scattered bobbing faces
Fixed on the Goddess, while along the shore
Young people laughed and shouted in safe shallow places,

IV

Pretending not to mark the undertow,

And gallant women prayed with strangled cries,
And old men smiled like babies nigh those breasts
But found no pity in those violet eyes,
Which gazed out over vast immensities
Sightless, or, seeming melting with soft fire,
Scanned, like a salt unbending admiral's,
The raging sea of insupportable desire.

V

And a voice cried out everywhere: "I am
"*Pandemos Aphrodite!* Though they drown,
"Their hope is set upon me. I will keep
"And I will keep their world from running down
"And seeding in obedient rote. The Noun
"Shall not debauch the Verb." And the voice ceased
And the Queen's soul rose to the plane of dreams
Which memory holds. Slightly her breathing's pace increased.

VI

And now the Goddess, in the form she knew,
Stood by her head, a Woman tall and fair;
And, as the sunshine on a summer's day
Sings in the blue beatitude of air,
So, in her snood, sang Cytherea's hair,
Gladdening the dreamer's heart by gleaming through,
Where, leaning over her, she wisely smiled
Stroking the Queen's hair, while she told her what to do;

VII

Coaching her as to a question which, that day,
She must make Perseus ask Bellerophon
And afterwards by every means delay
His bearing off the Head: and she must con
The words of it, till she knew every one:
"And I," said Aphrodite, "shall be near,
"Doubt not, to eavesdrop what the men will say,
"For all depends on what I trust to overhear."

VIII

At last the sun rose, and they all awoke
And sat there on the ground to break their fast;
But first Andromeda besought the King
Apart:—"My Lord, if ever in the past,
"When my poor folk grew malapert, thou hast
"Taken my counsel and been glad—now, pray,
"Ask this one question of Bellerophon,
"Before thou giv'st thy—giv'st the—giv'st our Things away!"

IX

He answered not. She knew he would obey.
And her memory of the promise in the dream
Flew Eastward, bee-like to the Cyprian's throne,
Who, mounting swift behind her feathery team,
Flashed back over the momentary gleam
Of ocean, thence along the northern strand—
And only Andromeda marked the Morning Star
Unusually shining over daylit land,

X

Or saw it flash, as Aphrodite smiled,
Well-pleased to watch the Gorgon-slayer wince,
Doing the Queen's will, when:—"I make no terms,"
He said, "need no assurance to convince
"That thou art called to bear this Armour, Prince . . .
"Look—when thou hast them, if—I say but *if*—
"Our Lady of Athens, by some word or sign,
"Herself should bid thee rise upon thy Hippogriff,

XI

"Say, wouldst thou *then* obey?" Bellerophon
Stared hard upon him: weighted words, and slow,
Reluctant then, he spoke:—"I am her Knight,
"Pallas Athene's—all I am and know
"Is hers . . . I cannot say—She could not so."
"Sir," said Andromeda, "the question stands:

"True heart will answer frankly:—Yes or no!"
His elbows on his knees, his cheeks sunk in his hands,

XII

Bellerophon sat silent, then at last
Muttered, still looking down:—"I cannot say."
And instantly the listening Goddess gathered
The reins in her white hands and flew away
To seek her Sister, whom she found that day
In windy Athens, where the free-born youth
Paced in their echoing gymnasium
And straight-nosed old philosophers were chasing truth

XIII

Through thickets of preposterous argument,
With pawky malice poked, to spike the chase;
And smiling flashed Athene's teeth, to see
How first the Idols of the Market-place
Stumbled and fell, too gross to stay the pace,
And next the Idols of the Cave fell down,
The Idols of the Cave that hide the light
From men—and she was holding out an olive crown

XIV

To grace the victor. First the Cyprian spoke:—
"Well may'st thou, Sister, spend thy godhead on
"This idle gossip, these old husbands' tales!
"And, whilst thou smilest on some hoary don
"Or soft youth, all the time Bellerophon
"Flouts unabashed thy will! The question-game
"Is swiftlier played, where Knights are battledores
"And the light-bandied shuttlecock thy sacred Name!"

XV

Therewith she told Athene what was spoken
Between the three upon the mountain-side;
Who, while she hearkened, scowled, and her face darkened,
And when at last she ceased, no word replied

But took towards Aphrodite one sharp stride
And, like a nettle, all at once, her hair
Grasping, thrust under her strong arm, and so
Hastened her off, protesting, through the Upper Air.

XVI

"Spinster of wish! Blind Hoodwinker!" she hissed,
"If thy deep purpose moles beneath my ken,
"I can at least force that this tale be heard
"Before the Father of all gods and men!
"*He* will not be deceived!"
      The two came then
To where the bright clouds around Olympus rolled
Beneath their flight: there all the gods, assembled,
Sate, each upright, alone on his own throne of gold.

XVII

Save where some few stood round, with curious looks
Examining the harp that Orpheus played:
And loud the thunder-laughter of the gods
Outrang, to see so firm the Warrior Maid
Grasp, that the Cyprian snood was disarrayed;
And louder still the shout, to see her frown
To hear the shout—for what can Beauty do,
Scanted for breath, with one looped elflock tumbling down?

XVIII

But, tortuous as the thoughts beneath that snood,
The old Myth doubles now, to find the three
Silent, at odds upon the mountain-side:
What follows next? Unless she find a key,
Andromeda must watch catastrophe,
Must see Bellerophon ride off the field,
Equipped victorious, leaving her stripped lord
With neither Pegasus, nor Gorgon's Head, nor Shield!

XIX

She did not falter now: she only knew

That all her heart was set upon delay,
That swiftly she must act. To fetch the Sack
Perseus arose; but ere he turned away,
Even as he spoke them, spinning words to say:—
"Wilt thou," she cried, "Sir Servant, ere we part,
"Allow (I know thou wilt) this lady free
"One more pert question, which still hives within her heart?"

XX

And she let the memory of her second dream,
Winning in on her, sweeten all her face
With Paphian courtesy, so that all seemed fair
(The very asking seemed to do him grace!),
But first she blushed and murmured low:—"In case
"My foolish chatter overburden thee—
"As there has been some show of it—I know
"Thou wilt forgive a woman's curiosity!

XXI

"Thou seem'st a tender and a gentle man—
"Why didst thou slay thy brother?"
                                        He replied,
Staring, unmoved:—"I found him with his slave,
"Lashing her naked back with the raw hide.
"Not that I came in time: she also died."
"A savage monster," said the King, "God knows
"Is miscreant—yet—and yet a brother's life
"Was weighty payment for a lawful owner's blows!"

XXII

"Because," the warrior muttered, "on the face
"I saw the grin—the nadir of man's shame—
"Sign-manual of damnation (mine own blood!)—
"The last lasciviousness that bears no name—
"All that I am leapt out of me, a flame
"To blast my brother's life—my sword had spelt
"Catastrophe, ere yet I knew it writ!
"I had felt before I thought, and struck before I felt!"

XXIII

Luck is the oldest of the gods; men fight,
They die: the good, or else the ill, prevails:
They pray, they labour, plan through sleepless nights—
And, in the end, what tipped the trembling scales?
A sauceboxful of wind in sagging sails,
Or four fine days, absurd, from Kent to France!
Nations demobilize, and statesmen sing
Of glory, while historians harp on circumstance.

XXIV

Silenced, the Queen gave up all hope. What now?
What farther thing, so answered, might she say,
To hinder the great Render? Silently,
Unasked, a little space she drew away.
"First thou and I, Bellerophon, shall pray—"
She heard the King's low voice, as she espied,
Along the way they had travelled yesterday,
Coming post haste and romage down the mountain-side,

XXV

A horse, a man, a mounted Nuntius!
Panting and eager, she ran back again
And bade them, if this act they went about
Were one no common fellow might profane,
They should a little longer yet refrain.
She pointed, and they turned and stood and waited
Impatient, till the dusty cavalier
Drew nearer and his horse's headlong pace abated.

XXVI

The man, dismounting, made obeisance low
Not more to Perseus than to Andromeda.
He told them he had ridden hard and long
With slender hope to cheer him on his way.
He had escaped from Aethiopia,
He said, no easy feat, but harder still

His task to find the King and cast their fate,
The nation's, on the bosom of his sovereign will.

XXVII

He said the younger Phineus, victory got,
Had fastened on the people each device
Invented to protect them from Medusa,
And had them gripped now in a closing vice:
There was a dreariness around his eyes,
That told of mineral depths beyond despair:—
"Wings—" he kept whispering, and upon his voice
Settled, like snow, a Mystery-hush—"Wings in the air!

XXVIII

"His first act was to close the frontiers
"And send the King's friends into banishment:
"None from without can enter: none within
"May leave on pain of death! So has he bent
"Their minds and pleased their flesh, that discontent
"Is unknown: peace and health are everywhere!
"No man is any longer poor or sick
"Throughout all Aethiopia—wings in the air!

XXIX

"His arts of war progress in peace far more;
"Those thin translucencies and carapaces
"Which once against the fearful Gorgon-ray
"Armed their keen darts and gloved their glowing faces,
"Are worn by women, to step up their graces—
"To waist and paste and lace them—lovers wear
"Tissues of thin Phinean assidue
"Between their flower-soft, mingling limbs—wings in the air!"

XXX

Poets, he told them, sang of the new stuff
In odes: they said its constancy was such
As kisses must adore—crystal as light,
Nor interfered with any sense but touch,

It was so tenuous—and that not much,
Being itself like smooth skin with no hair:
Constant, because no violent embrace
Its papery tenacity need fear to tear.

XXXI

"And those lithe tubes—the infants call them 'Mother',
"Sucking—and yet no bastardy is rife,
"For through their lissome distance the lewd father
"May swive a slave and fecundate his wife
"Living apart from him. The surgeon's knife
"Is guiltless of abortion—all is fair
"And cleanly done in baths and hospitals—
"Wings over Aethiopia—wings in the air!"

XXXII

Some harder products of those arts had kept
Pace with the soft, or even outstripped a little:
Timber and marble were almost unknown;
They had found a means of processing the spittle
Of bats to thin rigidities, unbrittle,
Much used in building homes—and everywhere
For statues of the Gods, and children's toys,
And lamps and vases stamped in shapes, and light as air.

XXXIII

"The flame on the high Altar of Athene
"Is quenched: the cackling priests that wear her cloth
"And draw their stipend from her Temple-treasure,
"Openly sacrifice to gipsy Thoth.
"The women pray aloud to Ashtaroth,
"Forsaking Aphrodite, and their prayer
"Is heard in Lesbos, while philosophers
"Proclaim to all that *Zeus* is an old name for air.

XXXIV

"O King," the Courier ended, "we well know
"Some god has made thee leave us in our plight;

"Yet (for we can no other) we beseech thee—
"There is no help for us, unless the flight,
"Renewed of dire Medusa! If it be right,
"Thou wilt not leave us sealed in hell! We pray
"Hourly for thy return, and, while we pray,
"We dream, we dream still of thine old Talaria!

XXXV

"And if they be no longer thine, the Shoes
"Thy youth had on—so be it! Yet some hold
"Even the Sandals Hermes wore too slight
"To save us now. Maybe some flight more bold,
"More ranging, more sustained than thine of old
"It needs! Oh, I but babble of these things!
"We know not how! My embassage is this:
"Save us and hover over us with sovran wings!"

XXXVI

Silent they stood up on the mountain-slope,
Silent—a breeze stole rustling through the whins—
Silent, like figures on a vase. Above
Phoebus was leading up the Heavenly Twins
Nigher the zenith; while upon the Prince
Silent, accusing, both with one accord,
Andromeda and Perseus bent their eyes
And "O Bellerophon," they cried, "what is thy word?"

XXXVII

And he:—"Have I not said I may not fly?
"How shall the Gorgon make the lewd less lewd?
"Rather *His* Levin purges! Therefore pray,
"Casting yourselves upon the Fatherhood
"Of Zeus, who giveth all. I have learnt that good
"Is not one man on wings, but each man's choice
"Instantly to obey: when lean wolves howl,
"The Mastiff cocks his ears up for his Master's voice!

XXXVIII

"Your people grow inhuman, sin, turn monstrous—
"There is one hope still! Send a fratricide
"On Pegasus! Unstrap the surcingle
"And monstrous wings come floating from his side,
"Being a horse—I say, a glorified
"Chimaera! scorning his dear law of kind,
"Twy-natured, dangerous! Chaos shall rule chaos
"And pride shall cast out pride! Ye crazy fools and blind!"

XXXIX

Then they besought him, by his knees, to go,
Because a god had made her Shield his own,
And, when he would not, Perseus' pitying soul
Went wandering out to Pallas, like a moan.
But She, on far Olympus, by the Throne
Of Aegis-bearing Zeus, where, ranged in place,
The grave-eyed gods sate watching, all that while
Stood facing Aphrodite, arguing her case.

XL

There first the Foam-born Queen had held the word,
Telling her story—whom Athene bade
(Fearing some trick) swear first by Night and Styx
To speak the truth: and next the Warrior Maid
Addressed the Father's throne with close-arrayed
Ideas: and beauty sat on all those brows,
Contemplating the self-articulation
And global counterpoint of archetypal Nous.

XLI

As in some Council Hall or Parliament
The bandied catchwords, 'communist' or 'tory',
Keep a quick twittering of ninny minds,
Until some Elder Statesman, firm and hoary,
Rises, and glaring round, takes up the story,
A doctor in a school of pastrycooks,

And history lights upon his lips and truth,
For well he knows men's cities and their minds and books,

XLII

And when he takes his seat again, he hears
A low, unwilling murmur of applause—
So cool Athene now their free assent
Compelled, herself the Fountain of men's Laws
Of Thought, with 'so' and 'now', sub-clause in clause
Of marshalled rhetoric subsumed; and all
The gods awaited, poised, with bated breath,
Her lapidary predicates effectual.

XLIII

She was demanding sanctions (aptly citing
The nature of Proof, to prove compulsive force
In free assent), to force Bellerophon
To rise obedient on the Wingèd Horse
Over Aethiopia, and what further course
She should prescribe for him:—"My Knight, my word,
"Surely! Thy thunders, Father, to compel
"Knight-service, which, not serving—what were more absurd?"

XLIV

A windy susurration filled the place
Of her ceased voice—innumerable gods
Nodding assent—the forests of Olympus,
Rustling, became the forest of those nods:
And like one man, who has laid fearful odds
On some great Boxing-Match or Public Game,
All the Immortals, as the silence deepened,
Awaited Aphrodite's eager counterclaim;

XLV

Waited to hear some fierce tirade—but She,
Honey-sweet Crookedglancer, not with pleas
Answered the Brain-born; rather upon the ground
Sank, like a seabird lighting on rough seas,

And nestled herself up to Zeus's knees
Daughterly, while she took and stroked his hand,
Twisting his ring, till closer than herself
The Father knew what twisting schemes her heart had planned.

XLVI

Then—as in some face-flowering concert-hall,
Through double-basses and sharp violins
And coy wood-wind, the theme-announcing Horn
Calls with an unassuming call, that thins
The blood and all the awestruck spirit dins—
So dinned the Father's voice, as he began:—
"Ye Gods immortal—and except these twain,
"Small heed, it seems, ye take what fate befalleth Man!

XLVII

"And you—ye Two, who strive to bend his will
"Each her own way—be still! Necessity,
"Who once wrought well with your old jars round Troy—
"Ye know it—reigns no more. No man will I
"Neither unhorse by force, nor force to fly.
"What follows then? Who knows? May be, I love
"This Prince Bellerophon, as men below
"Their spaniels—and all day beside his boot or glove

XLVIII

"They lie and never stir; but, when at eve
"He steps, and his dear hand the bolt unbars,
"They leap and bark about with abject eyes! . . .
"Whether he do some service in your wars
"And at the last be named among the stars,
"Lies in his choice; who not the less shall come,
"Guided and hastened by his god-like thirst,
"To some delicious inn of bland Elysium.

XLIX

"Therefore my word is: Let the Brain-born now
"Lay on the doubtful Prince her dire command

"To take up arms—her Shield, the Gorgon's Head,
"And fly the Wing'd Horse over the waste land.
"And if he will—but if he shall withstand
"Her godhead, then the Foam-born shall such part
"Perform as to her bosom seemeth good:
"And best she knows the wish that hives in my dear heart!

L

"And you, our Daughters, daughters both, both dear,
"Pay good heed to our words, for this we say:
"Since the last menace of the Dragon's breath
"From Gorgon-darkened Aethiopia
"Man only may avert—go now away:
"In some more sisterly accord agree,
"Lest your extreme jars wreck the theme they wrought
"And Earth fall down disastrous Troy's catastrophe!"

LI

He ceased, and They, with chastened flight and slow
Floated together downward to the root
Of forest-crowned Olympus; but by then
Their conversation swelled to bitter fruit,
With both their voices raised in fierce dispute
And angry looks between them. If to fly,
When roundly bid, Bellerophon declined,
Pallas (the Cyprian said) must wield authority,

LII

Nod her injunction, and as roundly bid
The recreant from Pegasus alight,
Never to mount again:
                        "By Truth will I!
"I—with a sasserara!—mine own Knight,
"To please thee, shall unhorse! To do me right
"The Father hath refused. He knoweth best,
"Doubtless," Athene cried, "who also said
"He would unhorse no man by force. Do thou the rest!"

LIII

Thus the two Sister Goddesses approached,
Bickering, the Mountain where the anxious four
Stood, and Bellerophon, with Sack and Shield
Piled on his steed, would listen now no more,
But turned to go. And from that far-off shore,
To meet them, iron-winged above the sea,
Roused by some waft of danger, flying low,
Bickering, the Gorgons groped—Stheno, Euryale.

VI

THE GORGONS

I

I feel the Myth beneath me gathering speed.
The actors crowd the stage, the end draws near.
How steep the way! if, after all, I made
An overweening start! I pause, in fear,
To speculate from this my belvedere
Of invocation, forward to my end
And back to my beginning: whom to call
To bless the uncompleted tale? What Muse? What friend

II

Among the affable and mighty dead?
I know they cannot teach me what to say—
Or was it a finger creeping down my wrist,
To check these unsure choices when they stray?
Would he, who long, long since Nausicaa
Sang, and the gods at loggerheads, or he,
Who that soft-hearted Son, of Venus born,
When enterprise was duty, sent to Italy,

III

Answer; or he, who joined baptised Ruggiero
With Bradamante dipped in Merlin's cave?
But, more than all, my perilous ending needs
Him, whose *Endymion* scooped the wide enclave
Of Greece in Hampstead: All these helps I crave
And yet, for inspiration, turn my soul
To you, O Uncompleted Tales, yourselves
And you, ye Constellations blazing next the Pole!

IV

Feebly I call upon the Myths and Stars!
For, whether thou look backward into time

Or outward into space, thou dost behold
Thy Architects, O Man, thy Muse, my Rhyme—
Paradigm on celestial paradigm!
While, baby'd in thy heart, the Fiery Zest
That flung them once, with thy voice calls:—*I am!*
Behold! thus art thou half-created, Man—do thou the rest!

V

As in some dreary time, ere Man was fleshed,
When Troy was jungle still—Meander's plains
A swift, black water roughing down a gorge—
Two pterodactyls, flapping broad membranes
Of creaky gristle, ribbed with bones for veins—
Obscene upraisers of their vast of sloth—
From island to Aegean island crossed
A shipless waste of waters—so those Gorgons both

VI

Came lumbering on what seemed their wings, yet touched
Or seemed to touch the horizon with their tips,
Roofing the hollow, oily firmament
With stifling haze; the sailors on their ships,
Hearing the mutters from their horny lips,
Hurried about their work, or glanced in fear
Up at the mast for weather signs, aghast,
And knew not if the lift were far away or near.

VII

Many many leagues of ocean underneath
The abomination of their passing ran
Backward, ere Stheno spoke—nor checked a second
The fall and rise of either swishing van
That bore her on. Between the two began
Parley in figured noises, wombs of words
(As Alphabeta sprang from mother-glyphs
Of Eyes and Roofs and Rising Suns and Looms and Birds).

VIII

A wolvish longing those rude shapes expressed
To batten down the wing-fog on the Earth
And nest upon it, all obscurely mixed
With shadow-shows of Pegasus's birth
And fears of his ascent—his bursting forth
And piercing through with arrowy upward flight,
Cracking with sunshine and a snatch of sky
The roof of their dominion, letting in the light

IX

On dreary, twilit columns of young men
With eager hair and automatic eyes,
Marching and counter-marching through the fog,
Mashing and mangling truth, and praising lies,
Till language rotted down to snarls and cries
And meaning perished. Comfort, too, they found,
For on the back of their dream-Pegasus
A dream-Bellerophon still pressed him to the ground.

X

Some sewers are too common for the Muse:—
Think thou hast heard two procuresses chat,
Eyeing a vestal—pause, and plunge as far
Beneath the squalor of their hints as that
Itself was meaner than Magnificat:
So shall thy fancy hear Euryale
Mutter, hear Stheno answer—hear that pair,
With nagging itch and scratching, sketch their strategy;

XI

Planning to play into each other's hands—
Self-immolating, soft Euryale
And the breastless Beak of nude, intrusive will,
Stheno—to undermine their Enemy,
To steal his arms, till all his strength should be
His weakness, to turn back the holy force

Of the very gods against themselves, to make
Bellerophon keep Perseus off the Wingèd Horse.

XII

Meanwhile, beside the mountain-track, the Prince
Sprang on to Pegasus and towered astride
And, even as he turned to say farewell,
Andromeda came running to his side
And murmured low, and he in wrath replied,
Then turned to ride away . . . So must have said
A watcher, but the core of what befell
In those short moments by the Myth must be outspread,

XIII

Slow-motioned over many stanzas—first
The bickering goddesses approached unseen
And stood on either side the Prince; and now
The Gorgons, walking up, slipped in between;
Now suddenly their wings shot out, a screen,
Wherethrough the Olympian influence must ray:
The soft disaster masking Aphrodite,
While Stheno, with her back to Pallas heard her say,

XIV

Without word, pointing to the Shield and Sack:—
"Think'st thou my Arms were given thee in jest?
"Or Pegasus to ride? Thy hands do hold
"The Golden Bridle—and thou falterest!"
And now the Gorgon heard the stern behest
Laid on Bellerophon, forthwith to soar
Astride of the Wing'd Steed, and through the sky
Speed to the rescue, or be her true Knight no more.

XV

But She, the steely, cunning Horror, filtered
Athene's voice and made it seem to be
The Gorgon's, not the Goddess's: bemused,
He swayed and, looking down and groaning, he

Prayed; but inside his heart Euryale
Stirred up a medley of those ancient fears,
Antea, Chimaera, and the cloud-vain voice
Of Zeus remembered ranting in his sensual ears.

XVI

He prayed, but made no motion to obey.
Above the Gorgon's wing—"O thou sole Fount
"Of Zeus-born Reason," Aphrodite called,
"I say the Father wills him to dismount!
"Surely thou art his Lady Paramount!
"It lies with thee!"
                   But vexed Athene burned
With wrath:—"Ah, let him go his ways!" she said,
"I have done with him for ever!"
                          Proudly she returned

XVII

Back to the School at Athens, where she found
All in disorder: some old man propounded
Ironical dilemmas to pert youth,
Confounding them—but they were not confounded,
But plucked his beard, and mocked his voice, and hounded
His weak old age, and clutched him round the waist
And rantipoled him up and down, still struggling
To argue, vexed with tears and stuttering in his haste:

XVIII

And all the time he thought how, on Seriphos,
He had taught a lad and watched his wits unfold,
Coaxed in the sunshine of Philosophy:
'Ah, where is Danaë's Boy, the quick, the bold,'
He thought, 'Where now is he? I am too old!
'If he were here with me, we would be strong!'
So, when Athene came, she strengthened him
And truth unclouded gleamed again, but not for long.

XIX

Meanwhile the Paphian Goddess, more adroit,
Practised in soft, exclusive whisperings,
Sent parley down to the Queen's heart. Too wise
To let it filter through the Gorgon's wings,
Rather her honey-breathing mouth she brings
Close to her heart, and prompts her what to say
Then feeling that heart shrink, she lets it drink
Of blossomy warm wish. Swiftly Andromeda

XX

Runs to the Prince, astride on Pegasus,
And shyly hints the Father's Will revealed
Miraculous to her—he must dismount,
Give place to Perseus, up to Perseus yield
The Wing'd Horse and the Death's Head and the Shield!
Bellerophon grew rigid in his place,
Like one who fancies far-off sounds, and then
Slowly he turned and stared into the Queen's fair face.

XXI

Who knows what passes in the heart of hearts?
Who sees the demiurge's demiurge?
Ask not who guard the Guards, but ask who steer
The Steersman—what centripetals converge,
Where indecision alters into urge:
Bellerophon was staring at the Queen:
Who knows what passes in the heart of hearts?
And, afterwards, who knows? Who knows what might have been?

XXII

Euryale said:—*Stheno, our trial is
Now!* Stheno, like a dream-pealed ordnance shot,
Voided—obscene: the spastic influence
Smote him, reversed in spirit—round one spot
Case-hardening his heart, that screamed white-hot,
Till it spat venom: forth the long flame leapt,

Lickerish, and scorched the woman with some name
Men use in scorn among themselves. And the Queen wept.

XXIII

"Thou sapient Queen," he snarled, "What knowest thou
"Of things equestrian, or how horse and man
"Are grown to be one flesh? When I am thrown,
"It shall be time enough. Let him, who can
"Unhorse me! For thee too I have made a plan:
"That thou shouldst turn thy care from things half-known
"Back to thy needle. What the Father wills,
"Fear not, but by the Father's self I shall be shown!"

XXIV

Then soft Euryale laughed in the place
That once had been a breast, and croaked:—*Well done!*
And clanged her iron wings, and tossed across
A kiss-worm to her dark companion.
Like some old harridan, she croaked:—*Come on!*
Let's get back now! Bellerophon will keep
The fat Cob grounded! Gorgon! Hoot! up Gorgon!
And, wing to wing, they sagged off home, to stink and sleep.

XXV

But Cytherea, whispering, comforted
Gently her darling:—"Darling, do not weep!
"This hour, even this hour, thou shalt prevail,
"I being thy helper—so thine arrows keep
"Their sharpness! And now maybe thou shalt sleep
"A little while!" So, when she ceased, the Queen
Wondered and brightened, and let fall her pride:—
'How small I am!' she thought, 'How silly I have been,

XXVI

'Pitting myself against the stately men,
'And talking, talking!' Now she seemed to hear
Her own voice, muted to a madding whine,
Droning its monotone in Perseus' ear,

Humming incessant on, year after year,
Lifelong: her very body tried to shrink
For shame of it: her arms into her sides
So close she pressed, the one in the other seemed to sink.

XXVII

She was amazed, it seemed so very small,
Her waist; and this was all; she slept, nor felt
Thin gauze wings from a vanish of slim shoulders
Uncrumple, neither saw the love-curls melt
Into antennae.... When the Goddess dealt
The stroke of metamorphosis, she dreamed—
Being a Gadfly now—she was the Queen,
Herself, alone with Perseus—only Perseus seemed

XXVIII

Also to be Bellerophon; the Man
Was sitting in a corner, playing chess,
Himself against himself: at needlework,
Exasperated by his thoughtfulness,
She sat and talked in vain; the Secret Press
Flew to her mind; she spoke; he answered not,
Or absently—and she, she thought at last
Desperately: 'All men nurse some tender, muffled spot!

XXIX

'I will touch his, who cares no more for me!
'I will get underneath that placid skin!'
So, without altering her tone, she murmured,
Piercing some soft cloth with a tacking-pin:—
"The milk—I wonder, might we store it in..."
And heard herself no more.... With giant roar
Perseus sprang up and knocked his table flying—
And the high vault cracked and rumbled and crashed on the floor.

XXX

The Gadfly, whining in the noonday heat,
Swift on the Wing'd Horse—in the waking world—

Dived, while she dreamed, and stung in some soft place,
And stung and stung: the startled creature hurled
His hoofs above his head so high, he whirled
Round, like a wheel—a crack, a shout, a tear
Mingled in one intense flash, while he hung
Or seemed to hang, a silver globe, self-poised in air.

XXXI

But when his legs had found the ground again,
The surcingle was snapped, the housing gone,
And two white pinions from his trembling flanks
Sprang arching. Like a catapulted stone,
Far off upon the ground Bellerophon
Lay still, and, swifter than the startled steed,
Perseus was by him, kneeling at his head
And would have helped him rise. He said:—"There is no need!

XXXII

"There is no fear of falling off the ground.
"I am glad, I am glad to stroll and be a fool!"
And he rose and limped across to Pegasus
And clasped his strong neck:—
                              "Farewell, Beautiful!"
He murmured, "Dost thou mind the Fountain Pool?"
And, while he fondled, Pegasus' great wing,
Like the strange love of woman, curved above
His bruisèd shoulders, nervous, awful, sheltering.

XXXIII

But he, when first he felt its feathery touch,
Stared, like a man remembering things: some old
Horror came over him, as though he heard
A stealthy serpent rustling to enfold
Flesh with its flesh: he ducked, loosing his hold,
And passed in front, below the Horse's head,
Hastening as best he might; then, turning not,
Alone for ever down the mountain, limping, fled,

XXXIV

Fled from his friends, who would have loved him well
Over the mountain-shoulder, out of sight.
So the Myth knows no more of him. Alone
He eked out his humdrum years, till kindly night
Of death caressed him—now an eremite
And now a wandering beggar; and was known
No more in courts; but the common sort of men
Would turn and say:—"There goes that old Bellerophon!"

XXXV

Passing him in the street, and gossips told
How with each added year they watched him grow
More full of crotchets, how the children mocked him,
How all things through the day must run just so
As he was used to them, or he would go
Grumbling to bed and blaming. Yet the Blest
Received him when he died—no fiery stars
Whirling, but steeped Elysium dowered his ghost with rest.

VII

THE TEMPLE

I

Before the Gorgon-slayer tired of gazing
After the Prince, the Goddess had restored
The Queen to her own shape, and far away,
Dove-borne, to seek out her great Sister, soared:
The Queen, awaking, called aloud:—"My Lord!
"There is no time to lose, no time!" and pointed
Toward Pegasus—"Oh, think no more of me!
"Thy people need thee now, for whom thou art anointed.

II

"As for my safe return, this faithful Squire
"Is warrandice enough. Make haste, make haste!"
Then for a moment Perseus gazed on her,
Still tender for his friend: and grew amazed
And for that beauty and devotion praised
The gods—but knew not yet how she was clean,
Restored in truth, the marmor purged, the bride
Sweet from the bitter rock a second time—the Queen!

III

He turned and leapt astride. With Sack and Shield
Before him piled, he clucked the coaxing sound
And rose to wave adieu; but Pegasus
Closed in his wings and obstinately downed
His knowing neck, and fingerpawed the ground
As though to be up and away he burned
And wondered why the naughty snaffle checked
His tender mouth. Then Perseus understood. He turned,

IV

Smiling, to face his eager Queen and cried:—
"Lady—behold!—he will not be gainsaid!

"He waits for thee to mount!" Andromeda
Hid, for her people's sake, how glad, how glad
Her heart within her leaped:—
                              "Lord, thou art mad!
"Thou must be free for this! I may not stint
"The swift manoeuvre! Go! And go!" she said;
And he:—"We may not overpass the gods' own hint!

V

"It is enough, I bid thee mount! Obey!"
He stooped. She sprang. The Wing'd Horse, with one bound,
Is off the ground; and, with soft-humming sound,
Slowly at first, and slowly, circles round
Over the Nuntius, who stands spellbound.
Look, as a good ship casts off from the quay
And noses round the shoals, but when the bar
Is crossed at last, the bell tings full speed up to sea,

VI

So Pegasus is gone! Betwixt his wings
The pair, like eager babes, now lay their heads
Whispering together, leaning now apart,
To watch, below, the streams, inlaid like threads
Of silver, vanish up to watersheds
Or fray to deltas. Yet not home their course
Is set. The King observed, but held his peace
And smiled, content to trust the great sagacious Horse.

VII

Now festering sores were stripped and washed and healed
With truth revealed; now sleeping dogs were woken
And thumped approving tails, as both confessed—
Her midnight journey first, and his seal broken:
His follies with the Mirror—griefs unspoken,
Unspeakable that seemed—old wounds that warped
Sweet amity to gall, hurt not at all,
As tediously they chimed and havered, harped and carped.

VIII

At last the Hippogriff, descending, made
A gentle landfall, letting them alight
Low on a sea-girt rock. A Temple stood
There, with no land or living thing in sight.
This was that Temple, where Medusa, bright
And vestal, once had served the Gray-eyed Queen
Of Truth with her clean youth, before Poseidon
Abused her, ere Athene wrought the change obscene.

IX

What passed within that Shrine I dare not say
I wholly know: such fragments I unfold
As I remember, walking once by night
Alone, a man who overtook me told—
A courteous man, as young as he was old,
And laughed because he loved; he said deep joy
Lay at the world's root, and the gods were gay,
And now he seemed a sage, now seemed a romping boy.

X

In attitude of benison (he told)
Both manifest to both, the Deities
On either side the Sanctuary stood,
And warmer rayed the Sisters, and more wise,
Atoned: What lightnings Aphrodite's eyes
Darted! What thunders rolled round Pallas' brow!
As on the longboat, when the leadsman calls
Soundings to steersman—fore and aft, from poop to prow,

XI

Two faces close on intervening space,
So, goddess-guided, now the Queen and King
Stood up, with all the hollow Temple's length
Between, and, praying, heard its silence sing
Like the sea, far-off, in a shell roaring;
But soon Athene stirred; she took the Shield

From Perseus' arm and paced and struck it down
Upright before Andromeda, who stood concealed.

XII

Then straight, returning down the figured pavement,
Raised from a bracket, where it hung, a Crown
Of Olive, fairly wrought with leaf and bark
And fruit, and still no wreath, a very crown
For triumph or defeat; she pressed it down
Firmly upon his forehead, who then smiled,
Seeing his image in the bossy Shield
A grimy beggar hallowed, yet most like a child.

XIII

Most like a child he seemed in his own eyes,
A child that played at kings. Meanwhile no less
The Cyprian tended her belovèd Queen,
Whom from her boyish weeds she bade undress,
But swiftly comforted her nakedness,
Draping her majesty all in its own
Epiphany: for low she stooped and slipped
From her blest Waist the Cestus, her immortal Zone,

XIV

And cast it round a mortal! When at last
The Goddess drew the polished Shield away
And raised it high above the woman's head—
Where shall I fly for strength? How shall I say
What Perseus saw, or what Andromeda?
Look, what thou sawest when thou wast in love,
They saw more clearly—how that one was dear
And shining bright with glory from the gods above.

XV

Not thus for long; for Aphrodite spoke
Low, and the Queen upon the ground inclined
Obedient eyes: she saw not Perseus now
Nor with what gesture Aphrodite signed

Swift to her Sister, who stood tall behind
The King, till Pallas gripped the Goatskin Bag
And ripped it wide, and grasped what lay within
And raised it slowly . . . Even as one awful crag

XVI

Out of low foothills, rises on the sight
Of one who glideth backward—like a star
Ominous in the east at dawn—arose
Medusa: then Love, pointing, cried:—"Thus far
"Lift up thine eyes! No farther! All worlds are
"Suspended, Lady, on thy steadfast will!
"Shoot straight, shoot straight the arrow of thy gaze!"
The Queen's eyes rose. As once a father's tortured skill

XVII

Winged, neither high nor low, the clothyard shaft
True toward the apple on the darling's head,
So, neither high nor low, but on his Crown
Her steady, loving eyes she riveted:
O double interchange of holy dread
And counterpoint of passion's dance! His eyes,
Challenged by Pallas, left the polished Shield
And sank to rest on those thrice-blest convexities

XVIII

Advanced as if to greet him, polished shields,
But soft, more soft than anything men knew,
Than pilèd summer clouds' high cumulus
Or drifted snow so white that it is blue
Or upland valley pastures, which the dew
Is joyful and the shadow gentle on.
Till, sounding in a sunbeam, down the Temple,
Two voices, clear, rejoicing rose in antiphon:—

XIX

"Perseus!" she called, and he:—*"Andromeda!"*—
"Thou art the Sword, the Saviour from the Beast!"—
"Thou art the Meaning of the Abstract Word!"—

"Thou art my Head!"—
                    "And Thou my Will released,
"The glory round the Head!"—
                    Be it increased!
"Thou art my King!" she sang, and he:—"Thou art
"Mine Impulse freed, the self-warm Deed, my Soul!"—
"I will not break thy seal!"—
                    "I will not break thy heart!"

XX

I faint upon my end: where is my friend?
If he were here for me, he would attest
What mystery there was done, how Perseus changed,
How deep within his heart the Fiery Zest
Awoke, how he himself into his breast
Magical, as on Pegasus uprose;
His potency of manhood, like a lotus,
Opened, and all the Congo bloomed, a Grecian rose.

XXI

Sudden the wind rose: round the white-walled Temple
Dashed the tremendous, the unbridled Sea.
Poseidon sought to enter in, resenting
Mortals from their mortality set free—
Daring again his old impiety
There in that holy Place, and listening fear
Thrilled through Andromeda, remembering
The sea-girt Rock, the monstrous Jaws; but Cytherea

XXII

Called to Athene, and Athene called
Divinely loud, and some God came across
The waste of waters, hasting to their need;
A sable-winged and youthful God he was,
Late-comer to Olympus—Thanatos
His name and, where he came, he stilled the waves,
Walking erect on them: where he passed by,
He poured on anger oil of the dear grace that saves.

XXIII

Time is: time was: the high solemnity
Is ended. Perseus, on the godlike Steed,
Is boun for Aethiopia—at the stirrup
Andromeda stands bidding him God-speed.
The Cyprian promises she will take heed
Over the Queen's return. Fixed in the Shield,
Medusa's visage glares—but how if Hard,
Tempered with Soft, be toughened to pure Strength—annealed?

XXIV

There, in its place of freezing, Lust's hard stare
Had rested, drawn with Perseus' ardent gaze,
On melting mirrors, whence it had received
Refraction, not of light, but vital rays
Of womanhood restored, Andromeda's.
And now half-human grown, half Gorgon still,
She was Destroyer and Preserver, bound
Henceforth to brace and strengthen whom she failed to kill.

XXV

So, on unconquerable wings, he came
Back to the Kingdom which proud Cassiopeia
Had ruled with Cepheus long ago—where now
Men watched each other and went home in fear.
Even when the whisper ran:—*The King is here!*
They looked not up: 'What can we do alone?'
They thought, but, as the Wing'd Horse rose and fell,
The Shield appalled true hearts to steel, and false to stone.

XXVI

What followed: how on Pegasus he cruised
Tireless, how fiery zest maintained the pace,
Till slippery subterfuges, unrenewed,
Perished, till even the adroit must turn and face
Medusa, naked-visaged, or give place—
Let others chronicle; I but record

Saturnian resurrection, how at last
An age of gold was born, (the learnèd said 'restored').

XXVII

The thymy turf round Aphrodite's Temple
Pastured the Wing'd Horse. When the war was won,
Lady Andromeda rose betimes one morning
And climbed the hill—but Pegasus was gone!
Time, in a shining golden stream, flowed on
Over their heads, and each returning spring,
At cuckoo-time, they looked for him—then years
Passed, and they ceased to talk about his tarrying.

XXVIII

The gods loved Aethiopia in those days,
For Perseus' rule was courteous and sedate.
His throne was each man's heart, and while the King
Indwelt there, Freedom walked inviolate.
Whole in each household, total in the State
Harmony reigned through all that golden time,
Because, harmonious in everyman,
Body and soul and spirit rang a triple chime.

XXIX

One night in June the Palace roses breathed
Such incense, midnight found the royal bed
Vacant; the casement open, where they stood,
Let in soft streams by Philomela shed;
And, welling down from warm stars overhead,
Now faint, now clear, there seemed a far-off humming.
Then the Queen whispered, like one in a dream:—
"Hush! Dost thou hear, Belovèd? Pegasus is coming!"

XXX

And, when the humming ceased, they hearkened still,
Motionless, hushed, her cheek against his knees,
To pindrop, garden stirrings . . . out of doors
A separate rustle, like to dawn's first breeze

Or Eleusinian Persephone's
Priest-whispered Name, shivered below their sill;
And they leaned over then, and saw white wings
Moving enough to hold a hovering body still,

XXXI

And understood the Sending. Soon the night
Quickened to voices flustering, wisps of air
That flashed, like meteors, back, as up they soared:—
Who rides?
                What! Saw ye not the happy pair?
Whither?
        High, circumpolar spaces, bare,
August, await them!
                So, from mortal gaze
They passed and did not pass. Lift up thine eyes,
Reader, now evening darkens on these autumn days;

XXXII

And dusk itself surprises the clear mind
Conditioned to undying summer eves
And gloaming midnight skies! Lift up thine eyes
Over thy little smoke of burning leaves
And wonder, while thy shaping ghost receives
Huge, ghostly shapes into it! Read, and mark—
Forgetting astro-physics and light-years—
What immemorial Diagrams prick through the dark!

XXXIII

High in the East, beyond those Louvre-pots,
Cassiopeia, the stately, on her chair,
Circles; beside her, toward the Cynosure
Holding her pride true-centred, lest it err,
Honest, broad-shouldered Cepheus whirls; and there
Low in the South, where damp November dims
With rising mist the prospect of deep heaven,
The monster Cetus round the sky's Equator swims;

XXXIV

And what between? What Power upholds the Throne?
What alien Giant, with what spritely head?
One arm upraised to flash the twinkling mirror,
And one to brandish Herpe's crescent blade,
One shoulder pouring down in a cascade
Swift to his heel that springs from the seven shy stars
Men call the Pleiads—bold—a shower of gold—
Perseus is marching, Perseus is dancing up the wars!

XXXV

And yet, how still, above Andromeda
Bending, adores her bridal carcanet's
Enchanting cirque, at Algol in his lap!
While westward, at the star called Alpheratz,
Her dainty foot on Pegasus she sets,
Egging him on, and Pegasus tips gay
And pranceable, and mad, and upside down,
Because he feels the foot of fair Andromeda—

XXXVI

Of fair Andromeda, who in her midst
Holds the great Nebula, that vast maelstrom
Extra-galactic, which the sage proclaim
A furious womb of Firmaments to come . . .
Ah, but the Myth would rather draw thee home
From vain surmise, imagination's way
To Pegasus from Perseus, down those three
Bright stabs of flame, which men still name *Andromeda*.

THE END

AFTERWORD

THE CHARACTERS AND THE MYTH

Perseus was the son of Danaë. Zeus took the form of a shower of gold, in order to visit Danaë in the brazen tower, where her own father, Acrisius, had imprisoned her; and Perseus was the fruit of that union. His youth was spent in the island of Seriphos, until the jealousy of its King Polydectes drove him forth to seek the Gorgon's Head.

Andromeda was the daughter of Cepheus, King of Aethiopia and his Queen Cassiopeia. Because Cassiopeia had boasted that Andromeda was more beautiful than the Nereids, Poseidon, the god of the sea, sent a sea-monster to lay waste the country. Deliverance was promised if Andromeda should be given up to the monster, and she was accordingly chained to a sea-girt rock. At the eleventh hour the sea-beast was slain by Perseus, descending from the sky on winged sandals lent to him by the god Hermes, and Andromeda became his bride. Her former suitor, *Phineus*, tried to prevent the wedding and was destroyed by Perseus with all his followers.

Bellerophon was the grandson of Sisyphus. He was so called because in his youth he slew his brother Beller. To be purified from the murder he fled to Proetus, King of Argos, whose wife Antea fell in love with him. When he rejected her offers, she falsely denounced him to Proetus whose subsequent efforts to compass Bellerophon's destruction resulted in his being sent to kill the female monster Chimaera—part goat, part lioness, and part serpent. Mounted upon the winged horse *Pegasus* he was successful in slaying Chimaera, but thereafter drew upon himself the hatred of the gods and wandered, lonely and sorrowful, avoiding the paths of men.

The two goddesses, *Aphrodite*, born of the sea-foam—mother of Eros—and gray-eyed *Athene*, who sprang fully armed from the forehead of Zeus, hardly need my gloss. Their qualities and their mutual antipathy have been celebrated too often.

Phorcys and *Ceto* (both born of a marriage between Earth and Ocean) had four offspring, namely, the *Dragon* who was set to watch the Gardens of the Hesperides and the three Gorgons, *Medusa*, *Stheno* and *Euryale*. Stheno and Euryale were hideous and immortal, but Medusa was a mortal woman of matchless beauty, until she committed fornication with Poseidon in the temple of Athene; whereupon Athene transformed her into a frightful creature with serpents instead of hair and a stare so appalling that it turned all living creatures to stone. Medusa is the best known of the three Gorgons and is commonly referred to as *the Gorgon*.

With the aid of a helmet of darkness and the Talaria (the winged sandals of Hermes), Perseus was able to approach near enough to Medusa to cut off her head. But he could only do so by using the Shield of Athene as a mirror; for reflected in the Shield the Gorgon's stare was harmless. The severed head retained its petrifying qualities and it was with this weapon that Perseus destroyed, first, the sea-monster approaching to devour Andromeda and afterwards her old suitor, Phineus and his followers, all of whom he turned to stone.

From the blood-drops that fell from Medusa's head sprang Pegasus, who immediately flew up to Heaven. From the rock which Pegasus struck with his glancing hoof there flowed the fountain *Hippocrene*. Either from these same blood-drops, or as the more normal fruit of Medusa's connection with Poseidon, *Chrysaor* was born, who was the father of *Chimaera*. Thus, Pegasus and Chimaera both owe their origin to Medusa and the curious may like to reflect that the fabulous creature from whose act the Greeks derived the Fountain of the Muses, was the nephew of three abominations and the uncle of a fourth. The ambiguous quality of his parent, Medusa, is one of several enigmas which caused the foregoing poem to be written.

In it I have taken the sort of liberties which seem to me permissible, or rather for which the dreamlike elusiveness of all but a few central dramatic moments and the astonishingly rich symbolical content of so many Greek myths seem almost to cry aloud. Thus, in the case of Bellerophon, the events either narrated by him or actually occurring in the poem do not extend the limits of the story of his life as it will be found in the sources, but substantially re-tell it. In the case of Perseus and Andromeda, however, I have presumed to continue their joint history from the time of the rescue to the event of their constellation. Perhaps the greatest liberty of all is the combining of the two stories. While I know of no tradition to that effect, there are, even apart from the Mother of Pegasus, three links which seemed to me to justify in some way the desire which had come upon me to bring Perseus and Bellerophon, and Perseus and Pegasus together.

First, Proetus, the King of Argos, who played such an important part in the life of Bellerophon, was also, according to Ovid, the usurper of the throne of Acrisius the father of Danaë, and was ultimately destroyed by Perseus by means of Medusa's head. Second, there is at least one version of the story of Perseus, according to which he flew to the rescue of Andromeda, not on the winged sandals of Hermes (the Talaria), but on Pegasus. The third, and for me most important, link is the position of the constellations in the sky. Bellerophon is not there, it is true. I do not think he will be found anywhere among the stars. But Perseus, Andromeda and Pegasus are inseparably, and by no means inconspicuously, linked. For this brilliant group, together with the Mother and Father of Andromeda, may fairly be said to dominate the northern heavens.

Introduction to *Medea*

Sometime in the 1970s Owen Barfield began writing a play entitled *Medea*. An end-date for this composition is indicated in the Bodleian archive for the play by a return letter from BBC Radio in October of 1980 rejecting the play as unsuitable "for any of our slots" and offering no other critique. There is also in the archive two letters commenting on the play from Martin Moynihan, a diplomat and linguist best known to Inklings scholars as the translator of *The Latin Letters of C. S. Lewis*—one earlier undated letter, and a later letter dated February 2nd, 1983. The handwriting of the letters is difficult, but great praise is apparent. The first letter begins: "Dear Owen, It is a most powerful piece! At first reading, there's much in it I don't altogether understand—and, within that, *there's much I shrink from understanding*. These two combined are both dramatic plusses." These striking statements say much about this intriguing and disturbing play on a foundational Classical myth. There are in Moynihan's letters analyses of themes and specific portions of the play—and particular mention of both Charles Williams and Tolkien. Yet, despite the BBC attempt and these excited reactions from a long-time friend and fellow scholar, the play seems to have remained unknown after this time. This is a truly great work, a fitting addition to Barfield's dramatic oeuvre and his several deep retellings of ancient mythology.[1]

In this late mythopoeic work, the tension between authentic development within the ancient mythos and postmodern transference is tilted a little more toward the latter side, and this is a signal that the text is more didactic, the rhetorical act more foregrounded. The "tentacle here and there" stretched towards social issues put aside for a metaphysical synthesis in *Orpheus*, are here brought more into focus, though still firmly in a mythopoeic frame. Indeed, the text is still greatly mythopoeic, and Barfield does not demure only as rhetorical device in his suggestions that the wisdom of the mythos may in time find more pointed meaning in his explorations, but the philosopher poet in his later vision is more turned toward coming disasters, and as convinced as ever that long term solutions come from movement toward more participated and less predatory figurations of consciousness. At the polarity is the tensile throb of meaning and also the locus of our leverage to more actively participated consciousness. Barfield's final reframing of the questions draped around the mythopoesis of *Orpheus* underscores the unity of all of these potential lenses, howsoever the tensions are drawn: "I wonder whether the play, taken as a whole, may not be hinting at a transition from, or rather through, Eros to Agape, neither as a Platonic transfer of attention from carnal copy to ghostly original, nor simply as darkness giving way to light, but rather as moonlight brightening imperceptibly into sunshine."[2] Consciousness is neither a metaphysical mitigation nor a waking switch; it is a luminous evolution guided by the poetic principle and inscribed in the meanings that fire figuration. This is the frame of understanding within which Barfield plies his mythopoeic skill.

The story of Medea is indeed centrally located in the ancient mythos in the marking and mapping of socially defining taboos—indeed, the central taboo that generates social structure itself, for Medea is paired with the Oedipus myth to define the proper connecting of families to form society. The marriage taboo at the heart of society is a rule fully stated as 'Exogamy but also Endogamy'—that is, marry outside the group but not too far outside, for the social bindings of exogamy are lost if the connection is too stretched in location or custom. If Oedipus inscribes 'exogamy', the rest of the rule, 'but also endogamy', is inscribed by the myth of Medea. As Euripides tells it, she cuts all connections, even betrays her family, to run off with Jason. Later when Jason is offered to marry into the royal family of their Greek polis, he happily accepts. He would still love Medea, but marrying into the royal family would give advantage to their children and put them in line for great social power—the epitome of advantage gained through exogamy. Medea sees only personal betrayal and responds by murdering the princess, the king, and her own children—and then escapes in a divine chariot with the help of her godly relatives. Barfield's play varies from this telling of the myth in many respects, but the symbols and themes remain and suggest rifts at the heart of the social construction of meaning.

The central theme of Barfield's *Medea*, of course, is not equivalent to the ancient mythic inscription of social taboo but a postmodern transference. Our consciousness focused firmly toward the empirical world with not even a nod toward participation is a mental marriage too far removed from the polarity in our participated generation of experience. And marriage it seems to be, for as Barfield and his adherents well know, positivism is a tenacious and tempting dysfunction, one that has ruled long by empirical power and personal disconnections and continues with increasing arrogance, violence, and dissolution of meaning and social stability. Two particular elements of the play may serve to suggest the general sense of mythopoeic tension and the postmodern turn of ancient motifs. The first is the insistent, niggling, misogynist wheedling, fully modern and familiar in its relentless vulgarity, that turns the empirical lens, sophist in bent, to dig out the slightest possible doubt of female integrity, inscribed in Jason's relentless interrogation of Photeus that dominates Scene One. The second is the strange casting of Medea into the werewolf motif. The biting link between these two elements unmasks the institutionalized misogyny that repeatedly undermines society, but more importantly it mythically inscribes the imbalance of empirical camera-consciousness that unleashes a cruelly reductive empirical lens against all meaning and human dignity.

This mythopoeic disaster inevitably inscribes the failure of meaning that lies at the root of social and environmental disasters. The result of the collapse of meaning includes actual self-poisoning, individually and collectively, as in Barfield's final novella, *Eager Spring* (1988), and allegorically it is life in the sewer, as in his previous novella, *Night Operation* (1975). Both novellas end with the possibility of the redemption of meaning and recovery of our long-estranged humanity, but both also starkly warn of the meaninglessness, nausea, and violence that otherwise awaits our rapid descent into viciously imposed empiricism. The ending of Barfield's *Medea* similarly suggests the golden path of plumbing the mythic foundations of meaning, mapping the evolution of consciousness, and transferring that power to a new consciousness configuration, Original Participation becoming Final Participation, but it also warns of the onward rush toward social collapse that we seem to be choosing instead. If Jason's uncertain veneration of the Golden Fleece at the end of the play is a mythic symbol for evolving consciousness, the suggested path would seem to be modeled by Vi, the protagonist of *Eager Spring*. We need to learn the paths of cultural meanings, discern the evolution of consciousness through shifts in artistic and poetic expression—even in the face of perennial critique and rejection coming from the prevailing consciousness of the day—and wield mythopoeic meaning to engender the evolution of conscious experience. We may also need various calls of social action to stop the greed and violence and replant healthy nature, but social action will not suffice if we do not also work to rediscover the polarity of being and our participated role in the production of self and world.

Notes

1. The Bodleian archive for Medea (Dep. c. 1097) includes an early draft of the play, a typescript with corrections, the BBC rejection letter, and the two letters from Martin Moynihan. Though the extant typescripts in the Bodleian archive are dated to the 1970s, this play is perhaps another example of Barfield reworking an older text. J. R. R. Tolkien in a November 1944 letter to his son Christopher reports on a "most amusing and highly contentious" Inklings evening which included a reading by Barfield of a "short play on Jason and Medea" (103). In his 1985 article "The Defiant Lyricism of Owen Barfield," Thomas Kranidas mentions that Barfield told him about this evening and the difficulty of reading his "Medea" due to the general "exuberance and friendliness" of the group (26-27). The relationship between the reading at this event and the current text is uncertain. It is notable that there is no "Medea" among the materials in the Wade nor other discussion of the text in the publications that consider Barfield's other previously unpublished works.

2. Owen Barfield, "Foreword," in Owen Barfield, *Orpheus: A Poetic Drama*, ed. John C. Ulreich, Jr. (West Stockbridge, MA: The Lindisfarne Press, 1983), 10.

MEDEA

NOTE: In his youth Jason led the expedition of the Argonauts to recover from Aeetes, King of Colchis, the fleece of a golden ram which the latter had formerly stolen from a visitor to his shores. It is well known how, with the help of the sorceress Medea, daughter of Aeetes, Jason vanquished various fabulous monsters and recovered the Golden Fleece. Medea accompanied him on his homeward journey and they eventually arrived as man and wife at the Court of Corinth, where I have supposed that Jason ascended the throne. There are many different accounts of the subsequent history and ultimate fate of Medea, and I have devised my own, following the main tradition since Euripides that, because of the hatred which she came to feel for her husband, she inflicted a horrible death upon her own children in his presence.

OWEN BARFIELD

MEDEA

Dramatis Personae

Jason   King of Corinth
Medea   his Queen

Mermerus   (aged 10)
Corilla   (aged 7)   their children

Photeus   an elderly Councillor
A Slave
Huntsmen

ACT I   Scene 1

(A room in the Royal Palace at Corinth. It contains a couch, chairs and other furniture and is lit by candles. The doorway is hidden by the thick curtains which project from the wall in a semi-circle far enough for the door behind them to be opened fully without the curtains being moved.

Jason reclining on the couch; Medea beside it on a chair.)

MEDEA

Sire, you must sleep! How fares the realm
If your hand falters on the helm
Palsied with watching? No drug's good
Since that strange poison took your blood,
Save this I brew.

JASON

     You call it strange?

MEDEA

Sire, the whole Court deplores the change!
Drink, and restore yourself!

JASON

      Begone!
Let the realm founder! I will none!

MEDEA

You are not your own to squander! Think—
You are your subjects'.

JASON

I'll not drink!

MEDEA

What have I done? Your sharp words break
My heart like blows—

JASON

         (*aside*)   Now, Jason, speak
Or never!   (*aloud*)   Stay! I think I seem
Better; but first . . . first hear my dream:
    Night blessed this land, the white moon shone,
But in my brain bright day lived on
When, with your help, I'd wrought so hard
That every nerve was fagged and jarred.
I could not sleep. Across this floor
The moon fell on an open door.
I could not sleep. At last I spoke,
Calling you softly, if you woke:
'My longing, my repose, my queen,
'Come to my threshold and be seen!
'My own, my goddess tall and wise
'Of the blue robe and the starry eyes,
'Come and bring with you the Fleece,
'Our golden grace of light and peace:
'One glimpse, one glimmer heals my sight
'And launches spinning through the night
'This planet, rock-bound with despair,
'Mantled in soft and sun-filled air—'
    But when you answered not, nor came,
I stilled all clamour, pressed no claim;
Only a little while I wept
And lay long patient—and then slept
At last, light, dreamlessly, till—hist!

(You burn strength, tugging at that wrist!)—
Merciful powers, I slept until
You, queen, you, you across my sill
Stole, like a thief, all gauze and lace,
And stood where they just touched my face . . .
I dreamed I woke; and I dreamed you
Were the whole world my senses knew :
"Lights ho! What hour is't? Where's Medea?"
"Hush! lest you rouse the guard—she's *here!*
"Called'st thou me not? Why frown you so?"
"If't be the King's will, I will go—
"Only—tomorrow . . . Kings must sleep!"
"'Tis true!"
          "I am therefore come. Drink deep . . ."
I drank. I dared not bid you go:
But what needs more? Sweet witch, you know
What sorcery lifted, light as air,
The load I only prayed to share
And how I followed, through your eyes,
And lay becalmed in paradise
Hours upon hours, till, tired of this,
You suddenly smote me blind with bliss
And thrust me off from you and smiled
To see me sleeping like a child
Clasping its doll, your morning-gift,
The scorpion bred beneath your shift!—

MEDEA

May I go now?

JASON

                    I have not done:
Then—when you deemed yourself alone—
You—you—

MEDEA

          I feel—

JASON   (*raising a trembling hand to his forehead*)

MEDEA   Perhaps 'twere best
Some other time to tell the rest,
If you must go?

MEDEA
                 I feel too dazed
To answer! That your sick blood raised
Unsavoury fantasies (since how men
Are made is not beyond my ken),
I hear and grieve for't. That you blame
Me in some way you do not name,
Are vexed with me—or so you seem—
For being an actor in your dream,
Takes my breath from me. But that you
Should *tell* me! Me! Oh pardon! I'll do
My utmost not to cause distress
By showing any! I did most wrong
To shrink so, when I heard your tongue
Approaching that—oh, were you less
Than liege, were we of equal estate
That candour how—indelicate!

(*Exit*)

JASON

No clearer! No way blasted out!
No lightning through these clouds of doubt!
They'll never break! Oh God, the pain
Of that resolve to speak out plain!
The naked anguish, when I heard
My own voice stake upon one word
Our future lives! The loveless lot,
The sword thrust through the wedding-knot!
Each kiss, each smile, each word a task!
The contract not to drop the mask
Day after day! No hope of sleep,
Sickness, her hatred—I held cheap
All these and more, would they but buy
Light of conviction, the clear eye
For the true way however hard—

So grieved! So startled! Ha! On guard!
Why did she struggle then—foretell
Your drift unspoken? You know well
She's stubborn and feigns! There's nothing new,
Nothing that need perplex your view,
Only the disconcerting shock
Of the first encounter—a girl to mock
The resolute will that piloted
Argo! When first we spy ahead
Too clear the perilous way mapped out,
Fear prompts us to pretend we doubt.
Oh then, if we pause, we doubt in fact
And find ourselves unfree to act
For ever after! My intent
(Should she be taxed and not repent)
To shrink from nothing, holds unshaken.
                    (Strikes bell)
But if I prove to have been mistaken,
What then? . . . That way damnation lies!

(Enter slave)

Tell Photeus, boy, I seek advice. *(Exit slave)*

(Enter Photeus)

PHOTEUS

My Lord?

JASON

Oh Phoetus—yes—I sent—
Maybe you are on some labour bent
On which my summons intervenes?

PHOTEUS

Can the end interrupt the means?
You are too thoughtful.

JASON

                    No, in truth
I must ask pardon here. The youth

Bore a false message; neither news
Nor counsel I seek: their plans to amuse! *(sighs)*
To be frank, my Lord, I hoped to find
In idle commerce with your mind
Peace for mine own! I am much distressed—
May we talk a little? And then I'll rest.

PHOTEUS

    Oh Sire, dear Lord, I feel ashamed—
The beggarly service you have named!
And then to ask pardon for't. When I
And hundreds more were glad to die,
Would that bring peace back to your mind!

JASON   *(brushing his eyes)*

Weakness does this for me! You are kind!
A man must needs be moved to find
Duty breeds love—love gives so much—
When, elsewhere, love—or what seemed such—
Gives sourly, or withholds instead
Even the bare duty covenanted!
    I often think such friends must find
Being loyal to a distempered mind
Uneasy labour. Should they tell
Or hide from him, to get him well,
Bad tidings—rumours if you please . . . ?
What does that phrase mean, "the King's peace",
When not the body politic
But the body natural is sick?
For instance—*(A knock at the door. Photeus goes through the curtains and opens it. He returns with a letter, which he hands to Jason.)*

PHOTEUS

For you, my Lord, from Her Majesty.

JASON   *(reading)*

"My Lord, as I have felt myself somewhat ailing since I left you, I will if you please

keep my apartments for the space of one or two
days. I have made all arrangements so that your
comfort may be maintained in the meantime and
will, as soon as I can, recover my spirits
sufficiently to attend to it once more myself.
I am most sorry that this should have happened,
while you yourself are ill."
(*softly to himself*): My poor darling!

PHOTEUS

Shall the slave wait, or come again?

JASON

I'll write a line now. Quick! my pen,
I fear she must be suffer—stay!
(*harshly and suddenly*) No answer! Send the boy away!

(*Photeus does so—and returns from the door*)

JASON

Well, is it so?

PHOTEUS

                So?

JASON

            Do you find
Perplexing problems of this kind?
And if so, how do you decide
What to reveal and what to hide?
(*A pause. Jason shows impatience*)

PHOTEUS

Forgive me! I do understand—
It might well be that in some land
Far otherwise disposed than this—
Some realm where much more was amiss
Than the King's health—the Court *might* hear
Some tale of which a man might fear
Lest speech should injure the King's reason,

Or reticence connive at treason—
Is that your meaning, Sire?

JASON

                Even so.

PHOTEUS

Then my answer is a plain, blunt No.

JASON

I am in earnest, Lord!

PHOTEUS

                And I!

JASON

Think! I shall trust you utterly.

(A pause, during which Photeus remains unmoved)

There's nothing then? However small?
Nothing—we'll say—

PHOTEUS

                Nothing at all.

JASON

No (what word?)—No strange doings seen
Or talked—we'll say, about the Queen?

PHOTEUS

Now my dear Lord, let me suggest
It is time for you to seek your rest.
You have talked enough. Will you not try?

JASON

I am in earnest, Lord!

PHOTEUS

                And I!

(approaching Jason and laying his hand affectionately on his shoulder)
She is acclaimed on every hand
As the first lady in the land—
A stately Queen, a sweet, true woman,
Noble and gracious, yet how human!
A hand how deft, a heart how quick
To help the poor and heal the sick—
How all now bless with thankful hearts
What once they feared, her magic arts!
To all, kind looks and courteous tones:
Most loving with her little ones,
With whom your subjects every day
Peep through the pales to see her play,
Childlike, at battledore or ball,
In the shade under the high wall—

JASON

    And do you swear you have never heard
One hint of scandal—not one word,
One breath?

PHOTEUS

              I do.

JASON

                  Look at me, Lord!
I trust you—*nothing?*

PHOTEUS

                Nothing—unless
But 'tis too trivial—

JASON

              Ha?

PHOTEUS

                You press
So narrowly, Sire, that if I rack
My brains for tattle—oh, good lack!

I *cannot*—

JASON

              Tell me!

PHOTEUS

                      Some weeks back
Our Bureau of Intelligence
Lapsed from its customary sense.
Some new-broom member of the staff,
Unskilled at sifting grain from chaff,
Passed to the Boulé, tabbed and checked,
Some winecup gossip to the effect
That she—

JASON

                      That she?

PHOTEUS

(shrugging his shoulders)   a thought too much
Affects the kennel, byre and hutch,
Gives to the stable her private hours
And loves rank odours more than flowers:
'Twas said—

JASON

           Eh? What was that noise? Hark!
Heard you it not? A yelp or bark—

PHOTEUS

I heard nothing.

JASON

              Nothing? Quick!
Open the door!

(Photeus passes through the curtains and is heard lifting the latch. After a slight pause he comes out again, shaking his head.)

                I am more sick
Than I had fancied. It were best

You left me now to take my rest.
I am too weary to talk more.
My thanks to you, good Councillor,
For your kind company. Good night!
Pray send the slave to dim the light.

(Exit Photeus. Jason paces once or twice up and down the chamber, deep in thought.)

JASON

(with bitter irony) "Indelicate!"

(enter slave, extinguishes all the candles save one, and exit.)
(Jason lies down on the couch, covers himself and closes his eyes.)

Light of this house, O shining Ram!
All I am good for, all I am
Is hers: thou know'st, who heard my vow
Long since in Colchis: hear me now!
Thy fleecy thickness of gold rays
Wrap me, through the evil days—
Too surely looming, and through this night,
In wisdom, gentleness—and might!

(He relaxes, as for sleep. After a short pause a noise of breathing, whining and scratching is heard outside the door. This is followed by two not very heavy thuds, the second of which is immediately preceded by a faint rattling of the latch and followed by a single sharp yelp. Jason starts up on the couch and listens intently, but the noise is not repeated, and he again lies down and composes himself to sleep. Soon the scuffling and whining begin again. This time there are three thuds, before the first of which the latch rattles faintly as previously, before the second rather more loudly, while the third is preceded by the sharper click which the latch has already made each time the door has been actually opened during the scene. The curtain in front of it stirs and lifts slightly near the foot and then again hangs motionless.)

THE VOICE OF MEDEA

    Husband! Hear'st thou my voice? Lie still!
Listen: I mean to have my will.
Be wise, be guided, meddle not!
No farther probe the angry spot
Betwixt us. Use not thy male might

To drag the unspoken forth to light.
Remember! Battle upon this field
How grim, how gray! Love, dear, and yield!

(Jason stir uneasily in his sleep and groans. The curtain falls.)

SCENE 2

(The same: three or four hours later)

(Enter Corilla in her nightgown)

CORILLA

Father! Father! Are you awake?

(She crosses to the couch and pulls his arm. Tearfully:)

Father!

JASON   *(Straining in his sleep)*

Hiloo! hoo! hoo! hiloo!
At her! At her! At her! Ah-h-h-!

CORILLA

Father! You've been dreaming!

JASON

What's this? What hour is it? Where's Medea?

(seeing Corilla)

Why, little one! My *dear!*
Whatever is the matter?

CORILLA

I had a nasty dream—I couldn't sleep—so I've come here.

JASON

Why, I thought you couldn't reach the latch. How did you get in?

CORILLA

The door was open.

JASON

What did you dream about? Why didn't you go into your Mother's room?

CORILLA

I was frightened. Mermerus has gone to Mother.

JASON

Why?

CORILLA

He couldn't sleep either after I woke him up.

JASON

Why did you wake him?

CORILLA

I didn't mean to. I woke up screaming, and it woke him.

JASON

My little one! Come!   *(caresses her)*   But if you were frightened, Mother would have made it right again! In her nice warm bed!

CORILLA

I was frightened to go to her.

JASON

Frightened?

CORILLA

I was afraid she might be angry.

JASON

Why, you little silly, how could she be angry with a little frightened morsel like this?

CORILLA

She might have.

JASON

And such a *kind* mother! The merry games I have seen you playing with her! The peals of laughter! Why, she is *never* cross with you!

CORILLA

Not very often.

JASON

Well *then* I expect you deserve it, you know! Corilla! Not *frightened*, surely! What does she say to you? *(Corilla hangs her head and is silent.)* What does she say to you?

CORILLA

It's not was she says, it's her voice.

JASON

What sort of voice?

CORILLA

I don't know. *(crying)*: it bites, daddy, it *bites!*

JASON

Come, come, this is nonsense! You love your mother, don't you?

CORILLA

Yes.

JASON

Well, then—

CORILLA

When she is angry, it suddenly sounds *like someone else!*

JASON

Ah! *(aside)* Why do I go on pretending not to know? *(To Corilla)*:
Well, but Mermerus has gone to Mother's room. So *he* is not frightened anyway.

CORILLA

No, father.

JASON

But she is angry with him too sometimes—when he is disobedient?

CORILLA

I don't know; he hardly ever is.

JASON

Well, well! You're feeling better now, eh?
(Corilla sobs; he caresses her. Enter Mermerus in his nightgown)

MERMERUS

Father! Are you awake? Is Corilla there?

JASON

Yes. Come here! Whatever is the matter with you both?

MERMERUS

Corilla woke up and woke me and we couldn't get to sleep again. Father—

JASON

What did your mother say?

MERMERUS

Father—she's not there. Her room's empty! Where is she?

JASON

(Sharply) Did you tell anyone?

MERMERUS

(Surprised) No! Everyone's asleep. Can we stay here with you, father?

JASON

What hour is it? Go to the window and draw the curtains.

MERMERUS *(at the window)*

It's just beginning to get light. Are you any better, father?

JASON

Yes, boy. So much so I think—yes—I will hunt again today.

CORILLA

Oh father, you are not nearly well enough! Mother said—

JASON

I must be well enough.

MERMERUS

Oh, take me with you!

CORILLA

And me!

JASON

Oh children, you are not nearly old enough! No. Listen; don't look so crestfallen. *I* am not well enough, and *you* are not old enough, to join in the hunt properly. But we'll have a glorious day all the same. What do you say to the old Hunting Box on the hill? There are plenty of things for you two to play with there, and I can watch the hunt from the windows. What do you say? Shall we go?

CORILLA

Yes, yes!

MERMERUS

I shall watch the hunt too!

JASON

Well—we'll see.

MERMERUS

What will they hunt, father?

JASON

Oh, there will be quarry. I—I dreamed there would!

MERMERUS

Can we start *now*?

JASON

What? Why, yes; the sun will be up in an hour. Go both of you and get dressed and send the slave for orders as you go.

MERMERUS

Come on, Corilla!

(Exeunt Mermerus and Corilla, as the curtain falls)

ACT II

(Scene: a large room in the Hunting Box. On one side a large window. The room is rather untidy, with hunting gear scattered about and a few children's toys. Enter Jason, Mermerus and Corilla)

MERMERUS

How musty this room smells! I don't believe anyone's been here for months.

JASON

Open the windows, Mermerus. *(Mermerus does so.)*
(He picks up a doll from the window-sill.)

MERMERUS

Hulloa, Corilla, here's old Lollia! I thought she was lost.

CORILLA

(Joyfully) She *was* lost! She *was* lost! Give her to me!
(She takes the doll from Mermerus and rocks it in her arms.)
Dear Lollia! *Go* to sleep, then! *(Sings)*:
   Sleep thou, my baby, on my arm!

Mother shall guard thee from all harm!
There! there! *(laying the doll carefully down again)*
She's asleep now!

MERMERUS

Is it more difficult to hunt a wolf than a boar, father?

JASON

Yes, boy, I should say so. It's not often done. Generally, it's the wolf that does the hunting.

CORILLA

Will the wolf get away, Mermerus?

MERMERUS

Of course not! Where shall we see them, father?

JASON *(pointing out of window)*

You see the little wood down there? I think they will start the quarry there. The huntsman said that was where the people who have seen her about the place think she comes from. Then the dogs will head her up this way. They went in on the other side. They ought to be coming out soon now. Let us see if we can hear them. Listen!
(Jason and Mermerus turn their heads sideways to listen.

Corilla goes to the window and looks out.)

CORILLA

There's a white tower in front of the wood.

MERMERUS *(looking out)*

That's not a tower, silly; it's a *person!*

CORILLA

What! So tall!

JASON *(looking out)*

It's a woman coming up from the wood. She's not so tall, Corilla.

CORILLA

Oh no! Nor she is! How funny!

MERMERUS

She's quite near. Why, I believe it's mother!

JASON

It is. Hark! *(a distant barking of dogs is heard)*
It sounds as if they will be some time in there yet, before they break out. *(Sits)*

CORILLA

Do you still feel better, father?

JASON

Yes, Corilla, thank you. I feel much stronger. *(She climbs on his knee. Enter Medea.)*
Good morrow, Madam!

MEDEA

                Was this wise?
I heard of this mad enterprise
And came to see if it were true.
You are unkind, Sire, when you do
These reckless things. *You*, who are still
Feeble and feverish and ill,
To venture through this morning air!
Are these your thanks for all our care?

JASON

Well, it was rash perhaps. . . . I too
have a question, Queen: how comes it, you
Are here yourself, when in your letter
You said—

MEDEA

           But I felt so much better
This morning, Jason—

JASON

          So did I.
So for us both let that suffice.
But, Queen, at what hour did you rise?

MEDEA

Why do you ask me? With the sun
I awoke, and, hearing you were gone,
I rose and dressed without delay
And came—

JASON

     Then why did Mermerus say
He found your room untenanted?

MEDEA

     When?

JASON

Long before the night was dead.

(Medea turns her face away from Jason and towards the audience.)

MEDEA

(aside, with a sudden vicious snarl): The fussing, babbling fool!
(Still facing the same way, she dissolves into tears.)

JASON

Was it not strange?

MEDEA   *(turning to Jason)*

      I cannot speak
For woe: what ails you? Why do you seek
And search and probe about it all,
As though I were some criminal?
What *right* have you?

JASON

     Was it not strange? *(Medea sobs.)*
You do not answer. Let us change

The topic then: an hour ago
I parleyed, you may care to know,
With several of our people, freed
And slaves alike, an all agreed
Reporting a thing stranger still:
The Bailiff (since I have been ill),
The Master of my Hounds, a nurse,
A guardsman, several gamekeepers
Besides the watchman on his rounds,
Have seen and heard about the grounds
Prowling and howling through those trees
(pointing at window) A She—

MEDEA

Oh man! What ails you? Cease!
If you *must* rave on in this way
Let us at least send *them away!*

(She indicates the children. The yelping of the pack is again heard faintly in the distance, gradually growing louder as.it approaches.)

Tell me the rest when they have gone, *Please!*

(lowering her voice, confidentially):

So you're scratching up my bone
I buried! You see what you'll get!

JASON *(horrified)*

Madam?

MEDEA *(aloud)*

I fear your mind is yet
Unhealthy: You look wildly, Sire!

JASON

What did you say?

MEDEA

(raising her voice a little, as if to make herself heard above the now somewhat louder barking of the dogs):

                    I said, you tire

Your brain too much. Even now you seem
Like someone haunted by a dream,
Stare, as if frightened by some Bug!
Why would you not accept my drug?

(Commanding shouts are heard outside, and the barking dies away. Medea crosses to the window and stands there looking out. Enter Photeus.)

PHOTEUS

Well, Sire, the dogs did all they could,
Yet we found nothing in the wood.
Where shall we—*(seeing Medea)* I intrude, I fear!
I had not heard my Queen was here.
Madam, your humble slave!

MEDEA *(turning abruptly from the window)*

Mermerus, come here!

MERMERUS *(going up to her)*

Yes, Mother?

MEDEA

Will you and Corilla run back to the Palace
And fetch me something I left behind?

MERMERUS

Oh Mother, need we? I want to see everything!

MEDEA

Oh Mermerus, I want it so much! Be darlings!
(Mermerus still hangs back) Shall I start you off?
I know! Come along! We'll have a laughing-race.
Remember, Corilla, you mustn't laugh—

CORILLA

No! *(Laughs. Mermerus also begins to laugh.)*

MEDEA

(laughing, to Corilla): You goose! You mustn't laugh till you *get* there!

If you do, you've lost the race. *(taking them both by the hand and moving toward the door)* You shall have a start, Corilla, because you're so small. You must go on towards the wood till I call out 'Stop!' Then wait till I—

(Exeunt, Medea still talking to them. Jason paces silently to and fro. Photeus crosses to the window and looks out.)

PHOTEUS   *(smiling)*

By Zeus, Sire, 'tis a pretty sight
The three there—how the morning light
Glows through Her Majesty's raised hand,
Ready to start them, where they stand
Eagerly waiting! Oh, Sire, pray
Look! It is better than a play!
Now she has dropped it. Off! The pack
Thirsting to join—she holds them back
With some slight motion of her arm:
By Sirius, she must have some *charm*! . . .
Good dogs! Oh wonderfully good!
Seem to be folded in her mood . . .
Like statues! Frozen on the ground!
Gods! Not a quiver, not one sound!
By Zeus, look at their nostrils, though!
He! And Corilla laughing so,
She's lost the race ten times already—
Do come and look, my Lord!

(Jason continues to pace moodily across the room. Outside is heard a single, short, terrible howl, half lupine, half human. Immediately the dogs break out into a deafening frenzy of yelping and barking, through which a rush of pattering paws is heard for a few moments before it dies away in the distance, where the yelping still goes on.)

PHOTEUS

What! *(He cranes out of the window with strained attention.)*
Oh! Oh! Oh! The children! They're on to them! The children!
The children!

JASON   *(dashing to the window)*

You fool! They're *playing!* *(He leans out of the window and utters a wild, despairing cry. Photeus rushes out of the door. Jason cranes further out of the window and yells.):*

Seize the witch!
The Queen! Stamp on the hellish bitch!
Gouge out her eyes! Where is she? Oh!

(He staggers back into the room with his hand on his eyes.)

JASON   *(breaking down)*

Corilla! *(Eventually he masters himself, starts toward the window and then stops short.)* Photeus! *You* tell me! What's out there?

PHOTEUS   *(craning out of window)*

Ho! *(The yelping and barking grow louder again.)*

VOICE OFF *(shouting)*

Breaking up a she-wolf, sir!

PHOTEUS   *(still leaning a little out of window)*

Breaking? No! What? By Cerberus!
Wolf-bred themselves, they're at a loss!
'Dog never eateth dog', they say.
Worrying it—dragging it this way—
Snarling like mad, half rage, half fear . . .
Two men . . .

JASON   *(rushing to the window and beckoning through it)*

You fellows! Yes! In here!

(Enter two huntsmen, carrying the bodies of Mermerus and Corilla, covered, on stretchers improvised from hunting spears and blankets. They pause, awaiting orders.)

Well? Lay them down! *(The huntsmen obey.)*
The Wolf! Where did she come from?

1ST HUNTSMAN

No-one knows, Sir. The wicked varmints (may their fangs rot in their jaws!) hadn't hardly finished their work with these here; the—the life was barely out of 'em, Your Majesty, when she tried to slink past, making for the wood, like. But one of 'em see 'er and give tongue, and they were after 'er like a flash.

JASON

Good for them! Let them rend their fill!
Go, bid the huntsmen, when they kill,
To lift the carcass . . . bring it—*here* . . .
Not slung but—that way *(pointing to the stretchers)*—is that clear?
And bid them see it covered well!
Stay! One of you run back and tell
The Day-Guard of the Golden Fleece
To send it hither; (show them these).

(He hands certain tokens to the huntsman.)

And hasten back with it.

2ND HUNTSMAN

Begging your pardon, Your Majesty, but we'd
like you to know how sorry—*(He stops in confusion.)*

1ST HUNTSMAN

Sorry! I'll go on till my dying day
seeing them little laughing faces change!

JASON

Enough! I thank you. Hurry now!

1ST HUNTSMAN

Ay Sir, no more! *(Exeunt Huntsmen. Photeus, after a pause, during which he looks anxiously at Jason, follows them.)*

JASON

Oh, bow, bow, bow,
Proud head, before the levelling wind!
Ye Gods, I know that I have sinned,
Being weak and soft: then flowed all this
From the first self-renouncing kiss?
Have I been mocked throughout? Our troth

Plighted, the calm Fleece blessing both
Hallowed it, made it seem most just
To join affection (ay, and *trust!*)
With fierce desire. And I could boast
(Oh fatuous) all the Olympian host,
Not Cypris only, when *we* wed,
Made glorious in our marriage-bed!

(The dogs are again heard approaching but this time only with occasional, spasmodic, irritated yelps. Jason stops his ears.)

    I shall go mad! *(He crosses to the window and looks out.)*

(Enter 3rd and 4th Huntsmen bearing a stretcher covered as before.)

    Well, have they finished her?

3RD HUNTSMAN

    Dead as mutton, your Majesty!

JASON

Can no-one quiet those yelping curs?
Lay it down here, fellows! *(indicating a spot on the opposite side of the room from the children's corpses)*

(Exeunt Huntsmen. Outside they are heard endeavouring to quiet the dogs and eventually succeeding. Meanwhile Jason has thrown himself down by one of the children's stretchers and buried his head in the covering blanket. Enter 2nd Huntsmen, carrying the Golden Fleece.)

JASON *(without looking up, in violent irritation)*

Go away! Get out!

2ND HUNTSMAN

Begging your pardon, Sir: strict orders not to put this here anywhere but in your hands.

JASON *(rising)*

Very well, Give it me. Now go!

(Exeunt huntsmen. Jason slowly approaches the third stretcher and lays the Fleece carefully over it. While he is doing this, one of the dogs, which has obviously been held quiet much against his will, begins to utter tentative

staccato yelps, which succeed one another with increasing frequency until they amount to a continuous bark. The other dogs begin to join in. JASON strides impatiently to the window and pauses there a moment, looking out. The Fleece is stirred by convulsive movements betraying a change in the position or shape of the object beneath it, and at the same moment the barking of the dogs dies away into a single long-drawn whine expressive of mingled fear and yearning. Jason turns sharply and gazes, speechless with horror, at the still jerking Fleece. The whining ceases.)

JASON   *(in a hoarse whisper)*

It—she's—coming—back!

(Suddenly he gathers himself together, runs across to the stretcher and strips off the Fleece and covering blanket together, revealing Medea lying apparently dead. He gazes down at her, trembling.)

Queen, wife and—werewolf! *(Medea stirs slightly.)*
        Ha! not even dead!
This was a kind thought, sweet! Hoo!
Let's to bed!

MEDEA   *(faintly)*
        Water, some water for my swollen tongue!
I have come back—

JASON   *(beside himself, pointing to the children's corpses)*
        To muzzle your own dung
And lap your vomit!

MEDEA
        Jason, it is I!
The wolf is slain—

JASON
        How do I know that! Why?

(He fills a cup with water and holds it to her lips, helping her to sip, as she speaks.):

MEDEA

I do not ask forgiveness. I have come,
Dragged by the Fleece, unwilling, to this home
Where our two lives were linked by erring fate.
I should have had a soldier for my mate,
Not you, pale boy, with your romantic wars
On bulls, and fairy men from dragons' jaws
All planted by yourself! My wiles and charms
Would have slept safe in tough Achilles' arms.
He would have quenched *Its* cravings: how his strong
Arm would have chastened me, when I did wrong!
But you, because you willed me to be free,
Could neither master It, nor let It be;
Whence all this ruin!

JASON   *(speaking low and slowly)*

                                      Yes. I know the Fleece
Lights the truth home . . . no older truth than this?

MEDEA   *(stirring uneasily as the Fleece is mentioned)*

The Fleece! *(coughs)* The blood is choking
me! Raise my head! Have mercy!

JASON   *(kneeling and raising her head on his arm)*

Medea! Is the pain—

MEDEA

Ah—h—h! Have mercy! Is there no physician?

(breathing with increasing difficulty and speaking between gasps)

In Colchis, husband, when I was a child
A prophet prophesied: he said, a wild
Wolf was my bane—and I should win release
Only by marrying the Golden Fleece
Through one who held it . . . So the King,
My Father, stole the fatal Thing,
And straitly charged me . . . I obeyed . . .
Beguiled you, when I was a maid . . .
Jason . . . d'you see how I was trying . . .
Jason . . . the wolf *is* dead, and I still . . . dying!

(She groans heavily and expires with her head still resting on his arm. Jason lowers her head gently on to the stretcher and rises to his feet, where he stands with bowed head, gazing down at her. At last he covers the stretcher again with the Fleece. The morning sun, which has been shining through the window, reaches the edge of the Fleece and lights it up, spreading further over its surface, as he speaks the following lines, slowly.)

JASON

I might still not go mad, could I but know
That in some far time, after much more woe
Wrought on ourselves and others, more blood spent,
It will seem so, that these four torn lives meant
Something, cut out some cancer, left some soul
Purer from deep-grown taint, more sweet and whole:
O Phoebus, if't shall ever with us two
Be well, and with these little darlings, do,
Merciful God, here in this hour, a sign:
Smile on the Fleece, oh smile, and bid it shine—
Curdle a thin crust over the mess of shame
And torturing memories, which bears Jason's name!

(Raising his head and seeing for the first time the shining Fleece):

I dedicate my life, my life of sane despair,
To guarding thee, to saving thee unstained and fair.
(kneeling): O holy Ram, wilt thou accept a coward's faithful care?

CURTAIN

Bibliography

Barfield, Owen. *A Barfield Reader.* Edited by G. B. Tennyson. Hanover, NH: University Press of New England, 1999.
Barfield, Owen. *A Barfield Sampler.* Edited by Jeanne Clayton Hunter and Thomas Kranidas. Albany: State University of New York Press, 1993.
Barfield, Owen. *Eager Spring.* Oxford: Barfield Press, 2008.
Barfield, Owen. *History in English Words.* Foreword by W. H. Auden. West Stockbridge, MA: The Lindisfarne Press, 1967.
Barfield, Owen. *Night Operation.* Oxford: Barfield Press, 2008.
Barfield, Owen. *Orpheus: A Poetic Drama.* Edited by John C. Ulreich, Jr. West Stockbridge, MA: The Lindisfarne Press, 1983.
Barfield, Owen. *Owen Barfield on C. S. Lewis.* Edited by G. B. Tennyson. Middletown, CT: Wesleyan University Press, 1989.
Barfield, Owen. *Poetic Diction: A Study in Meaning.* Oxford: Barfield Press, 2010.
Barfield, Owen. *Saving the Appearances: A Study in Idolatry.* Oxford: Barfield Press, 2011.
Barfield, Owen. *The Silver Trumpet.* Longmont, CO: Bookmakers Guild, 1986.
Barfield, Owen. *This Ever Diverse Pair.* Oxford: Barfield Press, 2010.
Blaxland-de Lange, Simon. *Owen Barfield: Romanticism Come of Age: A Biography.* Forest Row, UK: Temple Lodge Publishing, 2006.
Flieger, Verlyn. *Splintered Light: Logos and Language in Tolkien's World.* Revised Edition. Kent, OH: Kent State University Press, 2002.
Gibb, Jocelyn, ed. *Light on C. S. Lewis.* New York: Harcourt Brace Jovanovich, 1976.
Kranidas, Thomas. "C. S. Lewis and the Poetry of Owen Barfield." *The Bulletin of the New York C. S. Lewis Society* 12, no. 2 (1980): 1-2.
Kranidas, Thomas. "The Defiant Lyricism of Owen Barfield." *Seven: An Anglo-American Literary Review* 6 (1985): 23-33.

Lewis, C. S. *All My Road Before Me: The Diary of C. S. Lewis 1922-1927.* Edited by Walter Hooper; Foreword by Owen Barfield. London: Harcourt Brace Jovanovich, 1991.

Lewis, C. S. *The Collected Letters of C. S. Lewis, Volume III: Narnia, Cambridge, and Joy 1950-1963.* Edited by Walter Hooper. San Francisco: HarperSanFrancisco, 2007.

Lewis, C. S. *Out of the Silent Planet.* New York: Scribner, 2003.

Lewis, C. S. and Don Giovanni Calabria. *The Latin Letters of C. S. Lewis.* Translated and Edited by Martin Moynihan. South Bend, IN: St. Augustine's Press, 2009.

Potts, Donna. *Nemerov and Objection Realism: The Influence of Owen Barfield.* Columbia, MO: University of Missouri Press, 1994.

Sugerman, Shirley, ed. *Evolution of Consciousness: Studies in Polarity.* Middletown, CT: Wesleyan University Press, 1975.

Tolkien, J. R. R. *The Letters of J. R. R. Tolkien.* Edited by Humphrey Carpenter and Christopher Tolkien. Boston: Houghton Mifflin, 1981.

—. *Tree and Leaf.* In *The Tolkien Reader*, 25-112. New York: Ballantine, 1966.

INDEX

Aristotle, 31, 70
Auden, W. H., 9, 315

Barfield, Maud Douie, 5, 16
Barfield, Owen, "Death," 78, 82; "Introduction to *Light on C. S. Lewis*," 8, 171-73, 315; "Psychology and Reason," 78, 82; *Angels at Bay*, 4, 5; 77-141; *A Barfield Sampler*, 9, 13, 144, 171, 315; *Eager Spring*, 11-12, 79, 281, 315; Foreword to *Orpheus*, 5, 8, 10-13, 77, 82; *History in English Words*, 15, 16, 21, 29, 315; *Medea*, 4, 8, 11, 14, 279-313; "The Milkmaid and the Unicorn," 143, 144; *Night Operation*, 11, 281, 315; *Orpheus*, ix, 3-13, 77, 78, 81, 82, 171, 174, 279-80, 282, 315; *Owen Barfield on C. S. Lewis*, 8, 13, 171-73, 177, 315; *Poetic Diction*, 6, 15, 21, 29, 315; "Poetic Licence," 8, 10, 11, 12, 13-14, 172, 173-75, 177; Program Note for *Orpheus*, 5, 12, 13; "The Queen's Beast," 143, 144; *Riders on Pegasus*, 4, 5, 7, 8, 9, 77, 81, 143, 171-277; *The Silver Trumpet*, 3, 16, 315; *This Ever Diverse Pair*, 7-8, 13, 315; *The Tower*, 4-5, 15-76; *The Unicorn*, 4, 5, 143-69
BBC Radio, 11, 14, 279, 282
Bellow, Saul, 9
Blake, William, 79; *Jerusalem*, 79
Blaxland-de Lange, Simon, ix, 9-10, 13, 77-82, 171-72, 174, 177, 315

Browning, Robert, *Sordello*, 4, 15-16

Coleridge, Samuel Taylor, 3

de la Mare, Walter, 13
Dennehy, Frederick, 13

Eliot, T. S., 9, 10, 82

Flieger, Verlyn, ix, 145, 315
Freeman, Arnold, 5

Gibb, Joceyln, 171-72, 315
Goethe, 177
Gunn, Thom, 143

Harwood, Cecil, 16
Hooper, Walter, ix, 33, 316
Hunter, Jeanne Clayton, ix, 9, 12, 13, 171, 315

Keats, John, 48, 79
Kranidas, Thomas, ix, 9-10, 12, 13, 171, 174, 282, 315

Lamb, Charles, 174
Lavery, David, ix
Lewis, C. S., 4, 5, 7, 8, 9, 13, 15-21, 22, 25, 27, 29, 32, 33, 77, 80, 82, 143, 171-73, 174, 177, 178, 279, 315, 316; *All My Road before Me*, 15-22, 33, 316; *The Collected Letters of C. S. Lewis, Volume III*, 15-22, 27, 29, 33, 316; *Dymer*, 16; *Out of the Silent Planet*, 79, 82, 316; Note on *Orpheus*, 7, 13

Marlowe, Christopher, 17
Milton, John, 17, 79, 176
Morris, William, 144
Moynihan, Martin, 11, 14, 279, 282, 316

Nemerov, Howard, 8, 9, 13, 316

Oxford Inklings, vii, ix, 3, 80-81, 143, 174, 279

Piers Plowman, 78-79
Pitter, Ruth, 143-44
Potts, Donna, ix, 8, 13, 316
Psalms, 143-44, 147

Seven: An Anglo-American Literary Review, 9, 315
Shelley, Percy Bysshe, 48

Steiner, Rudolf, 3, 77, 81
Sugerman, Shirley, 7-8, 13, 316

Tennyson, G. B., ix, 13, 177, 315
Tolkien, J. R. R., 80-81, 82, 143, 145, 174, 279, 315, 316; *On Fairy-stories*, 145; *Leaf by Niggle*, 80-81; *The Letters of J. R. R. Tolkein*, 282.
Tripp, Raymond, ix

Ulreich, Jr., John C., ix, 3, 4-0, 12-13, 82, 171, 282, 315

The Wanderer, 29
Williams, Charles, 174, 279
Wordsworth, William, *The Prelude*, 4, 17

Yeats, W. B., 143

About the Author

Owen Barfield (1898–1997) is one of the twentieth century's most original and influential literary figures.

As an author and philosopher, he rallied against 'positivism' and was instrumental in bringing about a new awareness of the spiritual world that would eventually result in the "New Age" movement. He lived to see with satisfaction how alternative ways of thinking have begun to transform the limited positivist mindset.

Early on, Barfield developed his theory of 'The Evolution of Consciousness', based on an understanding of imagination as the highest human ability, *"as a vessel by which divinity passes down into humanity."*

His fellow Inklings C.S. Lewis and J.R.R. Tolkien are among the leading figures influenced by Barfield's work. Tolkien's linguistic and literary philosophy were influenced by Barfield's theories. For Lewis, he was a life-long friend and creative partner. Indeed, Owen Barfield was 'Romanticism' personified.

About the Editors

Leslie A. Taylor (PhD, Southern Illinois University, 1997) is an independent scholar who specializes in Classical and Renaissance Literature. She has published on the Greek and Hebrew translations of Boethius's *De consolatione philosophiae* and has co-authored with Jefferey H. Taylor a book on the influence of Boethius on Milton's *Paradise Lost*.

Jefferey H. Taylor (PhD, Southern Illinois University, 1994) is a Professor of English at Metropolitan State University of Denver. He is author of *Four Levels of Meaning in the York Cycle of Mystery Plays* and has published on the Dutch and Hebrew translations of Boethius. Dr. Taylor is recipient of the 2016 Owen Barfield Award for Excellence.

www.ingramcontent.com/pod-product-compliance
Lightning Source LLC
Chambersburg PA
CBHW031901220426
43663CB00006B/710